Fighting Words

STUDIES IN AMERICAN LITERARY REALISM AND NATURALISM

Fighting Words

POLEMICS AND SOCIAL CHANGE IN LITERARY NATURALISM

IRA WELLS

THE UNIVERSITY OF ALABAMA PRESS
Tuscaloosa

Manufactured in the United States of America

Typeface: Minion & Gill Sans

Cover photograph: *Stag at Sharkey's* by George Bellows, 1909. Courtesy of the Cleveland Museum of Art.
Cover design: Gary Gore

∞

The paper on which this book is printed meets the minimum requirements of American National Standard for Information Sciences—Permanence of Paper for Printed Library Materials, ANSI Z39.48-1984.

Library of Congress Cataloging-in-Publication Data

Wells, Ira, 1981-
Fighting words : polemics and social change in literary naturalism / Ira Wells.
pages cm. — (Studies in American literary realism and naturalism)
Includes bibliographical references and index.
ISBN 978-0-8173-1799-7 (trade cloth : alk. paper) — ISBN 978-0-8173-8677-1 (ebook)
1. American fiction—20th century—History and criticism. 2. Naturalism in literature. 3. Social problems in literature. I. Title.
PS374.N29W46 2013
810.9′12—dc23

2012042368

For Gillian

"Men were nothings, mere animalculæ, mere ephemerides that fluttered and fell and were forgotten between dawn and dusk."

—Frank Norris, *The Octopus*

"The highest possible stage in moral culture is when we recognize that we ought to control our own thoughts."

—Charles Darwin, *The Descent of Man*

Contents

Acknowledgments

Many of the arguments that follow will attempt, in one way or another, to extricate the American naturalists from the dense web of "historical determinism" that they themselves spun. Any merit granted to these arguments, however, could never be extricated from their own historical context. I consider myself exceptionally fortunate to have been able to write these chapters within an awesome community of scholars in the Department of English at the University of Toronto. I continue to extend my most sincere gratitude to Andrea Most, whose patience and intellectual generosity has been an extraordinary gift. I thank Paul Downes for his surgical close readings and exacting standards and Michael Cobb for his tireless enthusiasm and professional advice. I owe a special debt of gratitude to Jennifer Fleissner, whose penetrating comments will continue to influence my work far beyond these pages. Alan Ackerman read portions of this work at decisive moments and offered incisive criticism and encouragement. Neal Dolan has been a liberal source of intellectual nourishment, support, and sanity over the past few years. I'd like to thank Andrew DuBois for his conversation and friendship and for sharing some of his passion for the written (and spoken) word. Thanks to Julian Patrick for taking it easy on me in the squash court (and for much else). Nick Mount remains, to me and many others, a professional inspiration.

More people have contributed to these pages, and in more ways, than it is decent or possible to mention. Particular thanks must go to Sarah Wilson, Elizabeth Harvey, Jill Levenson, Brian Corman, Paul Stevens, and Alan Bewell. I'd like to thank my friends at Wilfrid Laurier University, especially Eleanor Ty, Jim Weldon, Maria DiCenzo, Markus Poetzsch, Tanis MacDonald, and Russell Kilbourn. And I'd like to thank my colleagues at the University of Toronto, Mississauga—especially Holger Schott Syme, Dan White, Jeannine DeLombard, David Taylor, and Richard Greene—for their continued generosity and support. I have benefited from the companionship and conversation of many friends, especially my fellow inmates at 503 Manning: Chris Trigg, Chris Hicklin, Donald Sells, and Tim Perry.

Generous funding from the Social Sciences and Humanities Research Council, the Ontario Graduate Scholarship program, and the Department of English at the University of Toronto has made this project possible. Material from chapter four appeared in *American Quarterly* (December 2010). Particular thanks must go to Dan Waterman at the University of Alabama Press. Finally, I must recognize the kindness of strangers: the patience and expertise of my two anonymous readers helped improve this effort in material ways.

On a more personal level, I would like to thank my father: the real origins of this book may be traced back to all those occasions when the *OED* was hauled out to settle a dinner-table dispute. Equal thanks must go to my mother for tolerating (and sometimes mercifully ending) those disputes. I'm grateful to John and Sally Hutchison for their constant encouragement and generosity. I dedicate this book to Gillian Wells. Thank you for the unending love and support you've given me in the writing of these chapters and for all those we'll continue to write together.

Fighting Words

Naturalism

A Polemical Introduction

Dubious Distinctions

"There are many strong arguments for keeping creative writers out of politics," exclaimed V. S. Pritchett in 1938, "and Mr. George Orwell is one of them" (qtd. in Atkins 51). Today, when literary critics are increasingly committed to demonstrating the political salience of their scholarship—to bolstering the ties between literary-critical praxis and an all encompassing "radical critique" of neoliberal Western democracy; to highlighting the political dimensions of race, class, and gender within an expanded conception of the literary "text"; to underscoring, in brief, the omnipresence of the political within the literary—Pritchett's interdiction can't help but have a faintly quixotic ring to it. Here was a literary critic who chose to defend his turf *precisely* on the grounds that it was apolitical. Aside from the fact that he was a creature of his New Critical times (and how times have changed), Pritchett could defend his stand for reasons that were both generic and specific. His assertion hinges on what he sees as the natural distinction between one genre (creative writing) and another (political commentary). Thinking about genres (as Pritchett well recognized) necessarily entails the discovery and policing of limits. "As soon as genre announces itself," Jacques Derrida writes, "one must respect a norm, one must not cross a line of demarcation, one must not risk impurity, anomaly, monstrosity" (57). For Pritchett, those norms and lines were perfectly clear. The creative writer must avoid a too intimate relation with politics, lest such miscegenation produce something "monstrous." Whether that word does justice to the overtly political writings of Pritchett's "creative" contemporaries—H. G. Wells, G. K. Chesterton, T. S. Eliot, George Bernard Shaw, and Ezra Pound, among others—remains an open question.

But the specific cause for Pritchett's generic injunction was George Orwell's

Homage to Catalonia, the work of nonfictional autobiographical reportage Orwell had composed about his experiences combating fascism in the Spanish Civil War. Of course, Orwell was hardly the only practitioner of "creative" writing who took an interest in the Spanish conflict. In 1938, the year Pritchett wrote the above-quoted review essay for the *New Statesman*—he titled it "The Spanish Tragedy"—the author of *An American Tragedy* toured Barcelona at the invitation of the Spanish Loyalist delegation in Paris. Theodore Dreiser lasted just a few days in Barcelona. The sixty-seven-year-old author wasn't about to take up arms (or risk being shot through the throat by a sniper) as Orwell had; he did, however, campaign for Franklin Delano Roosevelt and various titans of business to send food relief to Spain. While Dreiser's *Homage to Catalonia* went unwritten, he was Orwell's equal when it came to transgressing the partition separating the literary and the political. If George Orwell was one strong argument "for keeping creative writers out of politics," Theodore Dreiser was another.

This book is about the invention of the literary genre in America that was most conspicuously and energetically invested in overthrowing the genteel prohibition against the comingling of politics and literature. It's about authors whose creative writing was actualized by its persistent and meddlesome and unceasing engagement with "politics," most broadly conceived. That engagement came at a price. Their books were suppressed, censored, banned, burned, and vilified as immoral in the American mainstream. But the enduring significance of that political engagement, I argue, emerges most clearly when we step back to appreciate the highly polemical nature of naturalism in America. In the past century of literary criticism, the naturalists have been enlisted under any number of critical banners. But their first and last commitment—the literary commitment that underlies any of their more ephemeral political commitments—was to polemicism itself. Successive generations of critics have struggled to distill the essence of naturalism, to isolate the precise philosophical or aesthetic compound that separates it from literary romanticism and realism. That essence, I claim, resides most clearly in the polemical impulse that underlies naturalism and its texts. The present study takes up the significance of naturalism's polemicism within American cultural history.

Any extended discussion of literary genre must negotiate a few familiar hazards. Chief among these is the inherent instability of the concept of "genre" itself, as Jacques Derrida implies in the quotation above. Derrida's point is that genres necessarily include and are constituted by that which they formally resist. Naturalism is only "naturalism" insofar as it is steadfastly not "realism," "regionalism," "genteel," "aesthetic," "sentimental," "feminine," and so on; at the same time, as scholars have now established, American naturalism quite emphatically embraces each of these quantities. But while all genres are inherently unstable, all genres are not *equally* unstable. We may as well admit, along with June Howard, that "the fog rises more quickly here than with other forms" (94). Some underlying definitional uncertainty seems to have made the study of naturalism particularly treacherous.

This brings us to the second difficulty that inevitably arises in any attempt to consider "naturalism" as a coherent body of work. Specifically, we are forced to contend with not one genre here but two: the genre of naturalism—primary texts by Frank Norris, Theodore Dreiser, Stephen Crane, Jack London, Richard Wright, and the others—and the satellite genre of critical writing that hovers around and reports back from those planetoids of prose. That distinction may strike some as (pardon me) "academic," but it is crucial to recognize that the "primary texts" can no longer exist in any condition "prior to" their academic explication. This is only partially explained by the fact that the texts of the first genre are today selected, edited, introduced, and in some cases even published by combatants in the second. More crucially, we can no longer even pretend to apprehend a purely "literary," as opposed to a "critical," naturalism—a naturalism that can be understood to preexist critical explication. And perhaps we never could. Naturalism was always less a unified "school" or movement than a polemical construct: from H. L. Mencken's initial championing of Theodore Dreiser, the genre has continually been put to use in critical agendas of one stripe or another. As I'll detail in chapter 1, Mencken didn't admire Dreiser for his natural facility as a novelist—for his ability to render a character or turn a phrase. Far from it. But Mencken could grin and bear Dreiser's pachydermatous prose because Dreiser's work was a useful weapon to be deployed in what Mencken considered the most crucial culture war of his age, in which that ever-multiplying phalanx of superstitious, censorious, prudish, art-hating, self-righteous Puritans threatened to swamp the few remaining outposts of literacy and culture in America. Theodore Dreiser was the perfect comrade in such a contest. And while the terms of that contest would change dramatically over the course of the twentieth century, as consecutive generations of critics turned to the naturalists for support in their own cultural conflicts, the *fact* of the contest would remain. In chapter 2, I map the terrain of these shifting rhetorical battlegrounds, arguing that naturalism has always depended upon polemical reconstruction by its critics—critics who were themselves animated by the palpable polemicism of Dreiser, Norris, and the others.

But just what would it mean to consider the original naturalist authors as "polemicists"? I have just argued for the futility of recovering an "original" naturalism lingering beneath a century's worth of criticism. Nonetheless, understanding the polemical nature of naturalism does get us some distance closer to the spirit that animated this prose in the first place. Consider, to start, the argument Frank Norris outlines in his 1902 essay, "The Novel with a 'Purpose.'" After swiftly establishing the impossibility of the "purposeless" novel (for even amusement and titillation are "purposes" of a sort), Norris goes on to argue that the "highest form" of the novel is one that "proves something, draws conclusions from a whole congeries of forces, social tendencies, race impulses" (1196). Norris is quick to distinguish between the polemical agenda of the novel—the "something" to be proved—and the story itself; he recognizes the aesthetic failure of novels that make narrative entirely subservient to "purpose." The narrative thrust, the "page to page progress" of Harriet Beecher Stowe's *Uncle Tom's Cabin*, for instance, had to be "more absorbing to her than all the Negroes that were ever whipped or sold" (1198). The narrative architecture of a novel, in Norris's view, may start to seem like a Trojan horse for the author's political "purpose." Without it, the novel "degenerates into mere special pleading, and the novelist becomes a polemicist, a pamphleteer" (1197). Norris wants to be something more than a mere "polemicist." But deprived of his polemical "purpose," the novelist devolves into a purveyor of disposable amusements to be tossed out the rail-car window "together with sucked oranges and peanut shells." The novel, in its highest form, must constitute "a great force," "fearlessly proving that power is abused, that the strong grind the faces of the weak, that an evil tree is growing in the midst of the garden, that undoing follows hard upon unrighteousness, that the course of Empire is not yet finished, and that the races of men have yet to work out their destiny in those great and terrible movements that crush and grind and rend asunder the pillars of the houses of nations" (1200). Norris may rankle at the "polemicist" label, but the formal construction of his prose here confirms where his allegiances lie. It is a critical commonplace to disparage passages like this as "purple" or "overwrought," but I would suggest that those qualities are symptomatic of the essentially polemical nature of Norris's prose. The timbre of the diction, the catalogue form, the paratactic style, combined with the references to "race" and "empire"—even the inadvertent repetition of the word "grind," where Norris's style begins to slip away from him—all of this works to indicate the underlying "purpose" of Frank Norris's prose, a purpose that is quite detachable from the specific content of his argument here. That purpose is the purpose of polemic, an aggressive form of writing that seeks to establish its own supremacy and enflame the passions of the reader.

Norris's conviction here, that novels of the highest order are to be distinguished according to their capacity to "prove something"—their polemical purpose—combined with the conspicuous deployment of polemical prose in his essays and novels, constitutes the foundation of the literary aesthetic he shared with the other authors we refer to as "naturalist." The things they wanted to prove changed with the times; what did not change was their polemical impulse, along with their appeal to readers' passions. Norris was clear that this was a didactic mode: "The novel with a purpose *is*, one contends, a preaching novel" (1197). In its ideal form, this novel would perfectly imbricate its polemical purpose into its narrative action so as to convince readers without recourse of direct authorial intervention (in which case the "novelist" would be reduced to a "polemicist, a pamphleteer"). However, as Malcolm Cowley observed of the naturalists more than sixty years ago, "their books are full of little sermons or essays addressed to the reader; in fact they suggest a naturalistic system of ethics complete with vices and virtues" ("'Not Men'" 420). One thinks of the many small preacherly interjections and more fleshed-out Spencerian "sermons" delivered by the narrator of *Sister Carrie*, or of the extended essays Richard Wright incorporated into the trial of Bigger Thomas (one of which, issued by Bigger's Communist defense lawyer, occupies a staggering twenty-four pages of the 2005 Harper Perennial edition). These sermons and essays, then, do not so much represent the failure of the naturalist novel as they reveal the form at its most nakedly naturalistic. These are the moments when the underlying ideological machinery of the novel becomes manifest; when the polemical "purpose" of the novel shines through most conspicuously. Of course, as readers of these fictions, we are in no way obliged to accept the surface-level inscriptions of these purposes. No less than other fiction writers, the naturalists were often working at cross-purposes with their own conscious intentions. As I hope to show in chapters 3 through 5, which offer close interrogations of three polemical issues, careful analysis of naturalistic fictions often yields surprising and counterintuitive conclusions about the issues at hand. But recognizing the polemical intentions of these artists is a necessary starting point. The critic's work starts here.

Genteel Pursuits

Naturalism, to put the matter slightly differently, is literature that proceeds from a thesis. As Keith Newlin has recently observed, naturalism therefore shares at least some of its literary DNA with other species of propaganda. For Newlin, however, the "purpose" of the naturalistic novel is primarily indicative of its generic inheritance from melodrama. As Newlin sees it, the naturalists "employed the narrative device of melodrama as an efficacious means to convince readers of the truth of their theses and to elicit sympathy for their protagonists or even, as in the case of Hamlin Garlin, Upton Sinclair, and

London, to prompt readers to take action to redress social imbalance" ("Introduction" 6). Newlin argues that many of the supposed defects of the naturalist novel—the sensational storylines, the overreliance upon narrative coincidence, the authorial intrusions, the emotional overload—are in fact clear indications of the genre's debt to melodrama. In short, the naturalists used melodramatic techniques in order to further their various agendas.

While I find certain aspects of Newlin's approach compelling, particularly his underscoring of the naturalists' "theses" as constitutive of their method, this book will argue that naturalism's "agendas" are less indicative of the genre's debts to Victorian melodrama than they are of naturalism's immersion in a larger culture of polemic that would come to dominate American public discourse in the twentieth century. This is not to deny that polemic is, at bottom, a profoundly melodramatic rhetorical form. But the shift in emphasis brings with it two important advantages for the study of naturalism, which can be briefly stated. First, considering the naturalists as "polemicists" helps return them to the material culture and literary marketplace in which all of the major players were implicated. As Janice Radway observes, "virtually every writer in the pantheon now associated with naturalism apprenticed with essays in the columns of fast-multiplying newspapers and then went on to write for the monthlies" (215). The particular form of this literary "apprenticeship"—undertaken during the circulation battles between William Randolph Hearst and Joseph Pulitzer and therefore during the rise of both "yellow journalism" and what Matthew Arnold first called the "new journalism"—inevitably colored the naturalists' later novelistic efforts. The era of new journalism—"an innovative, commercialized, sensationalistic, and above all dramatic style of reportage," in the words of Karen Roggenkamp, was also the age in which "the ideal of entertainment" was embedded as a first principle of journalism (xii). The imperatives of the naturalistic novel (which must deliver a sensationalistic and marketable narrative without sacrificing Norris's prerequisite "purpose"—the foundational requirement to "prove something") are therefore the imperatives of journalism in the Gilded Age. Scholars have long noted how naturalism's plots are "ripped from the headlines," without much consideration of the ideological and rhetorical circulation between their fiction and reportage. The naturalists' fundamental polemicism, I argue, is the impulse underlying both their yellow journalism and purple prose. (I provide explicit treatment of the nonfiction polemics issued by my three principal authors in chapter 2.)

In addition to helping to bridge their journalistic and novelistic careers, the reappraisal of the naturalists as "polemicists" introduces a huge mass of new writing into the conversation about naturalism. Of the twenty-seven volumes Theodore Dreiser published over the course of his lifetime, just six were novels. He supported himself—particularly in later life, when he devoted himself unreservedly to his causes—with polemics like *Dreiser Looks at Russia* (1928), *Tragic America* (1931), and *America Is Worth Saving* (1941). Many traditional conceptions of naturalism continue to honor the strict separation between his creative and political writing (as Dreiser himself encouraged us to do) and therefore end up ignoring or marginalizing the majority of his literary production. But it bears repeating that the true significance of naturalism (for early champions like Mencken) resides in the genre's very tendency to collapse the genteel opposition between art and politics. Furthermore, recognizing the cross-pollination between Dreiser's "propaganda" (as he sometimes called it) and his fiction not only gives us a clearer perspective on the literary life he actually lived, it also goes some distance toward clarifying the novels for which he is remembered.

There is a second crucial advantage to foregrounding the naturalists' polemicism. In addition to situating the genre's principle authors more concretely in their own time, such a framework also emphasizes their points of connection with our own. Polemical speech, we are now in a position to recognize, has emerged as the lingua franca of public conversation in America. In their magazine features and newspaper columns, as much as in their novels, the naturalists addressed their audience (and their opponents) in cadences that a previous, more genteel generation of American author would have deemed coarse (if not downright churlish). Those cadences are more familiar to us; they are, for better or worse, the major and minor key in which so much of our public conversation is played. Just as pertinently, the specific polemical issues that gripped the naturalists are still very much with us. In short, the naturalists used their fiction to explore some of the most controversial political and cultural issues of modern American life. Previous conceptions of naturalism have devoted considerable attention to a limited range of naturalistic dissent: scholars have long noticed, for instance, how naturalism draws on the scientific theories of Darwin, Spencer, Sumner, Huxley, and others to challenge the prevailing Judeo-Christian cosmology. But the naturalists also charted the basic coordinates of a wide spectrum of issues. So, my third chapter considers Frank Norris's *The Octopus* in relation to emerging discourses of environmentalism and nascent anxieties over ecological despoliation. Chapter 4 considers the relationship between abortion and censorship in Theodore Dreiser's *An American Tragedy* and argues that the "tragedy" of Dreiser's text hinges upon our understanding how its protagonist, Clyde Griffiths, is himself a work of art. In chapter 5, I argue that *Native Son*'s chilling protagonist, Bigger Thomas, represents a distinctly modern figure for terror, and the novel elaborates a disturbing complimentarity between terrorism and lynching as the crime and punishment that exist outside the confines of the law. While this project considers each of these polemical debates within the cultural and intellectual climates in which they emerged, it is also an attempt to engage with these ideas in their own spirit—that is, to situate naturalistic novels, polemically, within the highly fraught contexts they helped to invent.

The constellation of texts and issues explored here is of course by no means exhaustive. Jack London is one author in particular who calls out for attention as a "polemical" naturalist. Ambrose Bierce is another. Both writers were ferocious combatants in their journalistic milieu and pursued similarly controversial topics in their fictions. In a similar vein, there are a whole host of issues that one could put into fruitful conversation with naturalism's major authors. Sexual ethics, poverty, financial speculation and the credit system, governmental corruption, women's suffrage, fascism, socialism (and the labor movement more generally), democracy, human rights—each of these topics should receive more detailed treatment in the context of American literary naturalism. I have chosen to pair these particular authors and issues because the combination of the two seemed particularly germane, counterintuitive, and, I hope, compelling. Many other permutations are nonetheless possible.

Any work of scholarship aiming to suggest a new approach to naturalism is entering a crowded field. Keith Newlin estimates that more than two dozen books on the subject have appeared since 1980 ("Introduction" 3). But while many of these individual studies work to clarify particular dimensions of the genre, the effect of the totality of this criticism is (to borrow June Howard's metaphor) akin to a rising fog. Competing schools of criticism—which have formed roughly along generational as well as theoretical fissures—don't so much inform as completely negate or ignore one another. A given naturalistic text can be read in two completely contrary and mutually defeating ways by two different critics—all the while corroborating the presuppositions that engendered those readings in the first place—to the point where the "primary texts" themselves come to resemble Rorschach blots for theoretical introspection. Toward the end of her review essay on three 2004 books on naturalism—John Dudley's *A Man's Game*, Jennifer Fleissner's *Women, Compulsion, Modernity*, and Eric Carl Link's *The Vast and Terrible Drama*—Lisa Long delivers the unsettling verdict that, taken in summa, the understanding of naturalism that emerges from these works is capacious or porous or downright vague enough to describe virtually any literary work published in an eighty-year span. Long's demonstration of how naturalism may be demographically overwhelmed inevitably opens up onto more existential questions concerning the legitimacy and longevity of this literary state. What most concerns Long as a literary historian, however, are the ways in which certain displacements or projections of the original naturalists' racist and sexist ideology are replicated by contemporary literary historiography. Long's critique returns, in the end, to the question of limits, to the borders of a genre that are under continual dispute: "In the end, naturalism turns back on itself, becomes the uncategorizable category, precisely because the taxonomic and evolutionary tendency of literary history is naturalist in and of itself—concerned in its own way with determining what nineteenth-century critic Hippolyte Taine theorized as the ubiquitous 'race, moment, and milieu' that have produced literary naturalism and other generic categories" (172). The problem, in short, is that we're all naturalists now. The impulse to hierarchicalize literary as well as biological "types"—to produce generic as well as genetic taxonomies—arises from a critical praxis that is "naturalist" all the way down. There is a moral judgment here, as well as an aesthetic one. The generic scaffolding that may appear to support even the most inclusive critical practice inevitably conceals and legitimizes prejudicial ordering practices and "identity-based segregation," in Long's words (173).

For a complex of reasons that are as much professional as ideological (insofar as there is any daylight visible between those terms), many literary scholars have been hesitant to meet head on the moral challenges posed by naturalism and its study.[1] All of the original naturalist writers were capable of taking stands and issuing proclamations that critics have been understandably reluctant to advertise; there is always the danger—is there not?—of a certain guilt by association. But if a polemical purpose is part of what makes naturalism "naturalism," to what extent is the genre compromised by the chauvinistic and occasionally sinister undertones of so much naturalist polemic? The fact remains that the naturalists found themselves on the morally questionable side of the ledger on almost all of the crucial political questions that shaped the course of twentieth-century life. Their attitudes toward race and imperialism are well known. Frank Norris was an unapologetic proponent of Anglo-Saxon superiority who hoped that "the course of Empire is not yet finished" (1200). (Similar assertions litter Norris's nonfiction prose.) In his 1904 essay "The Yellow Fever," Jack London warned that "the menace to the Western world lies, not in the [Japanese] little brown man, but in the four hundred millions of [Chinese] yellow men should the little brown man undertake their management" (346). London, along with Norris and occasionally Dreiser, were all fairly unambiguous proponents of eugenics and "racial hygiene," and the language of "fitness" and "defectiveness" or "superiority" and "inferiority" structures much of their thinking on race, criminality, nationalism, and social class.

The naturalists did little better in the clash of political ideologies in which they were forced to take sides. After a lifetime's worth of thinking and engagement with political matters, Theodore Dreiser joined the Communist Party in 1945. While Richard Wright recanted his youthful infatuation with communism in *The God that Failed*, the various seductions of totalitarianism, fascism, and nihilism never entirely vanished from his work.[2] The well-rehearsed rebuttal to all of this is that the naturalists were a product of their times. Chalk it up to "historical context." The original naturalists' thinking on eugenics, for instance, was undeniably bound up in emergent discourses of science and scientism, and their racial anxieties (particularly those of the Californians London and Norris) were part of a pervasive western American form of orientalist panic and xenophobia that was hardly unique to them (and one that still makes itself felt in contemporary debates on immigration and border control in some western states). To judge the naturalists by our own moral yardstick would be "ahistorical" and "universalizing." Why is it, then, that after their shared experience of the Spanish Civil War, George Orwell would go on to write the fiercely antitotalitarian parable *Animal Farm* (1945) while Theodore Dreiser would go on penning lines such as these: "The total of English unemployed in 1938 is probably about the same as the total 'non-Aryan' and concentration-camp population of 'Greater' Germany in the same year. Whether it is better to die quickly by torture or slowly by hunger—and unemployment in England means nothing less—is a question on which there will be differences of opinion" (*America* 129). These sentences, from *America Is Worth Saving*, attempt to enforce a kind of moral equivalence between Nazi Germany and England and insinuate that England was prosecuting a holocaust of its own—not on the nation's Jewry but on its poor. The moral distinction between Nazism and England under Churchill was for Dreiser a matter of "opinion." Churchill, Dreiser would go on to claim, "affords us no glimmer of what he has to offer humanity which is superior to what Hitler offers" (219). To his mind, World War II was a contest between "Hitlerdum and Hitlerdee" (222).[3]

The question, then, is whether these familiar eccentricities of naturalism are simply that—"eccentric" to the core concerns of the genre—or whether the reverse is true and naturalism's proclivities toward racism, sexism, and the abject worship of force are in fact central and constitutive, not only of the genre of naturalism but of the naturalistic construction of "genre" itself. And what, in either case, are the moral stakes of continued critical and professional investment in such a category? While entertaining John Dudley's assertion that the naturalist novel is "an aesthetic form that itself embodies the masculine force it depicts" (110), Lisa Long wonders aloud whether "naturalism is a genre worth keeping" (164). The implied answer to that question is impossible to miss. Naturalism is a genre that "hurts others" (164); it is "trenchantly racist" (171); its fictions naturalize the discriminatory practices "embedded" in genre (171). In sum, "we might also consider a new sort of study, one which will sometimes set aside generic and identity-based segregation and [African American] 'add-ons' in favor of a difference-sensitive yet more integrated critical practice" (173). It is no longer merely a question of the naturalists' eccentric politics; in the hands of their critics, naturalism has come to exert a deforming influence not only on generic categorization but also on the entire discipline of American literary historiography.

These are serious charges, and they deserve an answer. On what basis, if we are to discard the alibi of historical determinism, should we continue to enshrine in our literary genealogy authors who as a group were rather too susceptible to sexist, white supremacist, or totalitarian fantasies? Chapters 3 through 5 of this study represent an extended argument for continued engagement with the naturalistic novel, finding that the works themselves offer a more consistently nuanced, dialectical, and often counterintuitive rendering of the issues than is to be found in the headline-grabbing pronouncements of the authors themselves. The naturalists were certainly capable of rendering frivolous judgments on grave matters, but the naturalistic novel, more often than not, constitutes a deep, searching, textured representation of those subjects. Very frequently, as I suggested above, when exposed to even modest interpretive pressure, the novels reveal conclusions quite at odds with the explicit assertions of their creators. Just as crucially, the naturalists were helping to chart some of the fundamental coordinates of twentieth-century political and cultural life. The naturalist novel embodies and fictionalizes the debates—on environmentalism, abortion, and terrorism—that continue to shape the contours of American democratic experience. They show how we got here. Frank Norris thought that any nondisposable form of literature had better "prove something." This is our something. The naturalists must be studied because the world they invented in their "creative writing" is the political world we inhabit today.

A serious discussion of Long's deeper concern over naturalism—about how the hierarchicalizing and taxonimizing imperatives of naturalism come to structure the very category of "genre" in American literary history—is, perhaps, the subject of another book. The answer to such a question might begin by recalling the polemical "purpose" of the genre as it was originally constituted. H. L. Mencken cherished Dreiser and the other naturalists as "the beginnings of a revolt, or, at all events, of a protest" (*Prefaces* 282) against the pervasive cultural Puritanism of his age. Mencken's misreading of "Puritanism" represented the great strength, as well as a considerable weakness, of his cultural critique. Mencken's grasp of Puritanism (as we'll discover in the pages ahead) was unsatisfactory insofar as it has precious little to do with the American Puritans in any theological or historical sense. Its strength resided in the fact that it became, for Mencken, a highly portable concept.

"Puritanism" could describe, for the great critic of the booboisie, any atmosphere of overweening piousness, any culture too eagerly devoted to a "pursuit of bugaboos, a denunciation of heresies, a snouting up of immoralities" (*Prefaces* 213). Whether or not Long's critique—which finds generic criticism on naturalism insufficiently "difference sensitive," inadequately "inclusive," and insubstantial in its interrogations of the genre's inherent sexism—may constitute a denunciation of postmodern, multicultural institutional heresies is something on which Mencken would have had an opinion. Mencken's naturalism was useful precisely insofar as it traversed the genteel partition separating literature and politics: "literature," for Mencken's genteel opponents, was a realm too pure, too ideal, for the grit and grime of the political. Given this pedigree, it is perhaps not surprising that naturalism should remain a noxious quantity to those who would use literature as the gateway to a more ideal (inclusive, interracial, gender-neutral) realm. It is of course academic doctrine today that literary art is thoroughly politicized, but some "creative writers" are still unwelcome in (postmodern, multicultural) politics. The terms of the debate have undergone a revolution of sorts, but Pritchett's genteel assumption still echoes.

1
An Education

Coming by It Dishonestly

One day in the spring of 1927, a scrawny, nineteen-year-old employee of the American Optical Company slipped away during his lunch break to visit the Memphis Public Library. Richard Wright had never before attempted to check out a library book for himself—he had, in his capacity as "messenger boy," occasionally fetched reading material for others—but that was something he had determined to remedy. Given the racial strictures of the Jim Crow South, however, a measure of subterfuge would be required. First, there was the small matter of the library card itself, one of many public amenities that were prohibited to blacks. Wright appealed to a sympathetic coworker—an Irish "pope lover" who, Wright correctly intuited, felt no abiding solidarity with the Southern racial hierarchy—who lent Wright his card. Then there was still the problem posed by the librarian herself, the last line of defense separating the spoils of literacy and culture from a black boy who had tasted precious little of either. In *Black Boy (American Hunger)*, his autobiography, Wright describes how he attempted to appear as "unbookish" as possible while he loitered around the librarian's desk, waiting for her to finish up with the remaining white patrons. By the time the librarian got around to acknowledging his existence, Wright was too anxious to speak; instead, he silently passed her what he hoped would be a "foolproof" note: "*Dear Madam: Will you please let this nigger boy*—I used the word 'nigger' to make the librarian feel that I could not possibly be the author of the note—*have some books by H. L. Mencken?* I forged the white man's name" (235). The librarian, no push-over, accused Wright of wanting the books for his own purposes. But Wright's response—"Oh, no, ma'am. I can't read"—was evidently plausible enough to placate her concerns. When she returned with two volumes by Mencken, *Prejudices* and *A Book of Prefaces*, the librarian had no way of knowing that she had inadvertently jump-started the career of America's first best-selling black novelist. Wright never permitted himself (at least in print) the small vanity of imagining that this same librarian, reshelving a copy of *Uncle Tom's Children*, might somehow have connected that work with the illiterate "nigger boy" who had slipped her a note a decade earlier. But the trickster origins of Wright's literary self were perhaps appropriate for the kind of author Wright would go on to become and for the kind of stories he would go on to tell. No one handed Richard Wright the keys to American literary culture. He came by it dishonestly.

Wright's path to literary self-expression therefore began with a daring feat of literary self-concealment. Wright's somewhat belated professional journey commenced with his own act of audacious authorship, one that carefully masked the author's own blackness behind a blinding epithet. In essence, Wright's adult literary career began when he called himself a "nigger" in writing. Wright would explicitly return to the theme of authorship as self-concealment in his most important novel, when Bigger Thomas composes a ransom note for Mary Dalton, the white girl he has already murdered. The intense anxiety that pulses through Bigger in these moments—will his white oppressors accept the note as genuine or has he somehow bungled the note and implicated himself?—was Wright's own nervousness when he submitted his note to the Memphis librarian. Of course, Bigger employs a different epithet for fear and loathing when he signs his letter "Red," trying to direct suspicion away from himself and toward the Communist factions in the novel. At the same time, when he writes "*do what this letter say*," Bigger also signs his letter "black." As Barbara Johnson has argued, behind this grammatical slippage "lies the possibility—and the invisibility—of a whole vernacular literature" (67). In the end, Bigger's scheme is unsuccessful, at least in that he does not escape with Dalton's money. But Bigger's choice of signature does throw the investigators off the trail: Wright's protagonist temporarily hides behind his "redness," just as the author himself had successfully disguised his literary ambitions behind the fact of his own blackness.

Of course, the story of how Richard Wright tricked his way into literacy and authorship is also the story of his education into naturalism. Wright would become one of the most recognizable and most studied practitioners of the genre, and his involvement in the movement was initiated and guided by H. L. Mencken.[1] Wright's fascination with Mencken had been sparked by the editorial page of the Memphis *Commercial Appeal*, which had recently printed a savage rebuke of the Baltimore journalist; any white man who was execrated in the South, Wright had reasoned, was probably worth looking into.[2] Of the two volumes Wright found in his possession that evening, *A Book of Prefaces* had the greatest immediate impact. And of the four essays contained therein, two would seem particularly germane for the embryonic author. Mencken's chapter on Theodore Dreiser introduced Wright to one of his most important novelistic influences and to the naturalist author to whom his own works were most often compared. Equally significant is the last chapter of *A Book of Prefaces*, an eighty-five-page dissertation on "Puritanism as a Literary Force." Here, Wright found a capacious rubric for making sense of the profoundly repressive Southern Protestantism from which he had recently escaped, as well as a story that would function as the deep context for the rise of naturalism itself. This new literature would, Mencken promised, facilitate "the beginnings of a revolt, or, at all events, of a protest" (282). That was a message Wright was perfectly attuned to hear. But—to reveal my game plan more fully—the crucial discovery in *A Book of Prefaces* wasn't so much the message as the polemical tone or "mood" of Mencken. The polemicism was, for Wright, a revelation.

My hope is that by making naturalism strange again, by discovering it anew through Richard Wright's untutored reading of H. L. Mencken, we might make a fresh and corresponding discovery of our own, which is that polemicism has indeed always been an essential element of naturalism in America and the genre has continually refreshed and energized itself through the furious polemical activity of scholars who have taken up and extended the impulse toward revolt and protest that had animated the movement from the start. Norris, Dreiser, Mencken, Wright—these artists were terrifically energetic and engaged polemicists who drew promiscuously upon the scientific, political, and philosophical resources of their culture in order to change the world for the better and advance their own celebrity. But they were polemicists first.

By focusing on Mencken as the lynchpin of naturalism, I hope to suggest an alternative genealogy of the genre in America. Mencken did more than anyone in his time to consolidate and defend the genre and especially to define its polemical caste. He repeatedly singled Norris out for praise, he was Dreiser's friend and sometime editor, and he operated as Richard Wright's first important guide to the world of letters. Perhaps most importantly, he helped define the "Puritanism" that all of naturalism was supposed to be reacting against. But by invoking Mencken from the outset, I also hope in this project to reorient our expectations about "naturalism," to focus more on its polemical effects than its supposed doctrines. A brief look at two of Mencken's essays from *A Book of Prefaces*, "Theodore Dreiser" and "Puritanism as a Literary Force," will help shed some light on these arguments, in addition to providing a sense of just what Wright discovered on that first momentous evening, when he devoured his first portion of Mencken alongside his nightly can of pork and beans.

For all his considerable faults and foibles, Theodore Dreiser was, for Mencken, to be admired as a figure of monumental endurance. Mencken begins his discussion of Dreiser by celebrating what he considered the author's astonishing staying power. "There is something downright heroic in the way the man has held his narrow and perilous ground," Mencken (67) writes in 1917—a full quarter century prior to the publication of the last of Dreiser's original works. Furthermore, Mencken applauds Dreiser as an American original: he can find no precursor for the author of *Sister Carrie*, blithely dismissing the standard comparisons with Norris, Zola, Hardy, Balzac, and a host of others; even if Dreiser inherited much of his biological materialism from Huxley, he imported none of Huxley's elegant prose style into his own writings. Dreiser's literary paternity is therefore vague, and Mencken admires his singularity.

But here is where Mencken's unqualified praise comes to an end. Indeed, despite Dreiser's genuine importance in the "desert" of American letters, Mencken quickly concedes that the actual reading of a Theodore Dreiser novel is an often painful undertaking, largely due to the author's obsessive heaping up of apparently pointless detail—a habit that resulted in works of punishing length. Mencken draws our attention to page 702 of Dreiser's *The "Genius,"* a novel he finds particularly loathsome. There, after ninety-seven long chapters and (by Mencken's count) some 250,000 words, Dreiser lurches to a halt in order to provide the reader with an extended account of the apartment of one small character named Althea Jones. We learn, amid this interminable catalogue of detail that the house is "of conventional design"; that there is "a spacious areaway" between its two wings; that these wings are "of cream-coloured pressed brick"; that the entrance between them is "protected by a handsome wrought-iron door"; that to either side of this door is "an electric lamp support of handsome design"; that in each of these lamp supports there are "lovely cream-coloured globes, shedding a soft lustre"—and on and on to no obvious point or effect.

What riles Mencken is that these details appear to be mere window-dressing: they don't advance the narrative in any appreciable way; they don't open up onto any particular theme; they reveal nothing significant about the characters involved, all of which is for Mencken proof that *The "Genius"* "is flaccid, elephantine, doltish, coarse, dismal, flatulent, sophomoric, ignorant, unconvincing, wearisome"; the novel "is spoiled and made a mock of by a donkeyish solemnity of attack which leaves it, on the one hand, diffuse, spineless and shapeless, and on the other hand, a compendium of platitudes" (107, 123). To make matters worse, Dreiser's prose in *The "Genius"* is at an all-time low: "There are passages in it so clumsy," Mencken barks, "so inept, so irritating that they seem almost unbelievable; nothing worse is to be found in the newspapers. . . . The thing rambles, staggers, trips, heaves, pitches, struggles, totters, wavers, halts, turns aside, trembles on the edge of collapse" (87). All of this, and a great deal more of the same, is to be found in what is officially a "tribute" to Dreiser—a definitive summation of his career that was intended to concretize his position of preeminence in the American canon.

Fighting Words

In Richard Wright's Beale Street apartment, dawn had broken by the time he finally got around to finishing his can of beans. Dostoevsky, Maupassant, Baudelaire, Nietzsche, Flaubert—the nineteen-year-old could scarcely pronounce half the names he had discovered in Mencken's *A Book of Prefaces*; at first, he admits, he didn't even know whether these were supposed to be real people or figments of Mencken's imagination. But what immediately struck Wright, what stayed with him for days (and indeed, never left him), was the attitude of the book, what he repeatedly describes in *Black Boy (American Hunger)* as Mencken's "mood": "the mood of the book would not die," Wright reflects, "it lingered, coloring everything I saw, heard, did" (238). What impressed Wright, as his young eyes had first taken in the sulfurous sentences above, was not so much the content of Mencken's essays (which was largely a mystery to him, lacking any and all context for the debates and players involved) but their style—the spirit of elegant savagery that infused each stabbing sentence. Looking back, Wright recalls,

> I was jarred and shocked by the style, the clear, clean, sweeping sentences. Why did he write like that? And how did one write like that? I pictured the man as a raging demon, slashing with his pen, consumed with hate, denouncing everything American, extolling everything European or German, laughing at the weaknesses of people mocking God, authority. What was this? I stood up, trying to realize what reality lay behind the meaning of the words. . . . Yes, this man was fighting, fighting with words. He was using words as a weapon, using them as one would use a club. Could words be weapons? Well, yes, for here they were. Then, maybe, perhaps, I could use them as a weapon? No. It frightened me. I read on and what amazed me was not what he said, but how on earth anybody had the courage to say it. (237)

We tend to associate naturalism with any number of themes and ideas—including, but by no means limited to, philosophical determinism, environmental conditioning, heredity, degeneration, lower-class subject matter, aggressive masculinity, purple prose, industrialization, scientific objectivity, *le roman expérimental*, the city, statistics, force, imperialistic nostalgia, progressive liberalism, the displacement of the gold standard and the rise of paper money, the birth of the professions, and the dominance of finance capitalism. But Richard Wright, reading Mencken reading Dreiser, saw something else yet again. He saw a way of "fighting with words." He saw that words could function as "weapons," which is another way of saying that language could participate in the extratextual world outside of its own closed systems.

Reading Mencken, Wright had arrived at what was essentially a (slightly more coherent) rephrasing of Frank Norris's famous call for "life, not literature." More coherent, because Wright had intuitively grasped that the ideal was not life "instead of" or "separate from" literature but a literature that participated directly in the most crucial affairs of "life." In other words, Wright understood that the library door was a passageway into the realm of authentic experience and not just an escape route from it. The obvious objection, of course, is that the polemical "style" here belongs to Mencken and not "naturalism." But this is precisely my point: naturalism has always been a two-way street, depending upon polemical reconstruction by its critics, who were themselves feeding upon the palpable polemicism of Norris, Dreiser, and others.

If Mencken's interventions into various ongoing literary debates in the first chapters of his *A Book of Prefaces* must have struck Wright as hopelessly recondite, the argument outlined in the book's final chapter, an extended polemic against the forces of Puritanism in American life, would have hit close to home. Two years earlier, Wright had finally fled his grandparents' house in Jackson, Mississippi, where he had spent the previous five years living under the extremely repressive and "Puritanical" household regime invigilated by his maternal grandmother. Margaret Bolden Wilson, a former slave, had come to her Seventh Day Adventism belatedly, but what she lacked in experience she more than made up for in severity. As Wright's biographer Michel Fabre puts it, "she lived her faith and imposed it on her family with unbelievable force" (*Unfinished Quest* 33). Margaret Walker calls her a "religious fanatic" whose outlook was "Calvinistic to the point of asceticism" (33). For Wright's grandmother, religious piety appears to have hinged upon a categorical repudiation of secular art. Reading, music, movies—all were strictly forbidden in Margaret Wilson's household. Wright recalls how his illiterate grandmother would incinerate the books he brought home; once, upon discovering that

Richard had ingeniously fashioned a primitive radio out of household detritus, the grandmother promptly destroyed the devilish device (*Black Boy* 123). Unsurprisingly, Wright's early literary efforts were therefore met with solemn concern over the state of his soul. After he convinced the *Southern Register*, a black weekly in Jackson, to publish a short story (bearing the provocative title "The Voodoo of Hell's Half Acre") in 1924, Wright's grandmother pleaded with him to abandon "the Devil's work" (160). The problem wasn't so much the sensational subject matter of Wright's youthful output ("crudely atmospheric," [157] is how he would later describe it), but that the story was obviously not intended to exalt Jesus and celebrate and advertise his imminent return. In other words, the story was not "truthful," and Wilson wished that Wright would stop "making things up" and devote himself to loftier pursuits.

These and other experiences produced in Wright the ideal reader of Mencken's "Puritanism as a Literary Force," a livid, occasionally vicious attack on the joyless religiosity that had circumscribed his childhood. Later in life, Wright would come to appreciate how religion had constituted the sole cultural resource of profoundly impoverished Southern blacks like his grandmother.[3] At nineteen, however, Mencken's simple stabs against "the Puritan"—"his utter lack of aesthetic sense, his distrust of all romantic emotion, his unmatchable intolerance of opposition, his unbreakable belief in his own bleak and narrow views, his savage cruelty of attack, his lust for relentless and barbarous persecution" (201–2)—must have seemed tailor-made for Wright himself. Mencken is primarily interested in the ways that America's engrained moral prudishness had in his view strangled and deformed the nation's literary output, but he frames these concerns within a sweeping history of the relationship of art and morality in America since the Colonial period.

The story he tells is a simple one. The vast majority of Americans in Mencken's time were, he charges, incapable of judging a work of art (or a piece of legislation, law, or any other document of public life) by anything other than moral standards. "Puritanism," in Mencken's polemical corpus, refers less to any particular religious sect, dogma, or historical fact than it does to a generalizable impulse or "atmosphere" that pervades all aspects of culture and literature: "The whole atmosphere of our literature," Mencken says, quoting William James, "is 'mawkish and dishwatery.' Books are still judged among us, not by their form and organization as works of art, their accuracy and vividness as representations of life, their validity and perspicacity as interpretations of it, but by their conformity to the national prejudices, their accordance with set standards of niceness and propriety" (225). Ethics had supplanted aesthetics as the primary field for the consideration of literature. Authors who didn't denounce the transgressions of their characters, works that failed to reinscribe explicitly the decorums of genteel society, and words that were unfit for the consumption of virginal young women were excoriated and prohibited by the leaders of a peasant people who were (Mencken insisted) fundamentally suspicious and secretly contemptuous of art itself.[4]

Mencken's "Puritanism as a Literary Force" is most interested (and interesting) in elaborating the external, paternalistic expressions of Puritan force in the Progressive Era, but it begins with a more general account of the internal, psychological manifestations of Puritan bias. Mencken proceeds from the assumption that the Puritan divinity is a fundamentally jealous, Old Testament God who brooked no creative rivalry. In this view (adapted from Leon Kellner's 1915 study *American Literature*), Puritan "art" is limited to serene contemplation of God and his designs and eschews the trivial concerns of the material world—precisely the grounds upon which Margaret Wilson had objected to her grandson's first literary endeavors. Mencken believes that this conception of secular art as an affront to God was a Puritan import to America, which over time developed into a larger and more complex social apparatus for the containment of the Dionysian spirit. Americans were thus the unconscious inheritors of this original Puritan injunction against artistic creativity that had since evolved not only into a purely secular philistinism but also into the widespread national "prejudice against beauty as a form of debauchery and corruption" (225). The contemporary American "peasantry" had none of the formal education of their Puritan ancestors, but they had inherited all of their supposed sententiousness and hostility to aesthetic beauty and "stood as unmoved before its phenomena as a savage before a table of logarithms" (210). In the political realm, Andrew Jackson had been the first to wield effectively the prejudices of the philistine mob and glorify them as a quasi-official doctrine of the state; every election since, Mencken laments, has been "a pursuit of bugaboos, a denunciation of heresies, a snouting up of immoralities" (213).[5] The result was a style of politics in which complex social, legal, and economic problems (which included everything from temperance to abolitionism to foreign policy) were reduced to "ethical" issues; every other dimension of policy consideration was secondary to the moral one.

Among the most deplorable consequences of this profound tendency to Puritanism in American culture was the general strangulation of what Mencken considered "meaningful" literature, works that engaged with the serious moral, cultural, and political issues of their time. Artists who battled back against the prevailing Puritanism (Whitman and Poe are Mencken's examples; Melville might have done duty here as well) were neglected or despised by the cultural mainstream. Emerson's great celebrity, he felt, was the celebrity of the preacher, the theologian, and the metaphysician, rather than that of the artist:

he was a latter-day Jonathan Edwards. According to Mencken, nineteenth-century literature gradually divorced itself from the serious moral concerns of the nation, such that, "save one counts in such crude politico-puritan tracts as 'Uncle Tom's Cabin,' it is difficult to find a single contemporaneous work that interprets the culture of the time, or even accurately represents it" (214). Literature, as exemplary of all the arts in such an intellectual climate, was worth pursuing "merely as a hand-maiden to politics or religion," rather than as a viable pursuit in itself (215). America's preeminent authors habitually shrank from the large-scale debates and cultural clashes that constituted the highest calling of anything deserving the name of "literature." "Henry James," Mencken had written in *The Smart Set*, "would have been vastly improved as a novelist by a few whiffs from the Chicago stockyards," and in "the followers of Howells and James one finds little save an empty imitation of their emptiness" (218).

More urgently, meaningful literature (that is, literature that engages with the immediate social and political concerns of the times) was not only deformed by the Puritanism within, it was also violently suppressed by state-sponsored Puritanism entrenched "in a body of law that is unmatched in any other country of Christendom" (226). Beginning with the passage of the Comstock Postal Act of 1873, and continuing with the Mann Act of 1910 and the Webb Act of 1913, the federal government had inaugurated a new and more ferocious form of censorship and vice crusading. This shift from an inward-looking, deeply personal Puritanism to an outward-looking, institutionalized Puritanism (which Mencken attributes to the economic affluence that came with the industrial revolution) brought with it a new kind of professional: "the moral expert, the professional sinhound, the virtuoso of virtue" (243). With new, ambiguously phrased legislation on the books to ensure convictions, professional vice crusaders like Anthony Comstock had the power to orchestrate raids, seize "unwholesome" materials, ban literature from the mails, burn or otherwise destroy "obscene" or "immoral" works, and bring artists and publishers to economic ruin through frequent and aggressive prosecutions. Thus, the suppression of vice moved from a religious to a secular practice. Anyone who dared to oppose Comstock and his ilk was slandered as standing "for" obscenity, vice, corruption, and the despoilment of little girls. Mencken conveys his personal frustration at having been drawn into and made partially complicit in this state of affairs: in his capacity as editor of the *American Mercury*, Mencken admits regularly to rejecting serious and otherwise admirable works of literature for no better reason than the imminent possibility that "some roving Methodist preacher, self-commissioned to keep watch on letters, will read indecency in it" (277).

In the end, even the mighty critic of the booboisie was forced into line as yet another pillar of the very moral Puritanism that had so execrably deformed the culture he loved.

Mencken's long campaign against Puritanism ends with a final lament, followed by one small consolation. The lament is for what Mencken deems the pathetic vacuity of the brightest artistic lights of the age: "The action of all the novels of the Howells school goes on within four walls of painted canvas; they begin to shock once they describe an attack of asthma or a steak burning below stairs; they never penetrate beneath the flow of social concealments and urbanities to the passions that actually move men and women to their acts, and the great forces that circumscribe and condition personality" (276). The sole consolation, which must pass as a conclusion for the Mencken's *A Book of Prefaces* as a whole, is that "time is a great legalizer, even in the field of morals. We have yet no delivery, but we have at least the beginnings of a revolt, or, at all events, of a protest" (282).

Polemic or *Polemos*?

Mencken professed not to care for debates about literary labels, which he considered exercises in academic pedantry. He certainly knew of the arguments that were swirling over the generic status of Theodore Dreiser, for instance. Much critical ink had already been spilled on the subject: was Dreiser a realist, a naturalist, or was he some kind of atavistic holdover from the romantic period? "The debate is all sound and fury," Mencken decreed, "signifying nothing" (146). Despite his attempts to remain aloft of these vulgar arguments, Mencken's assumptions do reveal a noticeable generic predisposition. In the concluding section to his *A Book of Prefaces*, Mencken gestures (albeit in negative terms) toward both a style and a set of concerns appropriate for contemporary literature. The proper subject of serious literature, literature that would do something more than merely replicate or repackage the Puritanism of the past, lies in penetrating "the flow of social concealments and urbanities," which have had the dual role of masking the elemental passions that animate human affairs, and radically circumscribing the function of literature within American culture. (The less Puritanical societies of Western Europe, and particularly Germany, provide Mencken with a model vis-à-vis the correct relation of literature and social concerns.) The proper task of literature is to infiltrate these concealments, to puncture the "painted canvas" with which Puritan culture has papered over the authentic nature of experience. In style, this new aesthetic will necessarily constitute "a revolt" or "a protest." In order to withstand the constant incursions of a larger Puritan culture, in order to be heard above the pious din, this literature will have to express itself in the robust, muscular, defiant tones that Mencken has modeled for us over the previous three hundred pages. And as we have seen, it was this style—the "shocking" verbiage, the "raging," "slashing" stabs of prose, the "clear, clean, sweeping sentences"—that had made such an impact on the young Richard Wright. Ironically, Mencken's own polemical commitments (his insistence on the superficiality of labels) prevented him from actually labeling the literature that would be constituted by that polemicism. Nonetheless, what Mencken was championing, what he was calling for, was naturalist literature, and Richard Wright heard that call.

But it was not simply the call of the wild, as some of America's genteel critics evidently thought. A great many morally sensitive critics were on guard against the kind of literature Dreiser represented—and, Mencken felt, unfairly slandered him for representing "animal urges." But no critic was more vocal in his concerns, more spirited and persistent in his attacks, than Stuart P. Sherman, a professor of English at the University of Illinois. Mencken may have shied away from calling Dreiser's fiction what it was, but Sherman had no such compunction; in "The Naturalism of Mr. Dreiser," a 1915 essay for the *Nation*, he offered a sharp rebuke to the mind behind *The "Genius."* Concerned that a great change has recently taken place, not only in "the spirit of the age" but "in the literature that reflects it" (4), Sherman begins by identifying the signature rhetorical gesture with which this new school justifies itself: if the discerning critic dares to question the unbearably "grim," "shabby," "commonplace" world represented in these fictions, he is accused of lacking the necessary fortitude to "confront reality." "Perhaps you had better read the chromatic fairy-tales with the children," Sherman writes, ventriloquizing his opponents; "men of sterner stuff exclaim . . . 'Thank God for a Realist!'" (5).

In point of fact, Sherman contends, the "courage" to examine reality is "no more a characteristic of Theodore Dreiser than it is of John Bunyan" (5). Authors of the Dreiser school may claim that their writing forwards no particular ideology or "philosophy of life"; they may claim that they seek merely to represent life as it "really is." But Sherman encourages us to dismiss this empty claim. An artist may state that his work is "photographic," but a process of selection, composition, and shaping has inevitably organized and ordered that representation, regardless of what the artist may think, and it is therefore the responsibility of the critic to interrogate the naturalistic "philosophy" that underlies this supposedly neutral mimetic mode. And Dreiser's philosophy—the "naturalist" philosophy—is found by Sherman to be both artistically and morally lacking.

The main problem is that Dreiser has grossly reduced his characters to the level of "jungle beasts." "By thus eliminating distinctively human motives and making animal instincts the supreme factors in human life," Sherman laments, "Mr. Dreiser reduces the problem of the novelist to the lowest possible terms" (9). Far from dispassionately representing life as it actually is, Dreiser has become a propagandist for a faulty theory of life in which human beings are reduced to chemical compounds and for a faulty theory of art that refuses to situate problems within their proper moral contexts. Sherman appears quite scandalized that, in Dreiser's work, "the obligations of parenthood, marriage, chivalry, and citizenship have been quite withdrawn" (9). Where an artist of the first rank (Anthony Trollope is one of Sherman's examples) would consider the individual in his full moral context, Dreiser habitually falls back upon his jungle clichés (9). Sherman can't say for certain why Dreiser is so singularly ill-equipped to write about suitably "educated" or "brought up" people—characters who have discerned some proper sense of the "conduct of life"—although he surmises that it might have something to do with the fact that the author himself hails from Indiana (9, 10). Sounding a sole note of harmony with Mencken, Sherman is quite put off by the stunning length of the typical Dreiser novel, which he likens to "a huge club-sandwich composed of slices of business alternating with erotic episodes" (11). Sherman signs off by reiterating his profound misgivings over Dreiser's "theory of animal behaviour" and dismisses naturalism itself as an "artistic blunder."

When Richard Wright asks of Mencken, "why did he write like that?" one acceptable response is "Stuart P. Sherman." Indeed, Sherman's repudiation of Dreiser had at least partially occasioned Mencken's response in *A Book of Prefaces*. For Mencken, Sherman, and the moral Pecksniffery he peddles, is precisely the kind of Puritanism that Dreiser was to be applauded for resisting. More pointedly, however, Mencken accuses Sherman of simply misreading Dreiser. The thesis of Dreiser's work isn't that men are "jungle beasts"—to the contrary, the profound pathos invoked by novels like *Sister Carrie* and *Jennie Gerhardt* stems from the intensity of the conflict between humanity and our animal nature, the fact that we must constantly try for but cannot perfectly achieve transcendence. Mencken's *A Book of Prefaces* was therefore intended as a firm corrective against Sherman's misreading.

The young Richard Wright was privy to none of the context when he first cracked open *A Book of Prefaces* that spring evening, but what he was getting was one side of a dialectic that was already in motion. In his first serious literary encounter, Wright was already well inside the blast radius of larger debates over naturalism. Indeed—and to reiterate my theme—"naturalism" was instantiated through polemical contests, of which the Mencken–Sherman feud provides an early and representative example. Sherman (as Mencken never allowed one to forget) was a professor of English, but the dispute over naturalism was not purely "academic" at this stage; it unfolded in the pages of the *Nation* and the *American Mercury* and other mainstream periodicals; it was spirited and vicious and frequently quite personal—"degraded swine" was Mencken's preferred epithet for Sherman (*Letters* 211). (Jonathan Crewe points out that many academics believe that "polemic belongs to the sphere of public journalism" [135], and that is precisely where the original debates over naturalism unfolded. Some of that polemical spirit, however, has found its way back into "academic" discussions.) In any event, the point is not that history has spoken and Mencken was right and Sherman was wrong but that both profited from this mutually combative relationship, while establishing the pattern of polemicism and showcasing the antinomian spirit that would energize debates about naturalism over the next century. Naturalism, here, was nothing more than an ignorant and immoral "artistic blunder," or was nothing less than a force that would liberate American letters from a repressive tyranny that had gripped the nation from its birth. The terms of the debate would change, and I will demonstrate some of the later configurations. But the fact of the debate, along with its intensity, would remain, and my argument is that the genre feeds off of and produces and in some sense *is* that polemicism.

Subsequent scholars of Puritanism in America, from Perry Miller to Sacvan Bercovitch, would of course do much to challenge and point out the nuances of the deceptively straightforward account of the historical trajectory of Puritanism offered by Mencken.[6] And it perhaps goes without saying that Mencken's essay relies less on anything that could be called original scholarship than it does on reportage, on the polemical redeployment of existing material; he leans heavily on the work of German scholars, such as Leon Kellner, who present a version of America's past that conforms to Mencken's prejudices. Mencken hated Puritanism for its "gentility," but, as Malcolm Cowley noted more than fifty years ago, there was nothing particularly "genteel" about Puritanism; the Puritans "believed in the real existence of evil, which they denounced in terms that would have shocked William Dean Howells and the polite readers of *Century Magazine*" ("Naturalism" 300). Mencken's conception of these cultural movements is important, therefore, not for the historical light it sheds upon the forces of Puritanism in American life but because Mencken's conception of the nation's Puritan past constitutes the imaginative historical background for the emergence of literary naturalism.[7] For Mencken, the work of Theodore Dreiser is significant precisely insofar as it resists the manifestations of Puritan force that have determined the contours of American cultural life throughout history. To be sure, Mencken despised Puritanism for reasons that had little to do with "naturalism" per se. Artistic suppression and censorship were serious concerns indeed: Anthony Comstock, top vice hunter at the New York Society for the Suppression of Vice, famously boasted of the fifteen tons of books (and four million pictures) that he had immolated and of the fifteen suicides he had caused.[8] Careers, reputations, and lives were ruined. But Puritanism also represented the antithesis of the *Gemütlichkeit*, which, Mencken was convinced, was the foundation of civilized life (Hobson 190). In Mencken's thought, Puritanism is associated with Anglo-Saxonism and England in general, a locus of increasing animus for the Germanophile during the First World War, and with Woodrow Wilson, one of his most reviled political figures.

"Puritanism" was therefore a capacious target and an appealing one for Mencken for reasons that had more to do with the urgent realities of the publishing industry—and with the rising nativism and anti-German sentiment in wartime America—than it did with any doctrinal or ideological legacy bequeathed by the nation's Puritan ancestry. Mencken's claim that "morality" had achieved an unimpeachable primacy in the fields of politics and culture (and that this morality most frequently assumed a denunciatory form—the "pursuit of bugaboos," the "snouting up of immoralities," and so on) may perhaps be linked to a style of political language derived from Puritan jeremiads. But that was not a link that he cared to forge, and besides, Mencken was obviously less interested in close examination of the sermons of the Puritan calendar than he was in his own tub-thumping against the moralists and the professoriate, which he considered a wing of Puritan culture. Preachers require devils, and Mencken had indeed become a preacher of secular *Kultur*. More, in his fight against Puritanism, Mencken had ironically fashioned himself in the dual role of crusader and prophet, leading a younger generation of critics "in battle against false gods and false values," as he himself put it (Hobson 191). Still, Mencken's understanding of the rise of Puritanism in America offered a compelling narrative, one that seemed to make sense of a diversity of cultural phenomena (censorship, vice crusading, Germanophobia, moralistic political rhetoric, and so on), and more crucially constituted a powerful rubric under which to condemn writers who may have seemed unshakably ensconced in the literary establishment. In making a case for his favorites (Dreiser and others) Mencken also devoted himself to undermining the reputations of authors like Henry James and William Dean Howells—two writers who (along with Sarah Orne Jewett and other local color authors) would constitute the negative touchstones for American naturalism over the next century, in no small measure due to their associations with this nebulous cultural quantity. "Puritanism"—Mencken's Puritanism—provided the context for naturalism's first revolt.

The genre that Mencken intractably refused to call naturalism is the product of this polemical history, rooted in a powerful misreading of America's Puritan past, implicated in a chauvinistic, aristocratic Gemanophilia that led to not infrequent outbursts of anti-Semitism from virtually all of its major authors, and consolidated in a century of critical contrarianism and debate carried out in tones bordering on the rancorous.[9] Following Mencken's original insurrectionary structure—his polemical "use" of the genre—critics have been apt to frame naturalism as the national literature of disobedience. What is less than clear, surveying the diverse fruits of this project, is what, in the end, naturalism is supposed to be rebelling against. The place of "Puritanism" in Mencken's reading has been filled with any number of authorities and cultural regimes. In a century of criticism, naturalism has constituted an assault on "machine industrialism" (Parrington), romantic imagination (Trilling), literary realism (Pizer), sentimentality (Lehan), regionalism and local color fiction (Campbell), feminization (Douglas, Seltzer), capitalism (Michaels), European aestheticism (Dudley), and patriarchal hegemony (Fleissner). Rarely in the annals of American literature have so few stories and novels been burdened with so much insurrectionary work. Naturalism emerges as the literary rebel with every cause.

The "core concerns" of naturalism are, at this advanced stage in the literary-historical cartography of American culture, a constellation of familiar clichés. The naturalists, it is still argued, are to be distinguished by their commitment to Darwinian (or Spencerian or Sumnerian or Huxleyite) evolutionary thinking and by the corresponding challenge to dominant Judeo-Christian cosmologies that is assumed to have flowed from those commitments. Or, they are to be distinguished by their (proto)sociological, (proto)social-Darwinian fixation on social class as a function of environmental conditioning.[10] Or, they are set apart by their miscellaneous fascinations with urbanity, industrialization, racial degeneration. They were pessimistic determinists whose fictions analogized and advocated the necessity of, say, centralized government; or, they dramatized the conflict between our determined natures and our spiritual strivings, and in so doing they emphatically affirmed a liberal-humanistic perspective. The naturalists could stand (or could be made to stand) for or against just about anything. Part of the confusion no doubt stems from the fact that most of the authors themselves died young (Crane at twenty-eight; Norris at thirty-two; London at forty; Wright at fifty-two) and didn't live long enough to write the reflective, synthesizing work that sometimes comes with age and perspective. As a rule, the naturalists didn't survive to write anything that could be construed as their "last words" on the subject, and when they did, as in the case of Dreiser, matters only seemed to get muddier with the passage of years.[11] "Last words" would not have "solved" naturalism, but at least some of what Mencken called the "sound and fury" surrounding naturalism came from the fact that it was (self-consciously and performatively) a young man's game.

If its multiplying contradictions and seemingly infinite internal fissures mean that naturalism must now be understood in the context of what Sacvan Bercovitch calls "authorities of difference"—a critical culture of dissensus rather than consensus—the story of naturalism inevitably reflects the story of the development of "English" as a discipline and of American studies as a province of knowledge within it ("Introduction" 2). Naturalism came into being at around the same time as the institutionalization of "English" as a discipline in American universities, and it is tempting to view the definitional disputes surrounding naturalism as a kind of perpetual, freakish sideshow to the larger circus. But the image of naturalism as somehow "beside" or "marginal" to disciplinary centers, while common enough, is not entirely accurate. A near-obligatory trope of critical writing on naturalism (as I'll discuss in greater depth below) is the tendency to self-marginalize, to justify one's interest in the genre with the claim that it is neglected or undervalued by institutional centers. To a certain extent, my project necessarily echoes these claims for naturalism's exceptionalism, although for the opposite reason: rather than unfolding at the periphery, the definitional debates about naturalism have taken place in the very center of larger institutional attempts at definition (which will become evident at the intersection of, say, naturalism and New Historicism). Naturalism is less a circus sideshow than a barometer of the climate at the very center of the critical ecosystem. Disputes about the nature of naturalism are inevitably connected with disputes about the nature of "English" as a practice and as an institution, and the polemical intensity of these debates issues from the proximity of the two and not (as it is surreptitiously argued) from the fact that naturalism has been given the short end of the stick.

The naturalists were polemicists first. This is not to say that Norris, Dreiser, and Wright, the authors under consideration here, were not in fact deeply interested in biological or environmental conditioning or in the city as a new kind of imaginative space. But these interests were a result of polemical priorities that always superseded and produced them. These writers were not united by a singular or consistent aesthetic approach, philosophy, or politics; they were, however, united by a polemical spirit (or "mood" as Wright called it) that infused their writing and caused them to take polemical positions on aesthetic, philosophical, and political matters. To say that the naturalists were interested in the symptoms of industrialism and urbanization and so on is tantamount to the claim that they responded to different aspects of the world around them. Their crucial difference is the *way* they responded to that world, the highly antagonistic, contrarian, eristic tones in which they constructed their literary identities in relation to Gilded Age American society.

Doubtless, the original naturalists said some strange things and tended toward outright belligerence in their voice. But why should we think of them as "polemicists," and why is such a category useful in organizing our thinking about naturalism? To answer this, we need to begin with the word itself. Our word "polemic," defined by the *Oxford English Dictionary* as "aggressive controversy," derives from the Greek *polemos, polemikos* (war, warlike). Polemicism is writing that is animated by a warlike spirit; it is understandable, then, that the polemic would operate as the distinctive literary mode for a group of authors who felt that life itself was one long war. Frank Norris was apt to describe almost any "manly" pursuit (the only pursuit of which he would approve) as war. Mining, agriculture, writing—even love and courtship, properly conducted—were "war." Theodore Dreiser took the metaphor further: in the "chemic" theories he advanced in his essays and fiction, existence itself, extending all the way down to the molecular level, is figured as a kind of war. And Wright, as we've seen, was most interesting in "fighting with words."

The naturalist obsession with war was an effect with multiple causes. Certainly, their bellicosity emerged from a pervasive cultural militarism that had also produced Teddy Roosevelt's Roughriders and was at least partially responding to profound anxieties about new and enervating psychic disorders that threatened heteronormative constructions of masculinity.[12] But perhaps the simplest explanation of the naturalists' romanticization of the martial ideal is the generational one. The original naturalists could idealize war because they belonged to a generation that had never experienced it.[13] Norris, Dreiser, London, and Crane were born in the 1870s, came to artistic maturity around the turn-of-the-century, and (excepting Dreiser) died well before the eruption of hostilities on the Continent. Theirs was a generation sandwiched between the monumental atrocities of the Civil War and the Great War, and their relatively chauvinistic, gung-ho attitudes about war were produced or made possible by the interregnum of peace.[14]

For some scholars, of course, the polemic is a degraded genre (if it is a "genre") fit for journalists and hacks and those seeking to bring undeserved attention to themselves.[15] Many have been skeptical of polemic for reasons that have little to do with its "warlike" associations. Polemicism is easily dismissed as crankiness in older critics and self-serving arrogance in younger ones. Then there's the general perception that polemicism tends to warp critical thinking—that the negative passions that fuel the production of polemic must be inimical to the dispassionate work of the critic. But there are also more serious ethical considerations to be raised about "polemicism" as a habitual way of responding to literature or indeed the world. In a 1984 interview with Paul Rabinow, Michel Foucault put it plainly but forcefully:

> I don't like to get involved in polemics. . . . The polemicist proceeds encased in privileges that he possesses in advance and will never agree to question. On principle, he possesses rights authorizing him to wage war and making that struggle a just undertaking; the person he confronts is not a partner in the search for truth but an adversary, an enemy who is wrong, who is harmful, and whose very existence constitutes a threat. For him, then, the game consists not of recognizing the person as a subject having a right to speak but of abolishing him, as interlocutor, from any possible dialogue. (381–82)

Foucault seems to suggest that there is something profoundly unethical about the characteristic stance of a Mencken or a Norris. He hints at a disturbing adjacency between rhetorical violence and actual, obliterating warfare: he implies, in other words, that polemic is ultimately inseparable from *polemos*. In his essay, "Can Polemic Be Ethical?," Jonathan Crewe draws our attention to the affinities between polemic and entertainment. Polemicists personify themselves and their adversaries in the form of identifiable characters and, in Crewe's words, "recast polemic as robust comedy" (141). But Foucault would perhaps have us think twice about the entertainment value of passages such as the following: "There must be complete surrender to the law of natural selection—that invariable natural law which ordains that the fit shall survive and the unfit shall perish. All growth must occur at the top. The strong must grow stronger, and that they may do so, they must waste no strength in the vain task of trying to lift up the weak." Mencken (Nietzsche 68) published those sentences in his 1908 excursus on Nietzsche, but they could just as easily have been written by his close friend Theodore Dreiser, who expressed similar sentiments throughout his career. Indeed, a disturbing amount of Dreiser's polemic—whether it was aimed against religion (a primary source of charity), against America's participation in the First and Second World War (in which WASPs and Anglophiles had buffaloed the United States into fighting against the Germans), against the prohibition on birth control (which led to the preventable birth of countless white trash babies), or against capitalism (whose internal contradictions led to unhealthy perversions of the natural order)—relates back to his Teutonic conviction in the superiority of the Germanic peoples. This is not to suggest that the Teutonism that bonded Dreiser and Mencken was a sole source of naturalistic polemic; the examples of Norris and Wright prove that the polemicism could exist quite independently of aggressive Germanophilia. But it is to say that these polemics, entertaining as some of them were and are, must also be considered in the context of the looming *polemos*. Mencken penned a scrupulously impartial review of Hilter's *Mein Kampf* for the *American Mercury* in 1933, remarking that the general thrust of German expansionism was "sensible enough."[16] And Dreiser's career ended with a furious outburst of polemicism that was not so much "pro" the German side as it was "anti" the Allied one.

One reason why "polemicism" is an attractive concept for thinking about the naturalists is that polemicism itself is a critical orientation or impulse rather than a totalizing "theory" of naturalism. (We'll take a look at some of those theories in the following pages, and find that they, too, reflect shockingly polemical attitudes.) While not wanting to posit polemicism itself as yet another "theory" of naturalism, I will briefly describe a few of the key characteristics of polemicism as it relates to the authors under consideration here. Most conspicuously, as Richard Wright discovered in Mencken, polemic involves using prose as a weapon: the polemicist seeks to establish the superiority of his or her own position by exposing the failures of all others. When Henry James decided to formalize his thoughts on the construction of creative writing, he was content to build his famous house of fiction. That project did not, as far as he was concerned, involve bulldozing every other preexisting house of fiction in the neighborhood. Frank Norris, by contrast, wanted to bulldoze. However, that demolition was not undertaken merely for the sake of watching something burn but for the creation of a new edifice. Polemicism involves rhetorical violence, but it is not autotelic or purely nihilistic violence. Foucault was concerned that there was something inherently suspect about a rhetorical posture that relied upon violence to undo its opponents. But as Crewe argues, polemic also has a productive side: "without feminist, queer, or postcolonial polemics, some of it ad hominem, there would be no academic fields corresponding to those designations" (138). "Without polemic directed at the New Critics," Crewe goes on, "there would be no institutionalized post-structuralism in the U.S. academy." Contra Foucault, Crewe argues that in some cases polemic is not only morally justifiable but necessary. Once again, Mencken provides a case in point: Mencken's moral failings were more conspicuous in the polemics he failed to write than in those he actually did. The very fairness with which the polemicist dealt with *Mein Kampf* seemed to betray some underlying turpitude.

Polemicism, Louis Menand suspects, "is likely to be the product of what Freud called the narcissism of small differences" ("Kael's Attack" 173). The reason Norris attacked Howells with such vehemence was because of their ultimate proximity, not their dissimilarity. Above all though, polemicism is a *passionate* form of writing, one that contrasts strikingly with how the naturalists liked to frame their literary pursuits. These authors were apt to present their arguments and their fictions cloaked in a "scientific" guise: the overt goal of naturalism, they argued repeatedly, was to tell the "truth." Norris's model for "truthful" writing was Emile Zola, who, in *Le roman experimental*, had advocated a literary mode that was akin to the scientific naturalism of Hippolyte Taine, Claude Bernard, and Prosper Lucas.[17] The naturalist author, for Zola, was less an active agent in the creation of fiction than an impartial observer of his characters: he proceeds according to the requirements of scientific objectivity, investigating how his or her characters respond to the deterministic pressures of environment and heredity—the combined influences of evolution, atavism, degeneration, and so on. The naturalists espoused scientific objectivity and empiricism and were suspicious and hostile toward the "emotions" (which, in Norris's mind, were one reason why women were constitutionally unfit for novel writing.) But the polemical form of their writing ultimately overwhelmed their supposedly dispassionate substance. The naturalists' polemicism consistently privileges pathos over logos—even if logos is the explicit ideal. "Give us stories now," was the kind of thing Norris would write in his essays, "give us men, strong, brutal men, with red-hot blood in 'em, with unleashed passions rampant in 'em, blood and bones and viscera in 'em" (*Novels and Essays* 1113). Bigger's fear, Carrie's yearning, Clyde's frustration, Hurstwood and McTeague's pathetic descents—the power of the naturalist novel resides in the emotional amplitude of these characters and their plights. And for the authors themselves, all writing was fired by a passionate polemicism activated by their own profound feelings of injustice, discrimination, and chauvinism.

While the "realist" authors generally sought to engage the cerebellums of their readership, the naturalists (consciously or not) pitched their fictions toward the lower organs. Sure, they often espoused science and dispassionate inquiry, but the irrepressible passions of their own work consistently overwhelmed that empiricist message. And here, as always, Mencken—whose own "mood" had so enraptured the young Richard Wright—is exemplary. Mencken liked to espouse a hard, unsentimental, dispassionate view of American culture; yet it is hard to imagine a more passionately dispassionate writer.

Mencken's polemical prose is designed to provoke emotional responses from his readers. If the later naturalists occasionally differed from the content of Mencken's pronouncements, they almost always attended carefully to his method.

The Art of War

What Richard Wright discovered that spring night in *A Book of Prefaces* would change the course of his life. Having succeeded once, he found it increasingly easy to deceive that Memphis librarian. "I forged more notes," he recalls, "and my trips to the library became frequent" (*Black Boy* 238). As had been the case with his encounter with Mencken's *Prefaces*, the specific details of the books he checked out proved less influential than the overall mood they engendered. As Wright put it, the "plots and stories in the novels did not interest me so much as the point of view they revealed . . . all my life had shaped me for the realism, the naturalism of the modern novel" (239). The course of reading suggested by Mencken's *Prefaces* had inflamed an itch that Wright didn't know he had, one that he would spend the rest of his life trying to scratch. But he distinctly recalls that whatever highs had come with this new way of thinking had brought their corresponding lows. Whatever perspective or mood or way of relating to the world that Wright was discovering, in his reading and in himself, it did not offer a simple consolation: "In buoying me up, reading also cast me down, made me see what was possible, what I had missed. My tension returned, new, terrible, bitter, surging, almost too great to be contained. I no longer *felt* that the world about me was hostile, killing, I *knew* it" (239).

In reading Mencken and the others, Wright found a literary worldview that confirmed the most basic assumption about life that he had derived from the nineteen years he had spent in the South. Life was war. And "literature"—anything deserving of the name, anyway—was not an escape route from that war but a path leading back to where the fighting was most furious. In the century that has elapsed since its invention, naturalism has fought on seemingly every front, from the purposes of art to the origin of the human race to the proper use of American military force. It fights, in the end, to assert itself upon reality, to find upon reality some mark of its own impress, to flaunt and parade the red badge of its self-inflicted wounds.

2
The Polemical Nature of Naturalism in America

From the moment they were first uttered by English speakers in the seventeenth century, the words "naturalism" and "naturalist" have emerged from snarling lips. In 1642, the English cleric Richard Montagu warns his readers of the "atheists or men . . . who will admit of nothing but Morality, but Naturalismes, and humane reason." As early as 1612, one finds evidence of "those blasphemous truth-opposing Heretikes, and Atheisticall naturalists" (*OED* "naturalist," *n.* and *a.*, 2a). In the nearly two hundred years that elapsed before the word "naturalism" came to describe a fin-de-siècle mode of American fiction, the defining features of naturalism had no doubt mutated or pupated beyond any resemblance of that earlier entity. Scholars such as Eric Carl Link have distinguished carefully between the scientific, philosophical, and literary streams of naturalism; the American literary naturalists are not unproblematic "inheritors" of the other, earlier naturalisms.[1] And yet writers such as Norris, Dreiser, and Wright do perhaps bear something in common with the "blasphemous Heretikes" and "Atheisticall naturalists" of the past. From the start, it seems, the word "naturalism" has described a party dedicated to waging a kind of cultural warfare, and genteel literary critics, no less than seventeenth-century clerics, have seen fit to vigorously denounce this apparently subversive entity. "Naturalism" has always had a way of courting controversy.

This chapter seeks to unpack some of the controversies in which the American literary naturalists involved themselves and to explicate what I take to be the polemical essence of the genre. It is not quite right to say that writers like Norris, Dreiser, and Wright have been "drawn" or "attracted" to polemic, since their writings are more often the source of this eristic energy than a reflection of it. But the polemics of these naturalist authors always emerge in dialogue and argument with their society. To an extent not yet recognized, the naturalists took controversial (and frequently contrarian) positions on a wide range of literary, political, and social issues. Frank Norris famously declared the innate inferiority of female novelists and frequently wrote about literature in tones suggestive of racial warfare. Theodore Dreiser once advocated, with deadly earnestness, a program of state-run infanticide for disabled or unwanted children. (Imagine Swift's "Modest Proposal," minus the modesty.) Richard Wright praised the Molotov–Ribbentrop Pact of 1939, an agreement of non-aggression between Stalin and Hitler, as "a great step toward peace" (qtd. in Kinnamon and Fabre 25): America's first best-selling black author publicly supported a dictator who instituted a form of slavery in his own nation. While many of their arguments were irascible, attention-seeking, and self-consciously inflammatory, the polemical spirit that fueled these outbursts remained central to the canonical texts of the movement. Naturalism is less a coherent philosophy than it is an attitude, a posture of aggressive controversy, which happens to cluster loosely around particular philosophical themes. The naturalists were polemicists, and their novels were always soaked through with the same antinomian spirit that pervades their work as journalists and essayists.

In the following pages, I take a closer look at polemics by the three authors under consideration. Where possible, I endeavor to focus upon some of the lesser known polemics by these writers (such as Dreiser's *Tragic America* and *America Is Worth Saving*) or to bring to the surface the polemical undercurrents of more familiar works, such as Richard Wright's "Blueprint for Negro Writing." The concluding section of this chapter focuses on the polemical construction of naturalism within the academy. Here, I hope to show that the polemical impulse of the original naturalists has been taken up by critics who have, in this polemical sense, extended the naturalist project.

Frank Norris: Why Naturalists Should Write the Best Novels (And Why They Don't)

If polemicism is a constitutive ingredient of naturalism, it is perhaps appropriate that this polemical spirit is most conspicuous in the author who first attempted to formalize the movement in America. Benjamin Franklin Norris Jr. would, over the course of his abbreviated career, attack his literary subjects with a ferocious polemical energy. Harold Bloom quite accurately calls Norris "the most aggressive of our Naturalist novelists" (vii), although that aggression was hardly limited to the novels and would work itself out in a polemicism that would remain a crucial component of the genre as a whole. Where (as we'll see below) Theodore Dreiser would devote much of his polemical energy to political matters, and Richard Wright would similarly address racial and then philosophical ones, Frank Norris's polemical writings center on literary questions. Of course, Norris did craft polemical essays and arguments on a wide variety of topics for publications that included the *San Francisco Wave* and the *Chicago American Literary and Art Review*. But none of the original practitioners of naturalism wrote as much or as energetically about the nature of naturalism itself.

The writings by Norris that are typically taken as definitive of the initial phase of naturalism in America were written over a span of six years, from 1896 to the author's early death of peritonitis in 1902. One of Norris's first polemical piñatas was a target that would soon become a favorite object of derision for H. L. Mencken: the university English professor.[2] Norris published "The 'English Courses' of the University of California" in the *San Francisco Wave* in 1896, where he had recently been appointed as staff writer and associate editor. The twenty-six-year-old Norris had just returned from South Africa where he had written local-color sketches for the *Chronicle* and witnessed the Jameson raid in Johannesburg; he had then briefly enlisted in the Uitlander's militia in its mounted division.[3] Clearly, "experience" was already something of a fetish for Norris. Indeed, the tension between observing and doing, and the personal insecurities that tension caused, was an important wellspring of Norris's polemicism.[4]

The publication of Norris's first novel, *McTeague*, in 1899 was still years ahead of him, but it's easy to discern the "naturalism" nascent in "The 'English Courses.'" In this early polemic, Norris rails against the pedagogical methods he encountered in his English courses at the University of California. He disapproves of the overtly empirical emphasis employed by his instructors: counting the number of metaphors in a particular passage of De Quincey, for instance. "'Classification' is the one thing desirable in the eyes of the professors of 'literature' of the University of California," he writes (*Criticism* 6). (For a concise catalog of Norris's pet peeves, just follow his use of quotation marks in these sentences.) The English student "classifies 'lyrics' and 'ballads' . . . makes out 'skeletons' and 'schemes' . . . has learned to write 'themes' and 'papers'" (7). For Norris, the process of acquiring an education in English was inimical to the "enthusiasm" required to produce creative writing of one's own. And yet he did recognize the urgent need for some kind of professionalization. By the time he left Berkeley for Harvard in 1894, Norris, who was never a model student, had essentially given up the hope of ever receiving his degree; instead, he wanted to be "thoroughly prepared for a literary profession" (McElrath and Crisler 131).

Norris's anxiety over "professionalization" is reflected in the novel he started writing in this period. McTeague's degeneration into a murderous, subhuman brute begins when he loses his profession: San Francisco authorities discover that McTeague has been operating without a dental license and force him to stop practicing. McTeague had come by his dentistry according to the model of apprenticeship under which a previous generation of American authors had come by the literary craft: Howells and Twain worked as reporters, and James had toiled in private until he had "arrived." The naturalists would do their stints in journalism too, but not before most of them had done a stretch at university.[5] Responding to the forces of professionalization that were transforming the American workforce, the naturalists were drawn to the formal education offered in universities. Norris was perhaps representative, however, in finding the experience unsatisfactory. In fact, university English had exacerbated his anxieties about "the real world." He writes, "the conclusion of the whole matter is that the literary courses of the University of California do not develop literary instincts among the students who attend them. The best way to study literature is to try to produce literature. It is the original work that counts, not the everlasting compiling of facts, not the tabulating of metaphors, nor the rehashing of text books and encyclopaedia articles" (*Criticism* 7–8). The emphasis on the literary "instincts" of young authors; the stress on production as opposed to consumption; the concern with originality, with staying true to life itself—in writing against the pedagogical approach of his English courses, Norris was starting to define a set of aesthetic concerns that he would go on to formalize as "naturalism." Just as important, however, is the polemical tone in which he frames those concerns. Norris's polemicism resides in the way he attempts to establish the clear supremacy of his kind of literature over every other kind. He's not interested in forging connections or seeking common ground; he's interested in demonstrating why one point of view (his) is superior to all others. The essay then parodies and makes a mockery of his opponents; Norris ridicules the way graduate students and faculty would "read papers" to one another and then retire for "'discussion' aided and abetted by cake and lemonade" (7). This is a manifestation of cultural gentility that he would go on to associate with Howells and the school of realism, although its original associations are with the academy itself. Naturalism's vexed relationship with the academy is only natural, therefore, given that the genre partly arose in opposition to the way English was taught and authors were produced.

In subsequent essays, Norris shifted his polemical focus from the academy to his rivals in the literary marketplace. Howellsian realism supplanted academic English as Norris's negative touchstone in "Zola as a Romantic Writer" (1896).[6] "Realism," Norris complains, is reserved for characters who are "well behaved and ordinary and bourgeois" (*Criticism* 71), and the plots and sentences of such novels were as structurally and grammatically well behaved as the characters they described. Naturalism, by contrast—which Norris insists is not an inner circle of realism, but rather a form of romanticism—tells tales that are "twisted from the ordinary, wrenched out from the quiet, uneventful round of every-day life, and flung into the throes of a vast and terrible drama" (72). (Naturalism's syntactical constructions were frequently as "twisted" as its plots.) Zola's importance for Norris here resides in the way the "man of the iron pen" tore down the class barriers of genteel fiction; his naturalism was "the drama of the people, working itself out in blood and ordure" (72). Norris extends his assault on the Howells school in "A Plea for Romantic Fiction" (1901), where he states that realism is so superficial that for it "beauty is not even skin-deep" (76). Romance, by contrast, is a scalpel for probing "the unplumbed depths of the human heart, and the mystery of sex, and the problems of life, and the black, unsearched penetralia for the soul of man" (78).

The fervid tone in which Norris fashioned these arguments has as much to do with the "character" of naturalism as the "theory" they express. Even in Norris's original forays into definition, the "theory" of naturalism (or literature that "counts") could emerge in opposition to various adversaries. In "Novelists of the Future" (1901), naturalism provides a manly alternative to the overly rarefied work of the aesthete: Norris scolds contemporary writers for sequestering their art from the energizing chaos of the real world. He implores them instead to follow the hearty, lusty muse of American fiction, which "will lead you far from the studios and the aesthetes, the velvet jackets and the uncut hair, far from the sexless creatures who cultivates the art of writing as the fancier cultivates his orchid" (*Criticism* 14). "Damn the 'style' of a story," he wrote in "An Opening for Novelists" (1897), "so long as we get the swing and rush and trample of the things that live" (30). In "Why Women Should Write the Best Novels: And Why They Don't" (1901), Norris explains how, for reasons having to do with leisure time, education, and temperament, women should produce the best novels. The fact that they don't tells us less about women (who, Norris presumes, are sensitive, delicate, and nervous) than Norris's idea of the novel itself, which focuses its unwavering attention upon "the crude, the raw, the vulgar" (35). "The Frontier Gone at Last" celebrates the Grand March of the Anglo-Saxon race (animated by the "desire for conquest" [113]), and in various places Norris implies that naturalism is the correct genre for capturing the triumph of his race.

Norris's "polemicism," then, manifests itself in a few ways that are hard to miss. First, his polemicism is necessarily thesis based: it is intended to demonstrate why a naturalist mode of literature is superior to all others. He then turns his critical attention to the opponent in question and produces a grotesque parody of that adversary (usually in the image of an effeminate, vitiated, racially or sexually suspect artist figure), a straw man that he then proceeds to eviscerate. Often, he turns on the reader in the second person: "You—the truant little would-be novelist," or "You, the artistocrats, who demand the fine linen and the purple in your fiction" (12, 78). Norris could make his case for naturalism in any number of ways. Sometimes he opposed the genre to "English literature" as taught in the universities; sometimes he opposed it to the realists who, he felt, drained life of its enervating fluids; sometimes he opposed it to the inferior races who (he felt) had been justifiably flattened by the marching Saxons; and sometimes he opposed its ideals to the gender that, he liked to insist, was much too frail to properly execute the rigorous offices of the writer. But what did not change was the polemical tone and the corresponding idea that naturalism continually comes into being through vigorous opposition. One corollary, for Norris, is the idea that creation itself is the by-product of conflict, and in this sense alone one may try to unify the tone and substance of these arguments in a theory. More concretely, Norris demonstrated within his own body of work the process of rhetorical violence through which naturalism would generate and regenerate itself in critical contests throughout the century.

Theodore Dreiser in Love, Poverty, and War

It is immediately apparent that Theodore Dreiser's prose was by no means as consistently polemical as Norris's. Polemicism was not Dreiser's only note. His characteristic tone was far less openly belligerent than Norris's: he often assumed the manner of a shrewd, bemused spectator of the human comedy (an attitude that shines through in the more "philosophical" moments of narration in *Sister Carrie* and is suggested by his *Ev'ry Month* pseudonym, "The Prophet"). By Donald Pizer's tabulation, Dreiser wrote millions of words worth of journalism and occasional prose—vastly more than the combined total of his appallingly long novels. In his work as a freelancer (1897–1902), magazine editor (1905–10), and lifelong essayist, Dreiser penned thousands of newspaper articles, magazine features, editorials, Communist pamphlets and manifestos, celebrity interviews, philosophical noodlings, literary criticism, theater reviews, and travel writing. Still, a polemical attitude animated a vast amount of writing in each of Dreiser's five decades as a professional wordsmith.

Dreiser fought against cultural movements, social institutions, and art forms that he felt were weak or inadequate. He inveighed, for instance, against the "school" of art represented by Aubrey Beardsley and Oscar Wilde, which he found "weird" and "obscure" (*Prose* 66). All of the American theater, he wrote, was mere "mimicry" and "buffoonery" (100). The "Jury System," he decided, was "a rank and outrageous mockery," a "useless, idiotic, malice-infested and ghost-supported pest" (74). The medical profession was rife with quacks and incompetents, and an inept doctor "is to me as bad as a burglar or a murderer" (204). When it came to philosophy, his main theme was of human insignificance, and he was often moved to eloquence (if that is the word) while pondering the innate ignominy of our species: "the lever that moves the universe," he once said in what might serve as a summation of his worldview, "is pain" (85). He came out forcefully on the side of birth control (though not for "feminist" reasons) and just as forcefully against organized charity, which ran contrary to the "grinding" order of the universe. ("There is no hope for the man with the small brain," he had decided [168]). He followed this train of thought all the way to where it ended in an essay called "The Right to Kill," where he suggested that "greater selective judgement as to the character of babies worth rearing might well be exercised" (227). Surely it would be more efficient if the government established a panel of experts who could peremptorily dispose of all the weaklings and misfits whose lives were such a drag on society as a whole.

Clearly, Dreiser was never shy when it came to expressing polemical ideas in his essays, and his novels, too, often centered on controversial subjects, which is why they were so frequently suppressed by the publisher or banned from sale. Most of the controversy around novels like *Sister Carrie* and *Jenny Gerdhart* had less to do with their portrayals of violence or "sordidness" (the naturalistic portrayal of violence that had necessitated deep cuts to *McTeague* and, later, to *Native Son*), than they did with Dreiser's portrayal of love. There isn't much in the way of actual "sex" in these novels, but the fact that the female protagonist of *Sister Carrie* failed to be punished for her implied venery was extremely controversial. The period of Dreiser's most furiously polemical writing, however, did not arrive until the 1930s. Indeed, with the onset of the Great Depression, Dreiser essentially ended his literary career and abandoned himself entirely to his polemical activities. The fruits of this decision are two substantial volumes of polemical prose, *Tragic America* (1931) and *America Is Worth Saving* (1941). While these works are almost universally ignored by scholars today, no study of naturalist polemics would be complete without at least a brief glance at their contents.

Tragic America was Dreiser's answer to the financial collapse of 1930, events that the author interprets as the beginning of a long war between the masses and the financial oligarchs, which will be resolved either in the rule of one "financial Caesar" or a "people's central committee as in Russia, with full power over all construction and execution" (13). Dreiser offers snapshots of the deplorable living conditions of northeastern laborers, before guiding us through plethoric abuses of the financial system perpetrated by the banks, financial trusts, railroad companies, and other familiar adversaries of equality. He writes at length about preferential shipping rates given to the Rockefellers and J. P. Morgans of this world, while ordinary workers are hard-pressed to make ends meet. He refers to the U.S. Constitution as a "scrap of paper" and suggests that its protection of private property had become a gross perversion of what the framers intended. The only solution to the country's problems, Dreiser predicts, is the gradual adoption of Soviet-style communism. The Constitution must be rewritten to reflect as much; all aspects of governance must be centralized; private fortunes and inheritance abolished. The state must "have authority to confiscate such homes of the rich as well as other institutions, private, civil, religious, as might fit into any purpose of the state" (414); and of course it is only right that the state should also have the ability to dispense the death penalty according to its needs (418). The author is not timid about expressing his support for Stalin, who "rules his land for the utmost benefit of the workers" (411), and Dreiser enthusiastically awaits the arrival of Stalinist-style leadership in America. Contemporary commentators on Dreiser have found little of genuine interest in *Tragic America*. Jerome Loving calls the book a "cobbled-together screed" (355). Richard Lingeman admits that it was probably Dreiser's "worst-written book," but he does find some value in it "as a jeremiad" (*Journey* 368). In other words, if there is any consolation to be found in *Tragic America*, it lies in the sustained polemical attitude of its author.

As Roosevelt's New Deal policies gradually revived the American economy, Dreiser threw his polemical weight behind another cause: that of keeping American soldiers out of the Second World War. The bitter fruit of this effort was *America Is Worth Saving* (which a fearful publisher had at the eleventh hour retitled from "Is America Worth Saving?" [Loving 385]). Dreiser offers a multitude of reasons why the United States should stay out of the conflict: a lack of military preparedness, the enormous expense, the necessity of conscription, and the potential abuse of military power by those in charge. The author bemoans what he sees as America's "Save-the-World-Complex" and argues that America's participation in the First World War was also folly. But the main reason why America should remain neutral is that England simply isn't worth fighting for.

As Dreiser sees it, England is essentially the modern inheritor of all of the most atavistic energies of Old Europe. At times, Dreiser couches his case against England in anti-imperialist rhetoric. England "is out to bleed the world for the benefit of a tiny group," he argues, "and yet every effort is being made to trick the American people into fighting to save this world for this black widow of nations" (56). Rushing to England's rescue is a particular weakness for America: "For once in our national history let us refuse to be suckers; let us guard our own homeland—not England's decaying and criminal empire" (58). Dreiser would like to know why America should take the side of England as opposed to Germany, when England has such a high unemployment rate: "Whether it is better to die quickly by torture or slowly by hunger—and unemployment in England means nothing less—it is a question on which there will be differences of opinion" (129). In other words, Dreiser could perceive no moral distinction between England and Germany, "Hitlerdum and Hitlerdee" (222), and insinuates that England was perpetrating its own holocaust against the nation's poor. Dreiser's most basic point is that English imperialism was more destructive than Hitlerian fascism, and America's decision to enter the war would constitute "imperialist aggression on Wall Street's behalf" (236). While his ostensible target is "imperialism," Dreiser makes little effort to conceal his disgust for "Englishness" itself—the "pallid and stunted" people, the "dingy gray pigment which uniquely typifies the English scene," the "bug-ridden, wretched homes" (89–90). The true victim of these events, in his view, was Russia: Dreiser was convinced that England had been in conspiracy with Germany and Italy to stamp out the "semi-Bolshevik government" (45) in Spain, which may have proven useful to the Russians in the inevitable Anglo-Russo conflict for which the Second World War was simply foreplay.

Dreiser was perennially rumored to be a favorite for the Nobel Prize in Literature, but the closest he ever came to the award was when Sinclair Lewis briefly recognized the older writer in his own acceptance speech. Lewis, who was awarded the prize in 1930, praised Dreiser for breaking the shackles of Puritanism in America. "Dreiser more than any other man," Lewis said, "marching alone, usually unappreciated, often hated, has cleared the trail from Victorian and Howellsian timidity and gentility." "Without his pioneering," Lewis added, "I doubt if any of us could, unless we liked to be sent to jail, seek to express life and beauty and terror."[7] Surely, this is how H. L. Mencken had packaged Dreiser—the lonely, harassed, persecuted artist who fought tirelessly against the Puritan moralism that had hitherto asphyxiated artistic expression in America. Surely, too, this is how Dreiser had presented himself. Dreiser had "cultivated," in Donald Pizer's phrase, "the mythic role of the hounded American writer" (*Uncollected Prose* 19). But as the trajectory of Dreiser's career in the 1930s would imply, polemicism has its perils.

Being at the head of the pack is a virtue only if the pack ends up having followed you. "Polemic," Louis Menand writes, "is a retrospective term. There are many more would-be polemics—that is, pieces that are written with the intention of changing forever the conventional estimation of an artist or a writer or a school of thought, but that fail to do so—than there are pieces that, looking back, can actually be said to mark a distinctive cultural moment" ("Kael's Attack" 154). Frank Norris's turn-of-the-century polemics for naturalism did not simply burst the bubble of American realism; they also represented the first steps in a new direction. Theodore Dreiser's 1930s polemics, in which he championed Stalinist policies and claimed not to be able make a moral distinction between England and Nazi Germany, cannot be said to represent the start of anything new and were instead very much the end for Dreiser.

Richard Wright: Party of One

Richard Wright was a polemicist on artistic, political, and philosophical fronts, and each of these was deeply informed by his thinking about the question of race in America. Wright's most important early artistic statement came in "Blueprint for Negro Writing," published in the first (and last) issue of the black leftist journal *New Challenge*. The central plank of Wright's "Blueprint" was that black literature should be produced for a black audience, not for a select coterie of elite white liberals. To this end, Wright implored artists to draw upon the rich cultural resources of African American folk art, including the blues, spirituals, and folk tales (40). The black artist, Wright argues, performs a crucially important kind of cultural work: he is to "create values by which his race is to struggle, live, and die" (43). But the essay is also partly an attempt by Wright to bring this folk art into coherent relation with the Marxian theory that had invigorated his own social activism since moving to Chicago: in generic terms, this meant that "a simple literary realism which seeks to depict the lives of these people ["ordinary", that is non–petit bourgeois black subjects] devoid of wider social connotations, devoid of the revolutionary significance of these nationalist tendencies, must of necessity do a rank injustice to the Negro people" (43).

Wright's "Blueprint," therefore, wasn't just a plan for erecting a new edifice; it was also a call to tear down an old one. His polemical targets, Wright's version of the "Puritans" or "realists" for a previous generation of naturalist, were the writers associated with the Harlem Renaissance. Mencken's *Prefaces*, Wright later admitted, "served as a literary Bible for me for years" (qtd. in Fabre, *Books and Writers* 108), and there is more than a little of Mencken's polemical energy in Wright's barbs against the "parasitic and mannered" Harlem authors, who were sustained by "burnt-out white Bohemians with money" ("Blueprint" 37). Moreover, echoing Norris's obsession with vigorous, heteronormative masculinity, and anticipating the codependence between a viable black artistic identity and black masculinity that would be more fully theorized by critics like Philip Brian Parker, Wright complained that the artistic inadequacies of this Harlem bunch were connected to a more profound failure of manliness: these scribes had "entered the Court of American Public Opinion dressed in the knee-pants of servility, curtsying to those that the Negro was not inferior, that he was human, and that he had a life comparable to that of other people. For the most part these artistic ambassadors were received as though they were French poodles who do clever tricks" (37). Where Norris had tried to create an artistic space for naturalism by attacking the gentility and effeminacy of the Howells school, Wright had assumed the characteristic naturalistic rhetorical posture but with writers like Claude McKay, Langston Hughes, and Zora Neale Hurston representing the enervating cultural authority. In his review of *Their Eyes Were Watching God*, Wright found that Hurston's prose was cloaked in "facile sensuality" and that the novel "is not addressed to the Negro, but to a white audience whose chauvinistic tastes she knows how to satisfy" (qtd. in Rowley 137).

The second major site of Wright's polemicism was the Communist Party itself, whose ideals Wright had first internalized as a member of the John Reed Club in Chicago in 1934. Communism proved to be profoundly attractive to Wright for any number of reasons, not the least of which was its promise of racial solidarity: the party had come out strongly against racism in recent years and provided "a common vision that bound us all together" (qtd. in Crossman 141). Some Americans in the New Deal years evidently felt that communism was preferable to democratic liberalism because it constituted a more robust answer to fascism, although this cannot be said to have been part of the attraction for Wright—indeed, he remained fiercely loyal to the party even after the Soviet-German agreement of 1939.[8] The vast appeal of communism, for Wright, resided in its promise of a systematic solution to the profound racial, economic, and political problems that plagued America in that bleak moment. In these years Wright approached communism with a religious fervor and was not in the least shy about spreading its gospel: the party, he said, offered "the first total emotional experience of my life" (qtd. in Crossman 117).

If Wright's writings for Marxism had constituted an important locus of his polemical prose, his writings against it would prove equally crucial. In 1937, Wright had insisted that "it is only through a Marxist conception of reality and society" that black liberation would be achieved ("Blueprint" 44), but by 1944, there he was in print calling his former comrades "narrow-minded, bigoted, intolerant and frightened of new ideas which don't fit into their own" (qtd. in Kinnamon and Fabre 51). Two years after his official break with the party, Wright published "I Tried to Be a Communist" in the *Atlantic* and contributed (along with Arthur Koestler, Stephen Spender, and others) to Richard Crossman's *The God that Failed*, the watershed volume of anti-Communist polemic issued in 1950. Wright's essay in that volume is decidedly personal and biographical instead of theoretical or "political" in any abstract sense: Wright forgoes the opportunity to repudiate specific tenets of communism as political theory and instead narrates a series of very personal betrayals, slights, and enmities that finally drove him out of his union local and the party as a whole. He's less interested in communism as a system than he is in the behavior of individual organizers, whom he found to be overwhelmingly invidious, self-interested, and backstabbing. (Wright would later feel double-crossed by Crossman himself, when he discovered that the Congress for Cultural Freedom, to which Crossman belonged, was bankrolled by the CIA [Rowley 520]). Wright had arrived at the conclusion that the Communists were merely using the race issue as a cynical means of advancing their own interests, and the piece concludes with Wright's decision to strike out on his own.

Wright's alienation from the Communists, combined with his decision to permanently move to France in 1947, resulted in another shift in his polemical focus, this time in the direction of philosophy. The writings of the final phase of Wright's career detail his engagement with philosophical existentialism. The main artistic fruit of what Arna Bontemps called Wright's "roll in the hay with Existentialism" (15) was *The Outsider*, the novel Wright published in 1953. Wright's *The Outsider* is broadly metaphysical, informed by Kierkegaard's *The Concept of Dread*, Camus's *L'Etranger* and *The Myth of Sisyphus*, and by the writings of Sartre and de Beauvoir, whom Wright had befriended in the previous years. Where his previous essays and fiction (with the notable exception of Max's courtroom diatribe in the final section of *Native Son*) had eschewed the abstractly theoretical for what was often praised as the more authentic flavors of subjective experience—"no theory can take the place of life," Wright himself had affirmed in 1937—*The Outsider* constitutes yet another reversal, in which a stereotypically existentialist protagonist named Cross Damon is guided through a highly allegorical plot. After he is mistakenly reported as dead, Cross Damon reinvents himself with the aim of achieving an existentially authentic identity, one beyond traditional moral precepts. Cross takes full advantage of his new enlightenment by murdering four people, including two Communists and a Fascist. Wright's point in all of this, it seems, is that communism and fascism are two sides of the same coin, two complementary expressions of modernist alienation. Racial oppression, similarly, is just one more example of this apparently permanent state of affairs, in which the strong necessarily subjugate the weak.

Wright had spent his childhood under Jim Crow, had spent his young adulthood in close intellectual proximity to Stalinism, and had come of artistic maturity under the shadow of European fascism: he had evidently come to regard this full catalog of horrors as springing from a universal will to power. When Damon is finally tracked down and interrogated about what he found meaningful in life, his answer—"nothing"—is less a final artistic or philosophical statement by Wright than simply the latest (and, as it turned out, the last) stab of the pen that had been animated by H. L. Mencken. *The Outsider* would be Wright's final book. It was as polemical, in its way, as *Native Son* had been thirteen years before, although—in a fashion that recalls Dreiser's career in the 1930s—its polemical message did not win him many acolytes. Had he not succumbed to a heart attack in 1960, and instead lived to the age of W. E. B. Du Bois, Richard Wright would have lived to see the second invasion of Iraq in 2003, and there is no telling how many polemical turns his career might have taken in the interim. In a 1938 interview, Wright identified two possible paths historically open to writers in America: either they found patrons, or "they banded themselves together into informal groups and waged war upon their society" (qtd. in Kinnamon and Fabre 12). In his career of highly polemical prose, it's obvious that there was one party Richard Wright had never left.

Critical Differences: A Polemical History of a Contested Genre

Some measure of the naturalists' success as polemicists is perhaps to be found in the violence with which they were rejected by the culture at large. Their works were routinely cut, censored, suppressed, removed from libraries, banned from sale, and sometimes publicly burned.[9] But the hostility ran both ways. Frank Norris, Theodore Dreiser, and Richard Wright conceived of themselves and their artistic occupations in direct opposition to mainstream aesthetic, political, and cultural assumptions of their times, and this oppositional spirit went deeper than the kind of philosophy, deterministic or otherwise, that informed their fictions. It affected the most basic choices they made as literary artists: the kinds of characters they represented, the kinds of words they chose, the ways they put their sentences together. Their work is soaked through with polemicism—and it is this polemicism, I have been arguing, that sets their "school" or "movement" apart. Of course, words like "school" or "movement" seem ill-suited to the naturalists, perhaps because its central proponents and exemplars (excepting the close friendship and professional alliance between Dreiser and Mencken) never actually had all that much to do with one another, in the way that, for instance, the Beat movement grew out of a particular constellation of relationships. Aside from a single, oft-cited instance of fraternity—when Frank Norris urged Doubleday to accept *Sister Carrie* for publication in 1899—the naturalists did not operate as a cohesive group, nor did they constitute anything that might have been considered a "scene" or a "set." As a result, the creation of naturalism as a "genre" of work was in large measure left to their critics—critics who have retained or continued to cultivate, to an often surprising extent, the polemical spirit that had animated the initial project. The reasons for this vary over time and from critic to critic: in some cases, scholars are quite transparently using naturalism for their own polemical purposes; in others, critical work seems to be quite simply contaminated by the polemical spirit of the novel or essay under consideration. In any event, "naturalism" was instantiated by the polemicism of its original practitioners, but that polemicism has survived and thrived in the critical debates about naturalism that have raged since Stuart P. Sherman and H. L. Mencken first squared off nearly a century ago. In this section, we'll visit a few of the most important loci of polemicism over the past century—books and essays by Malcolm Cowley, Lionel Trilling, Donald Pizer, Walter Benn Michaels, Michael Fried, and Mark Seltzer—in order to get a sense of how the genre has generated and regenerated itself through polemical criticism and debate and how the naturalist project itself persists in the work of scholars who have continued practicing a crucial aspect of that which they study—and, in this sense, they have become the new naturalists.

Malcolm Cowley seems prescient when, in 1949, he stated that "theories and doctrines were not the heart" ("Naturalism" 300) of naturalism. Cowley's naturalism, like Mencken's, was reacting against an ideology that had claimed literature for the side of godliness and ideality (as opposed to "business," corporeal humanity, and, in terms borrowed from the naturalists themselves, "life"). "What bound them together into a school or movement," Cowley said, "was this native rebellion and not the nature of the help"—that is, the intellectual support of Darwin and Zola—"they summoned from abroad" (300). Cowley further echoes Mencken when he singles out the "timid but tyrannical rule" of the genteel tradition as the object of naturalism's rebellion, but he disagrees about the source of that genitility. Cowley begins his essay, "Naturalism in American Literature," by appearing to undermine one enduring aspect of the naturalist mythology, which is naturalism's reaction to "Puritanism." The naturalists were indeed rebels, but Mencken had been sloppy or misleading in assigning Puritan origins to the prevailing 1890s genteel culture: the "ideality" or "decency" naturalism was reacting against was actually born of a post–Civil War aversion to barbarism. But after puncturing this particular canard, Cowley quickly launches into some mythologizing of his own: "These new men, who would be the first American naturalists, were all in some way disadvantaged when judged by the social and literary standards then prevailing. . . . They were in rebellion against the genteel tradition because, like writers from the beginning of time, they had an urgent need for telling the truth about themselves, and because there was no existing medium in which they were privileged to tell it" (301–02). Frank Norris—Cowley's prime example of this "new man," who had been so "disadvantaged" that he had to invent a new medium "for telling the truth"—had been born into a wealthy and respectable family and had received a formal artistic education in Paris before his literary training at Berkeley and Harvard. Stephen Crane emerged from a similar social class, while Edith Wharton hailed from quasi-aristocratic origins. Theodore Dreiser came from humbler stock, but he had never had difficulty finding his way into print and for many years found reliable work as the editor of "ladies' magazines"—working successfully as one of the genteel cultural gatekeepers that Cowley posits as the very source of his oppression. There is something slightly mendacious about the word "disadvantaged" in this context, given how hard writers like Norris had had to work to achieve those disadvantages. By "disadvantages," Cowley seems to be referring to their polemical artistic inclinations, which drew the moral censure of certain stodgy critics. But naturalism was not "disadvantaged" by polemicism; naturalism *was* polemicism, and Cowley's turn of phrase is just so much added gauze on the lens of history.

Nevertheless, Cowley's "Naturalism in American Literature" helped concretize the coordinates of one phase of the debate. He traces the influence of Darwin, Huxley, and Spencer, and emphasizes the connection between these American "rebels" and their French forebearers—especially Zola and Balzac. Particularly important was Cowley's succinct explication of naturalism's "pessimistic determinism": "the naturalists were all determinists in that they believed in the omnipotence of natural forces," he wrote, and "they were pessimists in that they believed in the absolute incapacity of men and women to shape their own destinies" (313). Later, he makes the point more forcefully, claiming that for these authors "men are 'human insects' whose brief lives are completely determined by society or nature" (331). Despite the fact that he contradicts his own sensible opening claim (that "theories and doctrines were not the heart" of naturalism) by reducing naturalism to a series of "doctrines" and even suggesting that these authors "suggest a naturalistic system of ethics complete with its vices and virtues" (321), Cowley's essay in definition seems to contain much of what still commonly passes for "naturalism" in today's critical writing. And yet it is remarkable just how much writing by the naturalists Cowley is forced to omit from the genre in order to maintain the integrity of its "doctrines." He includes most of Dreiser's novels—but not *The Bulwark*, which is too religious, and doesn't mention his polemical prose. Approximately one third of Frank Norris's work is judged "naturalistic," and one work by Richard Wright makes the cut. "Jack London held the doctrines and wrote fifty books," Cowley states, "but only three or four of them" are properly naturalistic (327). In short, if one attempts to hold the naturalists to a definition centering on "pessimistic determinism," only a very small minority of works by the naturalists actually qualifies as "naturalist." Cowley seemed initially to grasp the inadequacy of these doctrines, although he ends by reaffirming them anyway. He signs off on a judgmental note, deciding that "Dreiser is the worst writer of all, but in some ways the least objectionable; there is something native to himself in the misuse of the language, so that we come to cherish it as a sign of authenticity, like the tool marks on Shaker furniture" (333). Despite the literary incompetence of its principal authors, and despite the fact that so little of its writing lives up to the "doctrines" of the movement itself, naturalism is judged by Cowley to have been a worthwhile experiment: he values the rebelliousness of authors who were willing to write against the grain and admires that the naturalists "tried to seize the life around them" (333).

The two features of naturalism that Cowley had singled out for approbation—that the naturalists' linguistic infelicity is actually an index of their authenticity, and that the real accomplishment of the genre lies in the way it captured "life itself"—were precisely the two points that Lionel Trilling had sought to demolish in what is perhaps the most widely read essay on naturalistic subjects in America. "Reality in America" is in some ways an important rupture in naturalist criticism, because Trilling was the first to problematize the implicit mimetic theory that undergirds naturalistic representation: specifically, that reality itself exists as something reliable, concrete, knowable, and external to the imagination, and that it is possible and indeed desirable that art should transcribe this reality. And although Dreiser—or, rather, Dreiser's liberal critics—will be held up by Trilling as the main perpetrator of this particular naiveté, it is sometimes easy to forget that "Reality in America" begins as a relentless polemic against Vernon Parrington, especially his *Main Currents in American Thought* (1932).

Trilling's assaults on Parrington in "Reality in America" are many and sustained. He takes issue with the title of Parrington's volume: cultures do not "flow," Trilling insists, nor do they exist as any kind of "confluence," and Parrington's faulty central image betrays a more fundamental misunderstanding of the way culture works. (One can only speculate as to the depth of Trilling's disdain for the title of Charles C. Walcutt's 1956 study, *American Literary Naturalism: A Divided Stream*.) Culture, Trilling insists, is struggle; cultures exist only in dialectic, and some of America's most important artists have contained large parts of the dialectic within themselves, "their meaning and power lying in their contradictions" (29). To reject authors like Poe, Melville, Hawthorne, and James because their works resist or won't fit conveniently with the political commitments of liberal-minded critics, or because they fall outside one's preconceived idea of American culture, "is to examine without attention and from the point of view of a limited and essentially arrogant conception of reality the documents which are in some respects the most suggestive testimony to what America was and is" (30).

The second part of "Reality in America," then, is animated by Trilling's contempt for the "doctrinaire indulgence" that liberal critics have always granted Theodore Dreiser. While Henry James (once again finding himself on the opposite side of the argument) was consistently derided by liberal critics because his works seemed to have precious little "practical" political value—which is to say that James's supposed zeal for the manners of the upper class appeared, to critics of this persuasion, hopelessly out of touch with New Deal political priorities—Theodore Dreiser's reputation was inflated beyond all proportion. More specifically, as Cowley has just shown, Dreiser's literary faults—his narrative deformities and lugubrious prose—were inexplicably transmogrified into aesthetic and political virtues. If Dreiser couldn't turn a phrase, that was because of his more profound rejection of "gentility" in all of its morally and culturally vitiated forms. Meanwhile, the vivaciousness, incisiveness, and above all the *wit* of Henry James were simply further proof of his bourgeois irrelevancy. Trilling chalks this up to the good old-fashioned American anti-intellectualism that Tocqueville had noticed on his celebrated tour: the real reason we prefer Dreiser to James is that Dreiser's oafish mind reflects the dullness native to his readership, or at least evinces less of the intellectual razzle-dazzle likely to attract their scorn.

But at least part of the problem was that James's work resisted polemical appropriation by midcentury leftist thinkers: whatever his novels are, they are decidedly *not* appeals for tax reform, labor unions, publically subsidized housing, and other policies geared to maximize social equality; James is emphatically not a "socially responsible" artist for liberal critics. Trilling's piece is, in part, a polemic against the "polemicization" (or, if that's too ungainly a coinage, the "aggressive politicization") of literature for the side of progressivism. It's not that the liberal critics had misread Dreiser's political intentions, it's that literature shouldn't be read for its political intent at all.

At bottom, Trilling's argument is about the place of art in American society, which he believes should be free to represent and traffic in that inspired realm that was derided as "romantic," "imaginative," or "unreal" by liberal critics concerned only with literature's most practical and obvious and straightforwardly polemical engagement with public life. The underlying problem, therefore, is what Trilling terms the "American metaphysic," in which "reality is always material reality, hard, resistant, unformed, impenetrable, and unpleasant. And that mind is alone felt to be trustworthy which most resembles this reality by most nearly reproducing the sensations it affords" (13). What Trilling opposes (with regard to Dreiser and Parrington) is the too easy dichotomy between "reality" and "imagination." And Trilling's version of Dreiser is always for "reality" in its most vulgar sense, which he supports with the following (uncited) quotation from the author: "What, cooking, eating, coition, job holding, growing, aging, losing, winning, in so changeful and passing a scene as this, important? Bunk! It is some form of titillating illusion with about as much import to the superior forces that bring it all about as the functions and gyrations of a fly." As a final slap in the face, Dreiser found God in his last novel, *The Bulwark*, marking an ultimate and decisive "failure of mind and heart" (20): "Our liberal, progressive culture tolerated Dreiser's vulgar materialism with its huge negation, its simple cry of 'Bunk!,' feeling that perhaps it was not quite intellectually adequate but certainly very *strong*, certainly very *real*. And now, almost as a natural consequence, it has been given, and is not unwilling to take, Dreiser's pietistic religion in all its inadequacy" (21).

The broad scope of Trilling's "Reality in America"—which attacked Parrington and Dreiser as part of a larger polemical confrontation with the liberal critical establishment and the mimetic assumptions about the relationship between art and politics that lay behind the entity Trilling called "liberal culture"—made it among the strongest midcentury polemical readings of American naturalism. And Trilling's relationship to an earlier generation of polemicist is easily spelled out. "Liberalism" in Trilling's essay occupies roughly the position of "Puritanism" in Mencken's original formulations: liberalism has become the all-pervasive ideology in American intellectual culture, the unspoken network of assumptions according to which all art is (inappropriately) measured. Mencken was outraged that "literature" was judged by its adherence to received Anglo-Protestant inscriptions of ideality—that literature had to constitute a fit guide for the behavior of young girls. Trilling was outraged that literature was judged by its adherence to the received economic, political, and social doctrines of New Deal liberalism—that literature had to function as a pamphlet or "blueprint" for leftist policy makers. Of course, by 1960, Daniel Bell was able to assert in his standard explication of liberal political theory that "few serious minds believe any longer that one can set down 'blueprints' and through 'social engineering' bring about a new utopia of social harmony" (373). In other words, liberalism itself had (in Bell's reading) repudiated the impulse toward social blueprints, the central failing of Trilling's "liberal" critic. Doubtless, Trilling's "liberalism" is every bit the polemical straw-man construct of Mencken's Puritanism, and one might even suggest that liberalism had invented and indeed necessitated the very space for dissent that Trilling now occupied. (At least that would be the retort of the modern liberal critic, for whom Trilling's critique of liberalism would be taken as further evidence that the system is working.) In any event, the fact that Theodore Dreiser had gone from the artistic pariah of Mencken's generation to the subject of habitual sympathetic indulgence in Trilling's is perhaps less a measure of the "success" of Mencken's polemical project than an affirmation of Trilling's dialectical conception of cultural movements—which, of course, implied a forthcoming countermovement, a further transformation of Trilling's "synthesis" into a new "thesis" to be opposed. The most forceful expression of that opposition would arrive in the writings of Donald Pizer.

"Dreiser's central theme," Pizer wrote in 1966, "sets forth the idea—Lionel Trilling to the contrary—that the physically real is not the only reality and that men seek something in life beyond it" (*Realism and Naturalism* 18). And with that single sentence, Donald Pizer had dispensed with Lionel Trilling. In the past fifty years, no single critic has done more to shape the genre of naturalism than Donald Pizer. In *Realism and Naturalism in Nineteenth-Century American Literature*, Pizer begins by establishing what naturalism is not. It is not an extension of realism, as is commonly assumed. And it does not involve a "philosophy" of pessimistic determinism.[10] Pizer's definition of naturalism unfolds according to a very strict scheme. The naturalistic novel, he says, contains two "tensions or contradictions." The first tension or contradiction comprises "an interpretation of experience," while the second is a "particular aesthetic recreation of experience." The first tension or contradiction or interpretation of experience is the "theme" of the naturalistic novel, while the second tension or contradiction or aesthetic recreation constitutes the novel's "form." When Pizer speaks of the "tension" in the theme, he means that naturalism appears to focus on the ordinary foot soldiers of working-class and quotidian reality, but that it finds in these subjects something heroic or sexy or violent—the "excessive in human nature" (11). The second tension (the tension of form) refers to the apparent contradiction between the pessimistic determinism that the naturalists intended to affirm and the compensatory humanistic or imaginative impulse to find meaning in an amoral universe.

Pizer then goes on to illustrate his definition by furnishing examples from *McTeague*, *Sister Carrie*, and *The Red Badge of Courage*, though (for our purposes) one may perhaps do duty for all three. The placidity and order and routine of McTeague's Polk Street, and the dentist's deeply habitual and ritualized way of subsisting within his community, symbolize the fragile equilibrium that is thrown into chaos when Trina arrives and activates the atavistic sexual impulses that had been dormant in McTeague all along. The thematic tension of the scenario involves a pull between the sexual determinism that rules over the dentist and ruins his life and the compensatory humanistic element that arrives in our knowledge of McTeague's representativeness: our tragic realization that we share McTeague's fundamental predicament, that our best attempts at creating an ordered world are so frequently subverted by an internal violence that lurks at depths inaccessible to consciousness. In other words, our compassionate involvement with the dentist offsets the plot's determinism; that the novel finds ways of nurturing our compassion for McTeague affirms his humanity rather than the opposite "naturalist" assumption of life's amoral worthlessness. The underlying motivation of Pizer's work, he would later write, was to "establish the fictional complexity and worth" of naturalism ("Introduction" 13). For Trilling, the equation of naturalism's stylistic ineptitude with "authenticity" was symptomatic of a more profound aesthetic ignorance endemic to 1930s and 1940s American liberalism. In recuperating a hidden thematic and structural complexity in the same works, Pizer was essentially making naturalism consumable again for the version of liberalism (the liberalism of Arthur Schlesinger Jr., Daniel Bell, and others) ascendant in postwar America.[11] Pizer offered a vision of naturalism as pragmatic compromise. Naturalism did indeed involve "a sense of man more circumscribed than conventionally acknowledged," but they also "[feel] deeply and powerfully and significantly. And that is their naturalistic condition in a tragic humanistic context" (*Theory and Practice* 39, 53).

Pizer's attempts to make naturalism palatable in this postwar liberal-humanistic context would meet a powerful countervailing force when Foucauldian conceptions of power, knowledge, and discipline were brought to bear on naturalistic subjects in the 1980s. Studies by June Howard, Philip Fisher, Walter Benn Michaels, and Mark Seltzer were not as conventionally polemical as what had come before (at least on a stylistic level), although all four, in their different ways, retained something of the polemical spirit: recall, for instance, Mark Seltzer's observation that "creation, in Norris's final explanation, is the work of an inexhaustible masturbator, spilling his seed on the ground, the product of a mechanistic and miraculous onanism" (124). What could be a more polemical (and naturalistic!) response to Frank Norris than to confirm the exclusive maleness of his vision of "creation," while at the same time radically deflating it by underlining its "masturbatory" nature? (Of course, it would be Norman Mailer rather than Norris who would explicitly pathologize the "miserable activity" of masturbation in naturalistic terms.)

The New Historicist criticism of the 1980s reinvigorated naturalism by unequivocally recognizing a host of important categories for study, particularly the dual interest of gender and economics. In *The Gold Standard and the Logic of Capitalism* (1987), Michaels outlines two gendered models of Gilded Age writing: feminine consumption and masculine production. The naturalists may have conceived of their project as one of opposition to consumer culture, but in its championing of masculine production over feminine consumption, naturalism turns the female form into a privileged site of the seemingly infinite exchanges in capitalist modernity. Put simply, most turn-of-the-century naturalism ends up endorsing, rather than undermining, the dominant economic logic of the age. In *Bodies and Machines* (1992), Mark Seltzer also provides a gendered model of production, in which masculine and feminine reproductive forces are "linked but competing principles of creation" (27). Seltzer's work argues that the industrial culture dominant in late nineteenth-century America reduced human bodies to statistically disciplined machines, and the resulting crisis of masculinity produced a compensatory drive toward a masculinization of the reproductive process: hence, "the unnatural nature of naturalism" (14).

The work of the New Historicists was by no means explicitly framed as a response to Donald Pizer, but it was intended to refute the liberal-humanist naturalistic metanarrative of which Donald Pizer had become the unavoidable personification. The New Historicists were animated by an implicit rejection of Pizer's structuralism, his liberal sense of art and history, his style, and, most seriously, his assumptions about the relationship between culture and aesthetics. Pizer's defense of naturalism lay in the revealed complexity of these authors' artistic reaction to different aspects of their culture. "The responsiveness of American naturalists to the pulls of change and temperament," Pizer said in 1978, constitutes one "link between the movement and humanism" (*Theory and Practice* 40). Michaels, on the other hand, states that "the only relation literature as such has to culture as such is that it is part of it" (27). In other words, the 1930s critics who had emphasized Dreiser's critique of capitalism were wrong for reasons that Lionel Trilling had only begun to articulate. Dreiser did not "approve" or "disapprove" of capitalism; he "desired pretty women in little tan jackets with mother-of-pearl buttons, and he feared becoming a bum on the streets of New York" (27), as Michaels put it. His objects of desire, like his most profound fears, are inextricable from the cultural logics that produced Theodore Dreiser and his writings. To see Dreiser as "responding" to capitalism therefore depends "on imagining a Dreiser outside capitalism who could then be said to have attitudes toward it" (Michaels 19). New Historicist critics like Michaels and Seltzer were interested in what naturalistic texts can tell us about Gilded Age American culture, but they certainly weren't concerned with rescuing or redeeming those texts, or in showing how they're "ethical" or "humanistic." While they weren't attacking Pizer by name, the differences were profound.

Even if the New Historicist turn in the study of naturalism had been more inwardly than outwardly polemical—that is, more invested in refuting the internal assumptions of more traditional text-based criticism than in ad hominem or otherwise external modes of attack—Donald Pizer did his best to turn New Historicism itself into a locus of polemicism in his extraordinarily rancorous review essays and counterattacks. One of Pizer's refrains in this endeavor has been that the "New" Historicism is not appreciably different from the "old" one: "the basic cast of mind underlying Michaels's essays closely resembles that of a 1930s literary historian," he wrote of *The Gold Standard* (*Theory and Practice* 205). For the most part, however, Pizer's attacks on the New Historicists were only peripherally concerned in their readings of particular naturalist novels; instead, he focused his critique on their *prose style* as a symptom of ideological confusion. In an article entitled "Bad Critical Writing," Pizer wonders why "we" (that is, university English professors) "have to put up with terrible prose seeking to pass as legitimate expression?" (68). To illustrate his point, Pizer draws upon works by three writers whose garbled prose and mangled syntax he finds particularly appalling: Walter Benn Michaels, Michael Fried, and Mark Seltzer. By no means has Pizer limited his scope to the study of naturalism: the epidemic of awful writing has metastasized throughout the entire body of academic criticism. Pizer has chosen these critics merely because they happen to be writing on a subject he knows something about. What is fascinating about Pizer's exercise, however, is that his own thesis about the New Historicists—that their deliberately inept writing can "serve a rhetorical purpose"(68)—echoes the arguments about "literary style" that Frank Norris had initiated in what Pizer takes to be the defining formulations of naturalism itself.

For Pizer, the problem with New Historicist readings is not the historicism—which allows the critic to appreciate not only a given text's cultural embeddedness but the symbolic economy through which the once separate entities of literature and culture are understood to constitute one another. The problem, instead, lies in the critical inclination of New Historicists to locate nodes of cultural transfer in ways that find little support in the texts but do confirm critics' a priori theoretical assumptions. Pizer's thesis in "Bad Critical Writing" is that the "turgid, mind-numbing, tortured prose style" of the New Historicists is in fact intimately related to the critical priorities of its practitioners. In the case of Walter Benn Michaels, "bad writing" refers to the "constant repetition of terminology" (73): Pizer cites a selection in which variations of the word "nature" appear six times, "represent" and "imagine" four times each, and so on and so forth. Pizer calls this strategy a "rhetoric of incremental repetition," arguing that the repetition creates "a fugue-like harmony" that conceals the faulty logic governing the passage (73). Michaels's argument in the selection (that Norris's *Vandover and the Brute* [1914] allegorizes a contemporaneous cultural debate over the gold standard, which itself stands in for larger tensions between symbolic versus essentialist patterns of thought) is largely beside the point. Pizer's complaint, rather, has to do with the *way* Michaels unfolds his claim: "the logical glue holding this allegory together is no more than the rhetoric of analogical connectedness" (75).

Michael Fried, Pizer finds, is also guilty of employing an extended analogical structure in order to compensate for weaknesses in his evidence and logic. Moreover, the critical "worth" of Fried's insights on Stephen Crane's upturned faces has more to do with its "imaginative insight and speculative ingenuity" than anything resembling logical probability. In other words, this is a mode of inquiry that demands to be read as poetry rather than criticism—which is perhaps appropriate for a critical methodology in which culture itself "is conceived of as a huge poem" (79). However, even if we consider *Realism, Writing, and Disfiguration* as a long poem, Pizer insists that Fried's work is still an aesthetic failure, because its "dense, leaden, and convoluted" prose falls far short of the standard set by Ezra Pound. Mark Seltzer presents a somewhat different variation on the same theme. Where the "repetitive and wooly language" of Michaels and Fried was deployed to obscure the unacceptability of their premises, Seltzer's dense prose functions in the exact opposite way, "mask[ing] the commonplace nature of his ideas" (79). Seltzer's thesis—that late nineteenth-century American culture reduced human beings to statistics and machines, and the representational strategies of naturalism constitute the "aesthetic machine" for performing that reduction—is, Pizer suggests, to be found more clearly expressed in the 1930s critical writing of Vernon Parrington. Other than "to note that it is hackneyed," Pizer has no wish to quarrel with Seltzer's thesis; the real problem is that Seltzer's argument is "puffed up into something fresh and insightful by new terminology, impressive but cumbersome logical alternatives, and verbal by-play" (81). In all three cases, Pizer charges that New Historicist criticism "is often based on weak evidence and logical improbabilities" and flouts the "clarity and precision of expression" that should constitute "the model attributes of departments of English" (79, 81).

The point of "Bad Critical Writing" is that there is an intimate connection between the style of New Historicist criticism and the critical presuppositions—the "habit of mind," as Pizer calls it—that underlie its expression. ("To the extent that Dreiser's style is defensible, his thought is also defensible," Lionel Trilling wrote in "Reality in America" [17].) In a sense, then, Pizer has been making my argument for me. The difference is that instead of arguing that the analogical prose style of New Historicism betrays its inadequate logic, I have been arguing that the frequent pugnaciousness of naturalist prose betrays a "habit of mind," a polemicism that underlies it. Just as Pizer insists that failings of New Historicism are most conspicuous in a "style," so the distinctive features of literary naturalism (whether they are virtues or failings will depend upon one's attitude toward polemic) reside at the level of prose style. And in his vitriolic and pugilistic essay, Pizer has given us yet another example of that style.

Pizer reflects upon this polemical stance—an "acerbic tone," is what he calls it—in the essay's penultimate paragraph, one that begins as an apologia of sorts but quickly transforms into yet another foray against his enemies: "I am troubled by the acerbic tone of this last comment and of several similar earlier remarks. The tone reflects my irritation at the display of intellectual arrogance represented by the prose styles I have discussed. The authorial self-importance and corresponding contempt for the reader implied by prose of this kind has stimulated in me a desire to help cleanse the critical scene by causing some hurt" (81–82). "Why did he write like that?" The question that Richard Wright had asked of H. L. Mencken is here the question that Donald Pizer asks of himself. Perhaps his "acerbic tone" is unsettling precisely insofar as it indicates, as is so often the case with naturalism, that pathos has overwhelmed the logos for which it had been enlisted. The desire for a linguistic expression of purifying violence—to "hurt" the New Historicists, to "cleanse the critical scene" of their ugly and polluting verbiage—is analogous to the impulse Wright had found in Mencken, for whom the primary function of words (in the young Wright's estimation) was to "cause hurt." "He was using words as a weapon, using them as one would use a club," Wright had written; "I was jarred and shocked by the style, the clear, clean, sweeping sentences" (*Black Boy* 237). Is Pizer not calling for a "clear, clean" style, a "sweeping" out of the syntactical clutter that obstructs and obfuscates the faulty logic underlying the New Historicist assertions? Indeed, in going after the New Historicist critics for insufficient "clarity" in their prose, Pizer implies that it is possible and desirable for prose to operate as a window into meaning: the responsibility of the critic—and of the institutions that support them, "departments of English"—is to use critical vocabulary in a way that accurately represents reality as it actually exists. The naturalist appeal to "reality" (or its synonym—"life") is of course integral to the movement from Norris onward ("life is better than 'literature,'" he often declared [*Criticism* 42–43]). But this vision of a presymbolic "reality"—what Trilling had called "material reality, hard, resistant, unformed, impenetrable, and unpleasant"—was not a reality endorsed or recognized by the New Historicists, and their "repetitive and wooly" prose styles constitute a repudiation of the realism/romance or reality/imagination binary structuring the American metaphysic.

In sum, "Bad Critical Writing" exemplifies how the naturalist project is picked up and extended by the genre's most crucial critic. In complaining that the New Historicists read life itself as though it were an endless poem, making promiscuous analogical transfers from one realm of meaning to another, Pizer provides a critical reiteration of Frank Norris's refrain of "life, not literature." "Their criticism," Pizer writes, "is asking to be read as a form of poetic exploration of a culture which is itself conceived of as a huge poem" (79). More crucially, Pizer employs (and then draws our attention to) an "acerbic tone," one explicitly intended to "cause hurt" to writers whose stylistic idiosyncrasies and mannered prose lead to misreadings. (The critic's final pull back to "English departments" as institutions reveals a corresponding naturalistic interest in professionalization, as well as in force.) In adopting the role of the polemicist himself—in drawing attention to his own minority status, and then refusing to stay silent in the face of overwhelming opposition—Pizer draws our attention to the way that the rhetorical tactics of the original naturalists have been adopted by the genre's critics and have become a conventional part of the academic construct of the genre.

Of course, Pizer is hardly the only critical polemicist in the naturalist canon; many naturalist scholars use polemical tropes to a greater or lesser extent. Among the most conspicuous of these conventions is the tendency toward self-marginalization that is evident in much of the genre's criticism. Simply stated, it has become customary in the study of naturalism for the critic to indulge in a short meditation on the ways in which naturalism continues to be critically maligned or unfairly treated in comparison to other genres. So, in *The Theory and Practice of American Literary Naturalism*, Donald Pizer states that "in the demonology of modern literary history, naturalism is usually the anti-Christ" (36), having noted earlier that "the movement has been attacked by literary journalists and academic critics since its origin" (13). "Naturalism," Catharine R. Stimpson writes, "has often been ignored or oversimplified" (ix), and Eric Carl Link says that "because the literary naturalists are often misunderstood, they are often undervalued" (165). John Dudley finds that the genre has been "dismissed by some critics as either an extreme outgrowth of realism or an unfortunate philosophical dead-end" (5). Lisa Long believes that naturalism "has always been a rather sketchy character in the ongoing drama of our national literary genealogy," and Lee Clark Mitchell strikes a note of ironic understatement when he observes that "literary naturalism has never enjoyed an easy time with the critics" (vii). Jennifer Fleissner contends that the genre "has remained mostly marginal to American literary and cultural history" (6).

Such a gesture serves the obvious purpose of rationalizing and justifying yet another incursion into naturalism, yet another reframing of the genre's main concerns. But it also reaffirms the embattled essence of the genre, suggesting that naturalism exists and thrives in a state of constant opposition. Naturalism construes itself as the central marginal figure in American literature, the official outsider of the canon, the established generic Other. The study of naturalism thus contains these countermovements: with each new book and article, the genre pushes further toward the center while simultaneously insisting upon its own otherness. For the naturalist scholar, this self-othering gesture, this claiming of minority status, serves a double function: it imbues legitimacy to the study of naturalistic texts within a broader academic culture in which marginality is frequently equated with authenticity, while simultaneously channeling the radicalism and revolutionary spirit of its subject matter, figuring its own scholarly praxis as a rebellion unto itself. Naturalism persists, heroically, in the face of the multitudinous forces that would cheer its demise. And because it is already operating from the subject position of the Other, the genre is then free to sidestep the ethical implications inherent to the use of polemic itself. The naturalists' marginal subject position becomes the source (in Michel Foucault's phrase) of "the rights authorizing him to wage war" (382). The viciousness of the tactics is justified by the prior victimization of the subject (a "victimization" that had been self-consciously courted from the start).

But what is at stake (particularly for writers from racial and sexual minorities) in propagating these pronouncements of generic marginality? Why are naturalism's principal advocates so invested in the vision of naturalism as liminal, peripheral, edgy? Is there not something risky, if not slightly paradoxical, in making Frank Norris—the patriarchal, nativist, bourgeois, white supremacist naturalist—the sign for a certain kind of "marginality" (or "disadvantage," in Cowley's phrase) in Progressive Era American culture? To what extent can a scholar today seriously claim that naturalism has been "marginalized," and what is at stake in such a categorization—for naturalism and for those who have been marginalized by it?

The Central Marginal Genre

How, in the end, are we to account for the polemical nature of naturalism? Before proceeding, allow me to make explicit three of the implicit suggestions that inform my analysis. The first relates to the economic situation of the writer in the Gilded Age, the second has to do with the internal theorization of the genre, and the third concerns naturalism's response to deeper cultural inclinations encoded in the symbolic construction of America.

First, and most pragmatically, the character of naturalist polemicism was shaped by the dominant turn-of-the-century mode of literary production: that is, the newspaper industry.[12] Virtually all of the first American naturalists, including Dreiser, Norris, Crane, London, and Harold Frederic, spent some significant portion of their time working as professional newspapermen. Their work as journalists offered them a high degree of social mobility, which was to inform their fictions in concrete ways—particularly in naturalism's oft-cited "sordidness"; in works like *Maggie*, *McTeague*, and *Sister Carrie*, naturalist authors showed their readership how the other half (and, they intimated, much more than half) lived. Their literary sensibilities were all, to some extent, forged at the city desks of newspapers in San Francisco, Chicago, St. Louis, Pittsburgh, and New York. As Dreiser put it in *A Book about Myself*, the newspaper man "is at least free of moralistic mush. Nearly everything in connection with those trashy romances of justice, truth, mercy, patriotism, public profession of all sorts, is already and forever gone if they have been in the profession for any length of time" (396). They liked to conceive of their role as that of the "detached observer"—but always, given the economic realities of the fin-de-siècle newspaper industry, with one eye toward the headline. The 1890s print industry was a particularly cutthroat enterprise: new dailies were constantly springing up to compete for market share, and editors of the period were famous for trying almost anything to attract new readers.[13] These market conditions drew them (under the guidance of editors looking for a leg up on the competition) to sensational subject matter and led them to write about such subjects in an empurpled style. Papers like Pulitzer's New York *World* and Hearst's New York *American* achieved large circulations by indulging in "vanity, self-glorification, and sensationalism," as Theodore Dreiser once phrased it (*Uncollected Prose* 51). The razor-thin line between covering the news and making it (as well as that separating polemic from *polemos*) was blurred and sometimes (as in the case of William Randolph Hearst's "coverage" of American military adventurism in Cuba, Puerto Rico, and the Philippines) completely erased. In *The Brass Check: A Study of American Journalism*, Upton Sinclair wrote that Hearst's reporters were "willing by deliberate and shameful lies, made out of whole cloth, to stir nations to enmity and drive them to murderous war" (94).

In their capacity as reporters, the naturalists interviewed politicians, preachers, and convicted killers; they viewed hangings and inspected autopsies. It was in this highly competitive, vibrant, socially mobile, urban, drink-soaked, cigar-munching, frequently ethically underhanded mise-en-scène that the polemicism of the naturalist authors was honed. This milieu conditioned the prose style of writers who were forced to produce an enormous quantity of words under severe deadlines.[14] Mencken's prose would emerge, in the early 1900s, as the distillation and the pinnacle of this style in its most learned mode; but the quick, sketchy, attention-grabbing, unsentimental, hard-edged prose of the Gilded Age newsroom was common to all naturalists. They could appear to be cynical, although this cynicism was usually the manifestation of a deeper optimism, a sense that things could be improved and were worth improving—and perhaps even sentimentalism. This is not to say that naturalism is mere sensationalism, that it is simply hack journalism in novelistic form. But naturalism itself is often geared toward the topical, often "issue-based," and written in attention-grabbing tones, all of which is constitutive of naturalism's polemicism. Most crucially, however, the proximity of naturalism and newspaper writing led to its signature understanding of the relationship between life and literature—between events that happen in the world and the language that writers employ to describe those events. Newspaper work was indeed writing, but it was a great distance removed from the genteel world controlled by (in Mencken's phrase) "old women of both sexes" (qtd. in Hobson 76).

In addition to their literary apprenticeships as "newspapermen," many of the naturalists also participated in the burgeoning magazine market for polemical discourse. As Frank Mott reports, the number of non-newspaper periodicals in America nearly doubled during naturalism's gestational period—from 3,300 in 1885 to 6,000 in 1905 (11). By the time the original naturalists arrived on the scene, serial publications had emerged as a crucial venue for aspiring young wordsmiths. Norris and Dreiser (along with almost every other writer associated with the naturalist canon) published essays, features, and fiction in a wide cross section of periodicals. Predictably, the naturalists' work generally did not appear in the more patrician magazines of the age. The *Atlantic Monthly*, *Century*, *Scribner's*, and *Harper's* tended to err on the side of conservatism and gentility. But a host of other magazine outfits—titles like *McClure's*, *World's Work*, the *Masses*, and Mencken's *Smart Set*—proved less squeamish, allowing the naturalists to broaden their scope and reach a wider readership (in addition to keeping them financially afloat while they composed their longer works). By and large, as Charles Johanningsmeier observes, the naturalists fostered an image of themselves as being unjustly persecuted by those with their hands on the levers of power in the publishing industry. He quotes Jack London's eponymous doppelganger, Martin Eden, who gripes about "the editors, sub-editors, associate editors, most of them, and the manuscript-readers for the magazines and book publishers" being, "of all creatures under the sun[,] the most unfit" and "the very creatures who decide what shall and what shall not find its way into print" (qtd. in Johanningsmeier 796). On balance, and a few pricked egos notwithstanding, the naturalists got more out of the magazine market than it got out of them. Theodore Dreiser found reliable work on the editorial staff of several different magazines and supported himself for many years editing the *Delineator*, *Ev'ry Month*, and the *Bohemian*. Frank Norris benefited materially from his relationship with S. S. McClure, who gave him an editorial post and funded some of the Western research that would find its way into *The Octopus* (Johanningsmeier 369). Perhaps most importantly, the magazine market allowed the naturalists to participate in a more national polemical conversation on issues ranging from foreign policy to immigration to gender roles. Serial publications expanded the spectrum of the naturalists' polemical engagements and encouraged them to think beyond regional contexts. And much of the initial "theorizing" about naturalism itself would be worked out in the pages of those same journals. Both newspapers and magazines were essential ingredients in the literary marketplace in which naturalism's polemical style was forged.

A second, related aspect of the polemical nature of naturalism, then, has to do with the theoretical assumptions through which the central participants of the genre made sense of their own enterprise. It will come as no surprise that critics are highly divided on the issue of whether naturalism can be said to operate according to anything resembling a "theory": Pizer answers in the affirmative, arguing that although Norris's critical essays are "poorly written, repetitious, and occasionally plain silly, they nevertheless contain a coherent critical attitude of some importance" (*Realism and Naturalism* 99). Michael Davitt Bell counters this by pointing out that "nothing in Norris's essays is sillier than the critical attitude that underlies them" (*Problem* 241). However one comes down on the issue of the "theory" of naturalism, Norris's essays do usefully distil a pervasive tension between performance and spectatorship in Gilded Age culture. In Norris's call for naturalism, writing itself is relegated to a sphere of pure spectatorship, which is at worst a kind of record of quotidian banalities ("tragedies involving cups of tea") and at best the observational work of, say, a crime reporter—someone operating nearer to the realm of "life itself." (Norris's "life," as Michael Davitt Bell and others have pointed out, is of course the crudest paracosm, "the fantasy of a writer haunted by the spectre of 'effeminate' irrelevance" [*Problem* 119].)[15] Naturalism, in other words, is the literature of authors who have thoroughly internalized the newspaper reporter's belief in reportorial "objectivity" and that the function of literary representation is to truthfully record the events of the "real world"—and those who attempt to balance these convictions with a compensatory desire to be "of" the world itself. In short, it was precisely the naturalists' "theoretical" belief in the effeminate or otherwise sexually suspect character of writing (and its corresponding "irrelevance" to the real world of masculine affairs) that generated a compensatory desire to produce literature that actively and irrefutably engaged in the "real world." The naturalists' polemicism was the product of this fear of irrelevance that underlies the "theoretical" musings of its practitioners. They wanted to prove to others (and to themselves) that literature could actively participate in the world of "big things"; they wanted to undo the barriers between life and literature that, paradoxically, had animated their literary efforts.

A final phase of naturalism's polemicism relates to the embattled position its writers and critics habitually assume within the American canon. In 1915, Stuart P. Sherman complained that there was something positively un-American about Theodore Dreiser and his novels. "Dreiser's field seems curiously outside American society," Sherman observed (9). It wouldn't be the last time Dreiser would be met with such a charge (and particularly when he found himself trumpeting pro-Germanic viewpoints during both World Wars). Indeed, there was something very slightly foreign about all of naturalism, what with its associations with Emile Zola and a host of other European writers and scientists. As I've been claiming, however, naturalism has always involved emphasizing one's own otherness to the majority. In *A World Elsewhere*, Richard Poirier writes, "to be outside 'American society' is of course to be in the great American literary tradition" (237). The naturalists and their critics adopt a self-effacing polemical rhetoric precisely to establish the genre as the outsider, the "central marginal" figure in the American canon. The naturalists' polemicism allies them with a well-established pattern in the American experience, in which one way of instantiating Americanness is to reimagine oneself through an act of opposition. This is partly to explain why American naturalism remains such highly contested ground, while the naturalisms of other nations have long been fixed. In constantly defining naturalism as outside the mainstream of American literature (or, in the case of scholars, outside the institutional mainstream), naturalism has, in effect, claimed it.

At bottom, the polemical core of naturalism may well result from a central contradiction. For many of its key authors, the very fact of their writing stands as a kind of repudiation of the thesis that naturalism is often taken to exemplify. Naturalistic characters, it is most often assumed, are animated by a constellation of environmental conditions that are external to them. But as Ralph Ellison famously pointed out, Richard Wright's very existence as an author seemed to rebut the main thesis of his naturalism. The material circumstances of Theodore Dreiser's upbringing allied him more closely with Wright's place on the socioeconomic spectrum than with the realists; Dreiser taught his own mother how to read. Naturalism is the natural (perhaps even the necessary) site of polemicism, insofar as the internal logic of the genre seems to contradict the possibility of creative imagination for so many of its practitioners. A polemical attitude was a necessary precondition for the naturalistic mentality. The traditional naturalistic milieu—where environment is pure force, capable of determining personal relations while remaining untouched by them—is a field of assumptions that (if the acts of reading and writing are to retain any of their traditional consolations) necessitates a contradictory orientation. The very act of writing in a naturalistic universe often seems to contradict its own premises, and the conscious or unconscious recognition of that fact precipitates a redoubling of one's efforts in the opposite direction.

The present study, however, is oriented less toward the historical causes of the naturalists' polemicism than it is toward the future polemical contexts they helped to engender. It is perhaps less than surprising, given the temperaments of the artists involved and the inclination of the genre as a whole, that naturalistic fictions went on to participate in (and help establish) the terms for some of the most polemical debates in modern American life. For as long as naturalism has existed, its authors have been understood to have been partaking in literary acts of cultural insurrection; along the way, the naturalists charted the basic coordinates of a wide range of issues. The naturalists changed the way Americans think about issues like environmentalism, abortion, and terrorism. The following chapters, which take up naturalistic encounters with these issues in a series of mutually illuminating case studies, is also an attempt to engage with these ideas in their own spirit—that is, to situate naturalistic novels, polemically, within the highly fraught contexts they helped to invent.

The chapters ahead, then, are not meant to constitute another in an already overcrowded field of "theories" of naturalism. My intention is not to use these texts to concretize yet another incontrovertible generalization, applicable to all instances, about the nature of naturalism in America. Instead, I hope to offer extended analyses of three provocative naturalistic engagements, each of which further elaborates on the attitude of polemicism that underlies the genre, and also make a case for why we should continue to take naturalism seriously. My argument here is not that the naturalists' novels are "polemics" in the same sense as their newspaper and magazine work, which often fought ferociously for one side in an ongoing debate. I'm not suggesting that every naturalistic novel can ultimately be reduced to an argument "for" this or "against" that. Rather, the novels under consideration here turn on complex, artistic treatments of polemical issues, and they respond to those issues in ways that are often surprising. In their extremities, the naturalists can strike us as culturally alien, atavistic figures from a more primitive age. But I hope to show how the naturalists participated in and helped to create our own polemical world, how they helped instantiate a wider culture of polemicism in place today as surely as it was in the age of Mencken.

3

Against the Grain

Ecology, Environmentalism, and Frank Norris's *The Octopus*

The "Nature" of Naturalism

Every generation, it is sometimes observed, gets the artists it deserves. Something similar might be said about nature. Today, we seem to exist in a profoundly neurotic natural environment.[1] Twenty-first-century climatologists and environmental activists have successfully created an image of the climate system as fragile, perishable, twitchy. Climate change, as we know, is exacerbated by various feedback mechanisms embedded within the system: to use an example provided by Elizabeth Kolbert, "once an ice sheet begins to melt, it starts to flow faster, which means it also thins out faster, encouraging further melt" (54). Feedbacks of this sort—the water vapor feedback, the permafrost, the ice-albedo feedback—amplify tiny changes to the climate system into large, unpredictable forces of nature. In our age of environmental crisis, nature is akin to the neurotic subject: the symptoms of climate change (glacial melt, the increased ferocity of hurricanes, genetic mutation in displaced insect populations) arise from self-reinforcing complexes, which are deeply suppressed within the system, and can be brought to the surface only through close readings of nature and its destabilizing complexes.

This image of nature, in which the stability of the system is determined by a powerful (if indirect, even mysterious) human influence—one that cannot be measured with precision but that must nonetheless be assumed if only to stave off an impending apocalypse—is a long way from "nature" as it was conceived by the naturalists. When Frank Norris invokes nature, he usually imagines something indomitable and immense, an entity not only impervious to human interference but determining the very boundaries of the human.[2] Far from neurotic itself, Norris's nature was a place from which to escape modernity and its crippling anxieties: for the central characters of

Norris's *The Octopus*, Presley, Annixter, and Vanamee (and for the author himself, who had suffered from a breakdown of some description in 1897), the West was supposed to represent a theater for masculine recuperation. Here, among the super-abundant wheat fields of the San Joaquin Valley, the vitiated and neurasthenic modern subject would tap into the spirit of the West and reconnect with his racial essence.[3] But why, then, does no one seem to be getting well in *The Octopus*?

It may appear counterintuitive to begin a study of naturalism's polemicism by focusing on *The Octopus*. Frank Norris could be a staggeringly antagonistic and polemical author, but *The Octopus* itself may initially strike us as one of Norris's least polemical efforts. Indeed, in the end, Norris's novel seems to negotiate a compromise between the hard-line naturalistic "world of force" and the traditional Judeo-Christian cosmology that the genre is often held to be rebelling against.[4] Pages from the end, the mystical shepherd Vanamee is given the task of distilling a moral from the sprawling plot: "The grain we think is dead *resumes again*; but how? Not as one grain, but as twenty. So all life. Death is only real for all the detritus of the world, for all the sorrow, for injustice, for all the grief. Presley, the good never dies; evil dies, cruelty, oppression, selfishness, greed—these die; but nobility, but love, but sacrifice, but generosity, but truth, thank God for it, small as they are, difficult as it is to discover them—these live forever, these are eternal" (1085). This sounds more like St. Paul's address to the Corinthians than the summation of a naturalist novel—a novel that, Norris had promised, would return "definitely to the style of MacT. [*McTeague*] and stay with it right along. . . . The Wheat series will be straight naturalism with all the guts I can get into it" (*Letters* 48). *The Octopus*, for Donald Pizer, amounted to "Norris's fullest and most elaborate attempt to translate the conventionally supernatural into the natural" (*Novels of Frank Norris* 145). It was, in short, Norris's *Paradise Lost*, the argument of which would justify the ways of the naturalistic universe to his fellow man. *The Octopus* was an affirmation of faith: despite the various social problems and rank injustices documented in the course of the novel, we may rest assured that love, sacrifice, and generosity are eternal truths, built into the natural order of things.[5] In the end, the wheat from California will fill empty stomachs in Asia. Norris had taken some controversial positions in his time, but this was not one of them.

However, despite a message that would have been palatable to constituencies normally opposed to naturalism, and a tone that bordered on the conciliatory, *The Octopus* is situated at the crux of what has become the most polemical issue of our age. In *The Future of Environmental Criticism* (2005), Lawrence Buell puts it forcefully: "W. E. B. Du Bois predicted that the great public issue of the twentieth century would be the problem of the color line. In the century just begun, that problem shows no sign of abating. But ultimately a still more pressing question may prove to be whether planetary life will remain viable for most of the earth's inhabitants without major changes in the way we live now" (vi). With its deep interest in nature, environmentality, and even sustainability, it is fair to say that *The Octopus* represents an early engagement with what has become "the great public issue" of our time. The novel manifests this environmental consciousness in a number of productive contexts, including biodiversity (Mrs. Derrick is appalled by the "unnatural" sight of ten thousand acres of wheat in direct contrast to her parents' farm, which was home to a diverse array of crops and livestock); globalization (the novel ends with an enormous shipment of wheat bound for new markets in Asia, and Derrick's "ticker" indicated price fluctuations in world grain markets); and a host of new farming technologies (including genetic manipulation of seed and other strategies that would fall under the umbrella term "industrial agriculture"). Doubtless, terms like "biodiversity" were unfamiliar to Norris, but his work explored the concepts without the nomenclature. The novel also hinges on questions of the artistic representation of nature and anticipates the central positions (and tensions) within environmental literary criticism. In short, if we want to discern a naturalistic attitude toward nature, there is no textual ground more fertile than that of *The Octopus*.[6]

But what would it mean to call *The Octopus* an "environmental" or "proto-environmentalist" or "ecologically oriented" text? How, exactly, did the naturalists conceive of "nature" and of humanity's ethical relationship to the natural world? Were they (as one might expect) gung-ho expansionists, or did they harbor a compensating "respect" for nature, an impulse toward conservation? Do their works develop anything resembling a coherent ecological ethic, responding to the moral claims of the nonhuman world, or do they repackage the timeworn dualist tradition, justifying human domination of the natural environment? Does naturalistic fiction bear out in practice what its authors so often affirmed in theory: that nature is indifferent to humanity—or, at a minimum, that nature had not been created for our own convenience? Or, are we obliged simply to accept Vanamee's Pauline wisdom as the official "naturalistic" position on nature?

Surely (to answer the last question first) a text's attitude toward the natural environment may run counter to the intentions of the author. But equally important to achieving a viable environmental literary criticism is the reader's capacity to read against his or her own preconceptions about what it means to read. Obviously, on some level, any text can be read "ecologically" given that, in Robert Kern's phrase, "their authors, consciously or not, inscribe within them a certain relation to their place" (260). But in order to consider the environment on its own terms, Kern advocates an ecocentric mode of reading that he calls "reading against the grain," which involves working "to recover the environmental character or orientation of works whose conscious or foregrounded interests lie elsewhere" (260). Because readers have been programmed to interpret ecological features of literary works primarily according to the narrative needs they fulfill, reading against the grain "depends upon our willingness as readers to marginalize, if not completely overlook, precisely those aspects and meanings of texts that are traditionally privileged or valorized, . . . mean[ing] a whole range of anthropocentric attitudes and assumptions whose authority and even hegemony in reading and criticism are often still taken for granted" (267). "Reading against the grain" is a polemical mode of reading, in that it sometimes involves the deliberate "marginalization" of precisely those elements—character, the autonomous self, perhaps even the concept of "narrative" as it is normally formulated—that have been crucial to the study of literature. In this chapter, then, I hope to "read against the grain" of *The Octopus*, a practice that in this case will have less to do with dragging environmental interests center stage (for they are already very much in the spotlight) than with exposing and deliberately marginalizing what is most often posited as Norris's own (masculine, expansionist, and illiterate) ethos. I engage this task in the hope of retrieving an alternative set of (feminine, sustainable, and literary) values that was already embedded in the novel, but has thus far been overlooked.

First, I will need to say a few more words about what "nature" means in this context and about environmental literary criticism in general. I'll then turn to *The Octopus* itself, taking up a question that seems to preoccupy many of its characters: precisely how much aesthetic "distance" is necessary for the proper apprehension of nature? Just how deep into nature can we expect to go without losing ourselves? *The Octopus* evinces a tension (a central one for today's ecocritics) between the desire to throw off the shackles of aesthetics and experience nature "directly" and a corresponding fear of nature's obliterating power when perceived without our familiar aesthetic frames. This tension between art and nature finds a corresponding tension between the form and content of the novel itself. The explicit argument of the novel—its less than polemical "content"—emphasizes the majesty and beneficence of natural power as symbolized by the wheat. The novel troubles its own thesis, however, by representing the wheat itself as a product of human agency—as an *un*natural commodity of industrialization—while it is simultaneously forced to bear its symbolic burden. Despite its overt skepticism toward aesthetic frames, I argue that the novel finally hinges on a highly artificial aesthetic unity of place (California), race (Anglo-Saxon), and form (epic). Rather than fully thwarting an ecological consciousness, however, these unresolved tensions in Norris's text are productive: in the end, the novel itself might function as a bridge between naturalism and an ecological ethic, in spite of the famous chauvinisms of its author.

Thinking Environmentally

To begin *How Fiction Works*, his 2008 collection of thoughts on writing, James Wood ventilates an old metaphor about the construction of literature. "The house of fiction," he says, "has many windows, but only two or three doors. I can tell a story in the third person or in the first person, and perhaps in the second person singular or in the first person plural, though successful examples of these latter two are rare indeed. And that is it. Anything else probably will not much resemble narration; it may be close to poetry, or prose-poetry" (5). For Wood, the house of fiction inevitably rests upon the foundation of a self, which expresses itself in a voice that is either godlike and omniscient (third person) or subjective and partial (first person). What Wood will go on to argue is that the most successful fiction manages to bridge first- and third-person narration through free indirect style, a technique that allows us to see through the eyes of various characters even as we see through the eyes of the author.

For Lawrence Buell, environmental writing and criticism must address the construction of fiction from its foundations on up. In *The Environmental Imagination: Thoreau, Nature Writing, and the Formation of American Culture*, Buell argues that one of the most fundamental tasks of environmental writing involves questioning "the validity of the self as the primary focalizing device for both writer and reader: to make one wonder, for instance, whether the self is as interesting an object of study as we supposed, whether the world would become more interesting if we could see it from the perspective of a wolf, a sparrow, a river, a stone" (179). One of Wood's most basic assumptions is that "as soon as someone tells a story about a character, narrative seems to want to bend itself around that character, wants to merge with that character, to take on his or her way of thinking and speaking" (8). This is exactly the sort of thing that environmental literary criticism refuses to take for granted. From an ecocritical perspective, narrative need not automatically bend itself toward character—in fact, environmental writing more often strives to bend itself toward natural settings or to blur the neat distinctions between characters and settings. If narrative must bend toward "character," perhaps that category itself can be opened up to include all manner of nonhuman agents. For Buell, the "I"—whether the explicit "I" of first-person narration or the concealed "I" of third—"has no greater claims to being the main subject than the chickens, the chopped corn, the mice, the snakes, the phoebes—who are somehow interwoven with me" (179). Therefore, while the house of fiction may have only two or three doors, one of the priorities of Buell's "environmental consciousness" involves admitting more than recognizably human characters through those passageways. Such is the more modest claim of ecocriticism: to let the chickens in the house. The less modest claim is that the house never really existed in the first place—at least, it never existed as anything more substantial than an anthropocentric delusion. Indeed, the very notion that the business of fiction takes place inside of houses, which can be shut up and sealed off from the external environment, is more or less inimical to a literary praxis dedicated to studying the ecology as an organic, profoundly interconnected whole.[7]

It perhaps goes without saying that *The Octopus* doesn't do very well when judged by Wood's aesthetic standards. Norris makes no serious effort to render his narrative world from any subject position outside of his own. When it came to free-indirect style, Norris was either uninterested or incapable (or both). Most of Norris's descriptive language in *The Octopus* bears no relationship to the actual thing being described. Here, for example, is how Norris described the ranchers' league moments after its inception: "It was the uprising of The People; the thunder of the outbreak of revolt; the mob demanding to be led, aroused at last, imperious, resistless, overwhelming. It was the blind fury of insurrection, the brute, many-tongued, red-eyed, bellowing for guidance, baring its teeth, unsheathing its claws, imposing its will with the abrupt, resistless pressure of the relaxed piston, inexorable, knowing no pity" (800). And here he is describing something completely different—the San Joaquin Valley after the harvest: "flagellated with heat, quivering and shimmering under the sun's red eye . . . the great earth, the mother, after its period of reproduction, its pains of labour, delivered of the fruit of its loins, slept the sleep of exhaustion in the infinite repose of the colossus, benignant, eternal, strong, the nourisher of nations, the feeder of an entire world" (1084). From Wood's formalist perspective, this language is a melodramatic mess: for instance, how, in the first passage, can a "piston" be "relaxed" while it exerts "resistless pressure"? Why is the crowd "red-eyed" in the first passage, while the sun is a "red eye" in the second one? The answer has less to do with the fact that crowds and suns have anything in common than it does with the way Norris used language itself. When he was describing anything with "Force"—whether a sun, a crowd, a railroad, whatever—he would very frequently capitalize the noun (the People; the Wheat), pile up the adjectives (irresistible, insatiable, inexorable), and, in a surprising number of cases, garnish the object in question with a cherry red eye.[8]

The Octopus may fall short of Wood's aesthetic standard, but that doesn't mean it fails according to Buell's environmental one. In fact, Norris's aesthetic inadequacy—his refusal to bend his narration toward "character"—could signal a resistance to the destructive modernist self-absorption that has (some ecocritics hold) contributed to the increasing marginalization of the nonhuman world.[9] The most fundamental criterion of Buell's "environmental consciousness" is a text's resistance to anthropocentrism, a recognition of the interpenetration of human and nonhuman worlds. In other words, the environment itself, in such a view, must not simply be a theater for human actions but an agent in its own right. Here, Norris's novel seems to strike an interesting balance: for while *The Octopus* obviously turns on irreducibly human conflicts and dilemmas, the inanimate topography in the various bioregions of the San Joaquin Valley also take on an active role in the narrative. Most obvious in this respect is the wheat itself, which is in some sense meant to operate as a central character in the text.

The Octopus, most critics concur, is structured around the wheat as a symbol of the natural process: the novel traces the cycle of the crop, the planting, cultivation, and harvest of the wheat. The wheat is a symbol of human life processes, a naturalization of the supernatural laws presiding over birth, death, and rebirth.[10] But the wheat is not only a symbol. In fact, the novel explicitly renounces this anthropocentric gesture. The wheat is not an empty signifier in some larger symbolic transaction, depending for its significance upon the ratiocination of an external human mind. Here is Presley's last look over the San Joaquin Valley: "there came to him strong and true the sense and the significance of all the enigma of growth. He seemed for one instant to touch the explanation of existence. Men were nothings, mere animalculæ, mere ephemerides that fluttered and fell and were forgotten between dawn and dusk. . . . Men were naught, death was naught, life was naught; FORCE only existed—FORCE that brought men into the world, FORCE that crowded them out of it to make way for the succeeding generation, FORCE that made the wheat grow, FORCE that gendered it from the soil to give place to the succeeding crop" (1084). In defining the "environmental imagination," Buell had suggested that the human "self" may in the end be less significant than "the mice, the snakes, the phoebes." Norris concurs. Men are "mere animalculæ." And while the individual, character-driven crises in *The Octopus* offer the reader a compelling way into this "Story of California," those crises must appear much less significant in the overall sweep of what Norris called "The Epic of the Wheat."

The Octopus was the first in a projected trilogy of novels that, Norris writes in a prefatory note, "while forming a series, will be in no way connected with each other save only in their relation to (1) the production, (2) the distribution, (3) the consumption of American wheat." The second volume, *The Pit*, was a bestseller when it was released in 1903. The author died before he could complete the final volume of this trilogy, which was to be entitled *The Wolf*. Nonetheless, by placing the ultimate focus of his trilogy upon a crop, rather than on the travails or triumph of a particular human being or community, Norris's work challenges the anthropocentric perspective that has more recently come under attack from environmentally minded critics. If ecocriticism, as Buell suggests, is on some level committed to questioning the self as the primary focalizing device of fiction, Norris's "Epic of the Wheat" presents a preliminary artistic exploration of that principle. The wheat is the sole connection between the novels, which is suggestive of the ways in which a crop can connect people, places, and stories that we might not normally think of as sharing a connection.[11]

And yet it would be simplistic to interpret "FORCE," in the above passage, as a synonym for "nature" as it is employed in contemporary ecocriticism. For Norris's "FORCE" could just as easily stand in for the railroad, for globalization, for larger apocalyptic energies that would eventually crush the ephemeral forms of nature into submission and extinction. If men were "mere nothings," then "the mice, the snakes, the phoebes" could simply count for less than nothing. To attack the innate dignity of the "human" is not, in itself, an affirmation of the innate dignity of nature, nor is it to recognize the profound interdependence between the two. Henry David Thoreau repudiated the anthropocentric cosmology, along with the corresponding encroachments of discipline and rationalization, in favor of the rhythms of the nonhuman world. But there is another option: a rejection of humanism combined with an *embrace* of discipline—a dual repudiation of anthro- and ecocentrism. It seems possible, at least, that Norris's Pauline affirmation of God in nature was also, paradoxically, a categorical rejection of everything in sight.

Some ecologically minded writers, Jackson Lears among them, have suggested a binary between Enlightenment humanism and environmentalism.[12] These writers would have us recognize that the seeds of our current environmental discontents, or rather the assumptions about human superiority that justified and produced wanton environmental destruction, were present within the Enlightenment project from its origins. A true ecological ethic is therefore incompatible with humanism itself: "By insisting on the interdependence of human and non-human worlds," Lears writes, ecological thought "challenges the sacred tenets of [Western] civilization—the drive toward mastery of nature, the obsession with economic productivity, the deep utilitarianism that dismisses spiritual and aesthetic concerns as mere decoration and defines human advance as more things for more people" ("Usefulness of Cranks" 35). The tendency to turn natural bounty into commodities, along with the drive toward systematic control of nature, was built into the Enlightenment from the start. But Frank Norris may be the writer to undo the humanism/environmentalism binary. At times, *The Octopus* seems to affirm the central tenet of environmental consciousness, that humanity is not simply the centerpiece of all creation. Simultaneously, in appearing to worship rationalization, discipline, and other incarnations of "FORCE," Norris seemed to exalt "modernity" in its most hideously destructive incarnations. A closer look at the novel itself, and the historical background it describes, will shed some light on this apparent paradox.

The Mussel Slough Massacre

The plot of *The Octopus* bears some resemblance to the creature for which it is named: the narrative unfolds along a number of tentacles, each of which appear to be writhing in a direction quite independently of the others, but all of which connect back to the central structural and thematic event in the novel, which is the growth of a crop of wheat. The main conflict in the novel is between the Pacific & Southwestern Railroad (P&SW) and a consortium of wheat ranchers who have banded together to oppose the extortionate policies of the railroad. The human embodiment of the railroad is the corpulent S. Behrman, the speculator and railroad agent who, for much of the novel, appears to be physically invincible. But much of the railroad's capacity to intimidate relates to the fact that, as a corporate trust, the P&SW is physically unrepresentable: it is more of a malevolent idea, whose maliciousness is suggested by the image of a pseudo-mythical sea monster.[13] The ranchers know that the corporation is larger than any one representative, and this unearthly quality is a crucial part of the power that seemed (as Norris never tired of putting it) "inexorable." To combat the monster, the ranchers attempt to create a kind of corporate entity of their own, their "league," although they never seem to complete the transmogrification—their interests are ultimately tied to an inescapable physicality, petition as they might to enter the higher, ideational realm of pure force.

Norris's naturalism, in theory, combined the treatment of vast, powerful themes—which he associated generically with romance—with the microscopic attention to quotidian detail commonly associated with realism.[14] So, while his novel is ultimately concerned with the production of wheat as symbolic of the larger, cyclical processes of life and death—cycles animated and fired by a kind of ineradicable life force coursing through the universe—Norris approached his expansive theme via a decidedly petty squabble over the short-hall shipping rates between two equally avaricious parties. Any rise in wheat prices is matched by a corresponding spike in the shipping rates imposed by the railroad, which makes the ranchers feel as though they are perennially on the verge of bankruptcy. This aspect of the ranchers' dispute with the railroad is rooted in the questions over railroad trusts that had been roiling in California since the 1880s. But as the ranchers soon realize, this dispute over the price of shipping grain is superficial compared to the much deeper issue surrounding the ownership of the land itself. And this issue, which leads to the novel's bloody climax, was rooted in an event known as the Mussel Slough Massacre, an extended political conflict that finally erupted into a savage gunfight in 1880.[15]

The events leading to the Mussel Slough Massacre can be traced back at least as far as the deal struck between the Central Pacific and the Union Pacific Railroads and the federal government in the 1860s.[16] The government had allotted every other section of land to incentivize the railroad construction, while the rest of the land was sold to settlers. In order to maximize freight traffic (and their own profits), Southern Pacific encouraged pioneers to settle on their sections, too. The railroad distributed circulars advertising land at prices ranging from $2.50 to $5.00 per acre. Southern Pacific further sweetened the deal with assurances that all developments of the property (irrigation ditches, buildings, and so on) would not be factored into the final sale price when the transactions were eventually completed. Withal, the settlers would have first right of refusal on the land. It was an attractive bargain, and people settled Mussel Slough in droves. And thanks to the prodigious effort of these settlers, the land itself underwent a significant transformation: "from its former barren status the district became a deep breadbasket of California, which was then one of the great wheat growing states in America" (Brown, *No Duty* 94).

By 1878, however, after Mussel Slough had emerged as "one of the finest garden spots in the state," the *Visalia Weekly Delta* printed a series of letters indicating that the railroad had every intention of charging the full market price of the land—a figure reflecting all of the development and cultivation made by the settlers—which varied from $20 to $30 per acre. In Norris's retelling of the Mussel Slough affair, this enormous jump in price is construed as an arbitrary move by the railroad, explicable only insofar as the P&SW itself is understood to be an insatiable colossus, an entity bent on mindlessly increasing its own profits. The historical reality is slightly more complex. As

Richard Maxwell Brown explains, the Southern Pacific was then involved in litigation over their ownership of the lands: some settlers had insisted that because the company had not provided a line from Tres Pinos, in the north, to Huron, in the west, the company had therefore forfeited its title to the land. The settlers intended to claim ownership of the land themselves under the federal Preemption Act of 1841. The railroad retaliated by raising the price exponentially, which was meant to send a strong signal to the farmers. Norris provides a vivid illustration of how the railroad reneged on their side of the deal, but he erases the inconvenient details about how the farmers had reneged on theirs.

As in Norris's novel, the ranchers organized themselves into a settlers' league in order more effectively to oppose the Southern Pacific. But while Norris uses this ranchers consortium as an entry point into a narrative involving political corruption (the business of "new politics," which Magnus Derrick eventually adopts, precipitating his moral downfall), the historical settlers' league was comparatively blunt in its tactics. As Brown characterizes them, the settlers' league was less interested in mendacious political maneuvering (or, for that matter, in their legal battle, which went all the way to the Supreme Court) than they were in prosecuting a campaign of vigilante justice, which consisted of masked night-riding activities, physical intimidation, and perpetrating what was described as a "state of terror" on the Mussel Slough region (Brown, *No Duty* 105). The settlers' militant response, the decidedly harsh and aggressive posture surrounding what was ostensibly a matter for the courts, emerged out of the homestead ethic that had flourished in the American backcountry since the seventeenth century. As Brown explains in "Back Country Rebellions and the Homestead Ethic in America, 1740–1799," the homestead ethic included three beliefs that were central tenets of rural life: "in the right to have and hold, incontestably, a family-sized farm; in the right to enjoy a homestead unencumbered by a ruinous economic burden; and in the right peaceably to occupy the homestead without fear of violence to person and property" (76). Brown sees this ethic as emerging from long-standing policies of free public land grants that had helped entice settlement in Colonial America. As one New Jerseyman had forcefully asserted in 1746, once a man has bestowed his labor upon nature, that land must be considered his to own, and "cannot be taken, without breaking thro' the Rule of Natural Justice; for thereby he would be actually deprived of the Fruits of his Industry" (qtd. in Brown, "Back Country" 78).

But just as the belligerent behavior of the settlers' league emerged out of a particular American ideological formation, the rationale of the railroad was similarly rooted in another, competing version of the American dream. The railroad represents the interests of capital in a newly industrialized market economy in which corporations were emerging as the major players. Land enclosures, such as those in the San Joaquin in the 1880s, were understood as necessary subsidies for the kinds of corporate investment that was driving this new economy. And while Norris certainly used the railroad as an occasion for some of his most flamboyantly melodramatic bursts of prose ("the galloping monster, the terror of steel and steam, with its single eye, cyclopean, red, shooting from horizon to horizon . . . flinging the echo of thunder over the reaches of the valley, leaving blood and destruction in its path"[617]), Norris was not, in the end, unambiguously sympathetic with the side of the ranchers. Our compassion for the ranchers must be somewhat qualified by the fact that they, too, are unrepentant capitalists: both Magnus and Annixter coldly fire and lay off employees early in the novel to maximize profits and exert their force upon the serfs beneath them. Moreover, Norris's innate tendency to admire paternal "force" led him to rationalize the perspective of the railroad through Presley's apparently uncritical acceptance of Shelgrim's doctrine of force at the end of the novel—the fact that the railroad just happens to be assisting, rather than pushing back against, the natural flow of the wheat.

The events that, in all likelihood, drew Norris's attention to this material in the first place unfolded in the spring of 1880. Judge Sawyer of the federal circuit court in San Francisco had found against the settlers some months before, which had led to the filing of twenty-three suits of ejectment by the Southern Pacific (Brown, *No Duty* 105). The last avenue of legal recourse having been stripped away, the settlers' league was now a militia in all but name. On May 11, when members of the league were occupied at a community picnic (which becomes, for obvious thematic reasons, a jackrabbit drive in the novel), railroad agents went to the home of one settler, rounded up all of his household possessions, and dumped them into the road. En route to their second stop, they met with a group of league members, and there followed an exchange of views. The historical record is less than clear on how the ensuing gun battle actually started, and on who fired the first shot; Norris portrays it as an unfortunate series of events in which characters mishear and misunderstand one another, and an agitated horse inadvertently knocks one of the settlers to the ground. "Instantly," we are told by Norris, "revolvers and rifles seemed to go off as of themselves. Both sides, deputies and Leaguers, opened fire simultaneously. At first, it was nothing but a confused roar of explosions" (993).

If the roar of the guns was "confused," so were the later accounts of the event, largely due to the fact that all of the participants in the gunfight died of their wounds. Most of the killing had been done by a pro-railroad settler named Walter J. Crow, who murdered five men during the episode—a greater one-time kill count than such legendary gunmen as Wild Bill Hickok, Wyatt Earp, John Wesely Harding, or Billy the Kid. Crow did not have long to enjoy his distinction, however; he was spotted later that day hiding out in a nearby wheat field, where he was summarily executed. Norris carried off the description of the gunfight with uncharacteristic brevity and efficiency. He expends much more effort on the consequences of the battle, which finds Presley, the poet, reflecting upon what he has witnessed. "Horror weighed intolerably upon him," Norris writes, "monstrous things, huge, terrible, whose names he knew only too well, whirled at a gallop through his imagination, or rose spectral and grisly before the eyes of his mind. Harran dead, Annixter dead, Broderson dead, Osterman, perhaps, even at this moment dying" (1005). Presley's reflections constitute a succinct summary of Norris's idea of good fiction, a more or less explicit reminder of what the novel was supposed to achieve. In one of his perorations to Emile Zola, Norris had insisted that the French naturalist's fictional universe "is a world of big things; the enormous, the formidable, the terrible, is what counts," in contrast to the "monstrous things, huge, terrible" that haunt Presley. Characters in a naturalistic tale must be "flung into the throes of a vast and terrible drama that works itself out in unleashed passions, in blood, and in sudden death" (*Criticism* 72). In witnessing a real gunfight (as opposed to reading about an historical one, which is how Norris came across his material), Presley, the aspiring writer, has discovered the perfect subject for a naturalistic tale. And yet he shrinks from it—he is unable to respond, artistically, to the horrific events he has witnessed.

When considered from an environmental perspective, the events of Mussel Slough, and Norris's naturalistic representation of them, raise some unavoidable questions. Were the ranchers themselves really on the side of rectitude when they took up arms to defend their land? Is the homestead ethic itself ecologically responsible—or is it the very root of the problem? What the ranchers were fighting for, after all, was not simply the land in itself; they were fighting for the integrity of their own labor. What the Mussel Sough affair reminds us is that the WHEAT that Norris rhapsodizes ("untouched, unassailable, undefiled, that mighty world-force, that nourisher of nations, wrapped in Nirvanic calm, indifferent to the human swarm, gigantic, resistless," [1097]) is in fact not "natural" at all—there was no wheat in Mussel Slough until the ranchers dug their irrigation ditches and made the valley flower. Norris claims that the wheat is "resistless to the human swarm," but the wheat's very existence depends upon that swarm to plant, nurture, and harvest it. As for the homestead ethic itself, and the rule of "Natural Justice" cited by the New Jerseyman (in which the addition of one's labor into a particular landscape makes it unimpeachably his own), one can see how such ideological formations were necessary to incentivize expansion and colonization. But it is equally easy to see how such a perspective also works to legitimate a perception of human superiority over the natural world, how it operates to justify unlimited human growth and reckless domination over the natural things that we "own" through the gift of our labor. "The wheat remains," as Presley says; but the characters who are most willing to fight to exert their ownership over it are ushered into an early grave.

Against the Grain

Questions regarding our ethical stewardship versus the simple exploitation of the land may seem ahistorical or even "presentist," but the first stirrings of the modern environmental movement were well underway by the time Norris came to the San Joaquin Valley. John Muir, perhaps the central figure of early American environmentalism, had first come to California nearly three decades before. An early conservationist, Muir overturned the widespread public opinion that California sequoia trees might as well be harvested to extinction, since they appeared to be going extinct anyway. In the process, Muir pioneered the notion that trees were a "renewable resource," permanently changing the way Americans conceived of one phase of their environment.[17] But modern environmentalism, in the eyes of many, had begun with the publication of George Perkins Marsh's *Man and Nature* (1864), which was the first work to articulate what scientists now call "dangerous anthropogenic interference": the idea that human activities are capable of altering the terrestrial world in ways that are unpredictable, irreversible, and quite possibly apocalyptic. Marsh argued that the ancient Mediterranean civilizations brought about their own demise through environmentally exploitative practices that led to deforestation, soil erosion, desertification, and other wanton destruction of flora and fauna. If Americans failed to recognize their own impact on the environment, Marsh warned, they could follow a trajectory similar to the Roman Empire. "Our inability to assign definite values to these causes of the disturbance of natural arrangements," Marsh warned—addressing the climate change skeptics of the Civil War era—"is not a reason for ignoring the existence of such causes in any general view of the relations between man and nature, and we are never justified in assuming a force to be insignificant because its measure is unknown, or even because no physical effect can be traced to it as its origin" (465). By the time science can adequately measure humanity's impact on the environment, Marsh cautioned, the damage will already have been done.

Ecologically minded thinking had therefore been around for decades, particularly in Norris's native California. And *The Octopus* itself—when read against the grain—does indeed register an ecological attitude, or at least the passions that would ignite it, although they are lodged within a character so deliberately marginalized and subservient that few have thought to give her a second glance. Annie Derrick, Magnus's wife, is a former teacher of "literature, music, and penmanship in a seminary in the town of Marysville" (623). Mrs. Derrick is the embodiment of all the feminine clichés that Norris liked to ascribe to her sex. She has a taste for "nice" things and for "fine" literature; she has a great appreciation for "style." She is nauseatingly delicate of constitution and is constantly nagging her husband about his morals and business. Her most pressing desire is to depart to Europe. But it is her attitude toward nature that is most striking. Near the opening of the novel, we learn that Mrs. Derrick had been living on the ranch, Los Muertos, for ten years. And still, Norris, writes, "Los Muertos frightened her" (624). Mrs. Derrick's fear of Los Muertos is not the fear of an essentially urban sensibility who has been forced out of her natural habitat. This is not a city woman who has been forced out of doors against her will. In fact, as Norris relates, Mrs. Derrick had grown up on a farm. Rather, Mrs. Derrick's fear of Los Muertos is the fear of one who feels as though she is living in the midst of what she considers a kind of natural obscenity. Her childhood farm in eastern Ohio, she recalls, was a neatly groomed, carefully cultivated stretch of some five hundred acres. This farm was home to a diversity of crops and animals, and every element—"the water lot, the cow pasture, the corn lot, the barley field . . . the wheat farm" (624) and so on—had its place. As for the actual operation of this modest enterprise, Mrs. Derrick recalls that the cultivation of the land had amounted to a kind of honest courtship of nature: the farmers had "loved their land, caressing it, coaxing it, nourishing it as though it were a thing almost conscious; where the seed was sown by hand, and a single two-horse plough was sufficient for the entire farm; where the scythe sufficed to cut the harvest and the grain was thrashed with flails" (624). Los Muertos itself, Presley discovers, was once home to a diversity of crops and livestock. In a conversation with an ancient Spanish-Mexican villager in Guadalajara, Presley learns that the Derrick ranch had once raised sheep, horses, and steers, and had grown grapes and olives in addition to wheat. Now, however, Magnus Derrick's operation consists of "ten thousand acres of wheat! Nothing but wheat from the Sierra to the Coast range" (593).

Critics have long concurred that the central conflict in *The Octopus* hinges on the large-scale transformations that were occurring within American capitalism in the Gilded Age—the advent of trusts, for instance, or the monopolization and incorporation of lands to incentivize railroad construction.[18] But the novel is also attentive to the new ways that grain was being brought to market—for instance, Norris tells us that Derrick's "ticker," which indicated price fluctuations in the world grain market, was "the most significant object in the office" (619). The ticker drew Los Muertos into a globalized market, where "a drought on the prairies of Dakota, a rain on the plains of India, a frost on the Russian steppes, [or] a hot wind on the llanos of the Argentine" (620) influenced the market value of the San Joaquin crop. Norris's ranchers are among the very first participants in a truly globalized agriculture industry. For all the purple prose about the wheat as force, the novel is also intensely aware of the wheat as a commodity, something that derives its value not from within itself but from the external forces of supply and demand.

With this change in the marketing and distribution of wheat had come an equally important change in the grain's *production*—and with it, a change in humanity's relationship with nature. As Annie Derrick's bucolic childhood reminiscences suggest, Magnus Derrick is representative of a hinge generation, one that marked a transition from the small-scale, family farm of Mrs. Derrick's parent's generation, and thus farming as it had basically been practiced for millennia ("where the seed was sown by hand . . . where the scythe sufficed to cut the harvest"), to the massive, industrial-scale agricultural practices pioneered on ranches like Los Muertos. The novel narrates the rise of what is now called industrial agriculture, a revolution in farming technologies that radically changed how food reaches American consumers. While Annie Derrick's father's farm had been home to an array of different plant and animal species, on her husband's operation there is only wheat. The transformation of agricultural practices registered by the novel was also a major contributing factor for the urbanization of American society. Indeed, until about the 1920s, 1 out of every 4 Americans lived on a farm, and the average farmer's crop output was enough to sustain 12 Americans in addition to his own family. Today, only 2 percent of Americans farm for a living, but the typical farm feeds 129 people. As Michael Pollan writes, "measured in terms of output per worker," contemporary American farmers "are the most productive humans who have ever lived" (34).[19]

Norris depicts the rise of industrial agriculture from a number of angles. These ranchers, we are told, are not humble agrarians, but have studied "scientific agriculture" at university (597). Consider, moreover, how the relatively minor character of Cedarquist becomes obsessed with the idea of opening up new markets for the consumption of American wheat; at the novel's conclusion, we learn that the capitalist has sold his defunct iron plant, the Atlas Works, to finance a new line of wheat ships for Pacific and Oriental trade. "We'll carry our wheat into Asia yet," Cedarquist proclaims (1094). Industrial agriculture also called for innovation in agricultural technology and farming methods, which Norris manages to capture in a subplot involving the Derrick's purchase of a new fleet of plows from an eastern manufacturer. The ranchers are also shown to have a rudimentary understanding of the genetics of wheat growing. Harran Derrick takes great interest in different varieties of wheat: the ranch has had its best results with the White Sonora and Propo varieties, but it is clear that the farm experiments with different varieties in order to maximize yield. Of course, it is on farms like the Derrick's that genetically modified fertilizers and hybrid crops will be introduced in order to supplement nature's bounty. In short, the Derrick ranch is the locus of political, technological, and economic innovations designed to achieve economies of scale in wheat production. The most conspicuous sign of this revolution is, of course, the ubiquitous presence of the wheat itself.

The later action of the novel unfolds within a vast, inescapable sea of wheat. There is perhaps some irony in the fact that a ranch like the Derricks', despite its immense productivity, would have had to import all of its food. Unlike the family farm of Mrs. Derrick's childhood, Los Muertos is not self-sustaining: its product is basically inedible without processing. This leads us to one of the central ambiguities in Norris's portrayal of the wheat. Much of Norris's melodramatic rhetoric in connection with the wheat—his frequent descriptions of the crop as an elemental, Nirvanic, "world-force, [a] nourisher of nations" (1097)—encourages us to view the wheat as a symbol of the natural order, as representative of a transcendent power, an ultimately beneficent divinity presiding over creation. But at the same time, the wheat is just a tradable product, one commodity amid a marketplace full of commodities, and subject to the same capricious market forces. The novel seems to want to have it both ways: Norris continually speaks to the wheat's transcendence, while his characters continually treat it as a mere commodity. Within the novel, there is no sustained critique of the practices of industrialized farming as instituted in the San Joaquin Valley. It is not clear that Norris himself had any problem with the relationship between humanity and nature as it was embodied by the ranchers and their crop. The only voice to the contrary comes in the soft, feminine protests of Mrs. Derrick, who is vaguely frightened by this "new order of things"—"a ranch bounded only by the horizons, where, as far as one could see, to the north, to the east, to the south and to the west, was all one holding, a principality ruled with iron and steam, bullied into a yield of three hundred and fifty thousand bushels" (624).

Mrs. Derrick's sense that the land has been "bullied" into overproductivity is instructive. For while farmers of the previous generation "coaxed" the crop up from land that they had "nourished" and "loved," the present generation of farmers are reliant upon sheer, masculine force to get the job done. Nowhere is this clearer than in the titillating descriptions of the plowing of Annixter's land, which the author represents as a monumental ravishing of nature. As Norris describes it, this military-like operation consists of thirty-five separate plows, each of which requires a team of ten horses to move. Each of the plows consisted of five shears, so when the entire contingent was in motion, "one hundred and seventy-five furrows were made at the same instant" (678). "Steadily," Norris writes, "the hundred iron hands kneaded and furrowed and stroked the brown, humid earth, the hundred iron teeth bit deep into the Titan's flesh" (679). Norris explicitly intends this agricultural set piece to represent the primal convergence of "the two world forces, the elemental Male and Female, locked in a colossal embrace, at grapples in the throes of an infinite desire, at once terrible and divine" (680). But the undertone of sexual violence continually rises to the surface. Each unrelenting male plow is "insistent, eager, imperious" (677); Norris describes their combined action as the "heroic embrace of a multitude of iron hands, gripping deep into the brown, warm flesh of the land that quivered responsive and passionate under the rude advance, so robust as to be almost an assault, so violent as to be veritably brutal" (680). Norris represents the plowing of the earth as an epic raping of the land. But what is especially troubling, from an ecocritical perspective, is the extent to which Norris describes the land itself as desiring to be raped.

Norris continually characterizes the land as "offering itself" to the plow, the soil as "demanding to be made fruitful" (677, 678). Norris shifts pronouns to bring the reader into this scene, to make him or her feel the land's desire: "One could not take a dozen steps upon the ranches without the brusque sensation that underfoot the land was alive; roused at last from its sleep, palpitating with the desire of reproduction" (677). Here, it is the farmer, rather than the land, who is coaxed, tempted by the land itself, urged on by "the enervating odor of the upturned, living earth" (680). The land is practically begging to be plowed: "It was the long stroking caress, vigorous, male, powerful, for which the Earth seemed panting" (680). Surveying the scene, Vanamee is amazed at the sheer size and scale of this operation. The neighboring ranches, those of Broderson and Osterman, are fully engaged in the same brutal operation. But Vanamee marvels at the certain knowledge that all of the ranches beyond them are similarly occupied, even though he cannot see them: "far off there beyond the fine line of the horizons, over the curve of the globe, the shoulder of the earth, he knew were other ranches, and beyond these others, and beyond these still others, the immensities multiplying to infinity" (680). Here is a molestation of monumental proportions, a massive subjugation fit for the bottomless appetite of the Anglo-Saxon. Norris renders the plowing of the earth as the most prodigious gang rape imaginable.

Again, if there is one character in the novel who sees this tremendous rape of the earth as anything less than a majestic exhibition of masculine puissance, that character is Annie Derrick. Hers is the only voice in the novel that seems to be unsettled by this "new order of things," this new way of bullying nature into what she deems an unnatural, perversely homogenous super productivity. Interestingly, however, the novel registers these attitudes (and marginalizes Annie's perspective) less through her response to "nature" per se, than through her beliefs about art. As we know, Annie Derrick felt that there was something "unnatural" about her husband's operation: "The direct brutality of ten thousand acres of wheat, nothing but wheat as far as the eye could see, stunned her a little. . . . There was something vaguely indecent in the sight, this food of the people, this elemental force, this basic energy, weltering here under the sun in all the unconscious nakedness of a sprawling, primordial Titan" (624). When Mrs. Derrick is "revolted" by the thought of Presley's proposed epic, the "Song of the West"—with "its swift, tumultuous life, its truth, its nobility and savagery, its heroism and obscenity"—her response to the "savagery" and "obscenity" of the art is shown to be directly analogous to the "brutality" and "indecency" of the wheat itself (624). We are therefore meant to disregard Mrs. Derrick's perspective not only for its smallness, for the fact that it comes from a "one-time writing-teacher of a young ladies' seminary," and not even because of the pathetic daintiness of the body that produced these opinions, with its "pretty deer-like eyes and delicate fingers" (624). Mrs. Derrick's opinions on nature are depicted as inadequate because they violate a basic tenet of Norris's *aesthetic* credo: Norris insisted on the distinction between "literature" and "life," and he privileged the latter over the former in all respects. But Mrs. Derrick, it seems, cannot separate life and literature. Indeed, she seems to judge the landscape by the same standards she would use to judge a poem: symmetry, balance, proportion, restraint, and so on. The very aesthetic sensibility ("of the delicacy of point lace") that led her to condemn Presley's poem (as "not literature") is also the root of her revulsion toward the (industrialized) nature that she perceives as indecent.

What little critics have had to say about Annie Derrick and her response to nature has basically served to marginalize her further. Regarding the passage analyzed above, Donald Pizer states that Norris had depicted "a timid, withdrawn, and frightened person, one whose timidity and whose lack of the 'larger view' prevent her from sensing the fundamental benevolence of [nature's] power. To Mrs. Derrick, the railroad and nature are equally destructive because of their power" (*Realism and Naturalism* 163).[20] From an ecocritical perspective, however—that is, if we are prepared to read "against the grain"—we can perhaps interpret Mrs. Derrick as something more than a "timid, withdrawn, and frightened person" lacking in the "larger view." For it is precisely in the larger view, one which takes the entire novel into account—and the even larger view, which considers the long history of human cultivation of nature in relation to the very short history of industrial agriculture—that Mrs. Derrick emerges as a figure of survival and endurance. Throughout the text, Mrs. Derrick opposes the kind of political corruption and backroom dealing that will ultimately destroy her family. She repeatedly enjoins her husband to stay out of the settlers' league and to stay true to his honorable political instincts. In scene after scene, Mrs. Derrick functions as the conscience of the Derrick family, a moral touchstone opposed to both the impulsiveness and hotheadedness of her son Harran and to Magnus's overwhelming ambition and sense of self-importance. The ruination of her family occurs thanks to decisions she forcibly and vocally opposed. And then, at the end of the novel—after Lyman's betrayal has torn the family apart; after Harran's murder and her husband's collapse and degeneration—it falls to Mrs. Derrick to support her family, which she does. On his final visit to the ranch house of Los Muertos, after it has become the property of the P&SW, Presley is shocked to find Magnus in a state of collapse, looking "nearer eighty than sixty"; he notices that all of Magnus's "old-time erectness was broken and bent." Mrs. Derrick, the timid, delicate, powerless woman, is now the sole breadwinner: "it happens that my old place is vacant in the Seminary," she tells Presley, and she is "going back to teach—literature" (1074). In the end, it is Mrs. Derrick's literary sensibilities—"of the delicacy of point lace"—that will sustain what remains of her family, long after the grandiose dreams of the forty-niner, beholder of the "spirit of the West," have crumbled.

From the environmental perspective, too, Mrs. Derrick's point of view is looking more sensible and responsible with the passage of time. Her humbleness and humility in the face of nature, her privileging of the "local" as opposed to the "larger" view, is precisely what makes the vision she represents a more responsible ecological perspective. Mrs. Derrick's sense of proportion, her desire for balance, her dislike of "brutality"—these were supposed to be the qualities that disqualified her opinions as frivolous. These same qualities, we can recognize today, might well form the affective basis for an ecological ethic. For which of us has not, when confronted with the grotesque images of industrial-scale farming (which we now know to be environmentally deleterious, to put it mildly), felt some sense of disproportion, of imbalance, of brutality? Mrs. Derrick's response, ridiculed as it is, models for us one form of ecocriticism, in that she reminds us that factory farming and other causes of environmental despoliation should be confronted not only in the form of "scientific" argumentation but also on "artistic" grounds: in addition to the fact that it contributes to an empirically "measurable" environmental catastrophe, factory farming is also an aesthetic nightmare. Writers bear some responsibility to confront environmental despoliation if only because the refusal to do so would represent an astounding *artistic* failure.

Reading Nature

The character who most obviously operates as a foil, or rather a corrective, for Mrs. Derrick's aesthetic pronouncements is the poet Presley. Presley is in many respects our way into the narrative, and the plot tracks his artistic development in response to the growth of the wheat and the human conflicts around him. Despite the fact that he comes from some eastern university (it was his enervating experience there that necessitated his sojourn to the West in order to recuperate and replenish his masculine essence), Presley still recognizes the "weakness" of Mrs. Derrick's attitude toward art. "The 'Marble Faun,' Raphael's 'Madonnas' and 'Il Trovatore' were," Presley learns, "her beau ideals of literature and art" (623). To her overly refined taste, "art" is something that comes to us from foreign lands and aspires to those rarefied cultural heights achieved in the Renaissance. But her husband had always found cause to defer their Italian sojourn, and so Mrs. Derrick "obliterated herself" in the literature she had taught at the seminary. "Her taste," Norris writes, led her to "'Marius the Epicurean,' 'The Essays of Elia,' 'Sesame and Lilies,' 'The Stones of Venice,' and the little toy magazines, full of flaccid banalities of the 'Minor Poets,' were continually in her hands" (625). Mrs. Derrick had once engaged Presley in conversation on literary topics, but she was thoroughly dismayed by the young man's sensibilities, which here approximate those of the author himself. For one thing, Presley claimed not to care for "literature" at all, which "shocked her beyond words." "His indifference to 'style,'" moreover, "to elegant English, was a positive affront. His savage abuse and open ridicule of the neatly phrased rondeaux and sestinas and chansonettes of the little magazines was to her mind a wanton and uncalled-for cruelty" (625).[21] Presley had once attempted to convey to her the fierce, tumultuous spirit of his "Song of the West," but she was aghast: "'Presley,' she had mur-

mured, 'that is not literature.' 'No,' he had cried between his teeth, 'no, thank God, it is not'" (625).

In his conversation with Mrs. Derrick, Norris has Presley take up the side of "life," while Mrs. Derrick is made to represent "literature." An earlier conversation with the mystical shepherd Vanamee, however, revealed that even Presley's conception of "life" was not uncontaminated by the literary. After the death of Angele, his young lover, Vanamee had simply evaporated into nature. It has been suggested that Vanamee represents a figure of Thoreauvean simplicity, insofar as he seems to have relinquished the material and social comforts of civilization in favor of a more authentic and direct communion with nature.[22] Norris figures the relinquishment of Vanamee's social self as an almost physical transmutation: "He had melted off into the surface-shimmer of the desert;" Norris writes, "he sank below the horizons; he was swallowed up in the waste of sand and sage" (603). (The image of Vanamee being "swallowed up" by nature prefigures the way S. Behrman will be swallowed up by the unstoppable wheat in the hold of the *Swanhilda* at the novel's conclusion.) Upon his return, Vanamee recounts his travels to Presley—a succession of unfamiliar places and names recited as though from "a steadily moving scroll" (608)—which inspires Presley to tell the shepherd about his poem, the "Song of the West." Presley's artistic desire, he tells Vanamee, is to put the West "into hexameters," to "strike the great iron note; sing the vast, terrible song; the song of the people, the forerunners of Empire!" Hearing this, Vanamee "nodded gravely" (which is perhaps appropriate, given that he will spend the majority of the novel meditating on Angele's grave). Vanamee approves of Presley's choice of subject matter in Norrisean terms: "'Yes, it is there,' the shepherd declares. 'It is Life, the primitive, simple, direct Life, passionate, tumultuous. Yes, there is an epic there'" (609). Presley fixates on that generic classification, deciding that it is indeed the "epic" that he's been after all along. But he worries that he was born too late: "Ah, to get back to that first, clear-eyed view of things, to see as Homer saw, as Beowulf saw, as the Nibelungen poets saw." Presley longs for an awareness of nature that is untouched by the aesthetic residue of previous poetic perceptions. He believes that we latecomers "have been educated away from it all. We are out of touch. We are out of tune" (609). Vanamee listens to Presley's concerns, "his grave, sad face thoughtful and attentive," before suggesting an alternative route to his epic. For there is indeed an epic to be found in the West: "But why write? Why not *live* in it? Steep oneself in the heat of the desert, the glory of the sunset, the blue haze of the mesa and the canon" (609). Once again we find the binary distinction between life and literature, but this time, Presley finds himself on the side of literature. He admits that he could not live life in the manner of

Vanamee. "I want to go back," he says, "but not so far as you. I feel that I must compromise. I must find expression. I could not lose myself like that in your desert. When its vastness overwhelmed me, or its beauty dazzled me, or its loneliness weighed upon me, I should have to record my impressions. Otherwise I should suffocate" (610). Without the ability to externalize his impressions, to produce a record of the encounter between his self and the natural world, Presley would "suffocate"—which is to say that he would share in the fate of S. Behrman, who is choked and buried by the unstoppable flow of wheat in the hold of the *Swanhilda*.

This triad of characters—Vanamee, Presley, and Mrs. Derrick—represent the full spectrum of possibilities for conceptualizing the relationship between literature and the environment—the main business of environmental literary criticism. On one side is Vanamee, a pastoral figure who simply dissolves into nature: he argues that the environment is best appreciated directly, without literary mediation. On the opposite end of the spectrum is Mrs. Derrick, whose artistic sensibilities seem to be completely separate from nature and from the "West" (and emanate instead from some idealized version of Italy). Presley wants to occupy some middle ground: in his conversations with Mrs. Derrick, as we've seen, he takes up the side of life, but when he is faced with Vanamee—a "poet by nature," whose very life is his poem—Presley is equally unsettled: without his art, without some form of mediation, Presley would "lose himself" in nature. He yearns to stand "inside" with nature, rather than "outside" with art, and yet he fears that if he goes too deep, nature will consume him: that he will cease to exist. He seems to suggest that without the framing artifice of art, the "naturalness" of nature (qua Mrs. Derrick) becomes something unnatural, something obscene and devouring.

The Octopus is therefore pulling in a couple of different directions at once: it wants to bury itself in nature, but at the same time it is reluctant to relinquish its aesthetic frames. We might frame this contradiction as a tension between form and content. At the level of content, the novel makes a case for the inexorability of nature and the futility of "form." Put simply, the wheat cannot be stopped. As representative of nature's FORCE, the wheat will "get through in the end"—and it does. (It should be clear that this argument requires us to repress the obvious fact that Norris's very symbol of natural force is also a highly unnatural product of industrialization; that is, the wheat is transparently a product of the human agency that it is then meant to disavow.)[23] Philosophy, politics, economics, art—all cultural forms that are designed to package this truth, to process it and render it consumable to the human mind, are fundamentally without substance. Artistic formalism, aesthetic "style," and other forms of cultural compartmentalization, are all basically impotent, "meta-level," derivations of natural force: aestheticism is a way of framing or distancing ourselves from nature. But at the same time, Presley's fear of consuming nature (and the novel will express this anxiety in the final, primal scene of S. Berhman's "consumption," his reverse birth back into pure "nature") betrays some recognition of the necessity of form, of mediation, of frames. Without some way of framing experience, one risks losing one's senses and melting into nature. In spite of the content of its own argument, therefore (celebrating the inexorability of force and the futility of frames), the novel hinges on a very strict formal alignment of place (California), race (Anglo-Saxon), and form (epic). We might consider this three-way alignment as a kind of naturalistic "unity." Of course, there is nothing "natural" (in the naturalistic sense) about the idea of a "unity"; indeed, Norris's argument about the inexorability of nature sits uneasily with the highly artificial, highly constructed "unities" upon which the argument is structured. Norris's unities are not Aristotelian, per se, but they grow out of a transcendental belief in formal "propriety" that is every bit as abstract or artistic or unnatural as Mrs. Derrick's neoclassicist beliefs.

Early in 1902, shortly after *The Octopus* had appeared in print, Norris published in the *Boston Evening Transcript* a riposte to one William R. Lighton, who, in his own article, had evidently cast aspersions on the ubiquitous genre of "adventurous" western fiction in general, and with the stereotypical red-shirted, cliché-spewing backcountry adventurer, in particular. Lighton was fed up with the sensational swashbuckling and derring-do that had monopolized the pubescent vision of the authors of western fiction; it was time for a more sober, less melodramatic portrayal of the region west of the Mississippi. Norris's response to Lighton recollects Presley's desire to write a song for "a whole epoch," in "the voice of an entire people": "in the fictitious presentation of an epoch of a people," Norris replied, "the writer must search for the idiosyncrasy, the characteristic, that thing, that feature, element or person that distinguishes the time or place treated of from all other times and all other places" (*Criticism* 105). The ultimate goal of fiction, Norris suggests, is to capture the essence of a locality, to demonstrate how the particularities of local fruit are the natural and inevitable products of their native soil. "Thus if one were telling a story of a Southern plantation one would not choose as the main feature of the narrative a pirate captain of the Caribbean, but rather the typical planter. If the story were of Wall Street it would be inappropriate to introduce as chief actor a Maine Yankee" (105). Norris makes the argument for a kind of "natural" unity between place and character.

Different places produce different kinds of people, and it is the business of fiction to put people in their places. While the West was undeniably crawling with just the sort of docile, housebroken members of the middle class that were for Lighton the appropriate subjects of fiction, the crucial point, as far as Norris was concerned, was that the West had not *produced* this mild specimen. New York had produced its financiers, Maine had produced its traders, Boston its men of letters—but the West had produced an altogether heartier type, the adventurer. For Norris, the distillation of this spirited type was to be found in the forty-niner, "whose work since the beginning of the nineteenth century has been the subjugating of the West" (*Criticism* 106). Norris self-consciously used the western landscape to express the virtues—the fortitude, the impulsiveness, the inner strength—of a particular sociopolitical community. In the case of the forty-niner (of which Magnus Derrick is the chief representative), the gold discovered in the California landscape animated an innate drive for conquest, which manifested in what Norris calls "the spirit of the West," a spirit that is "unwilling to occupy itself with details, refusing to wait, to be patient, to achieve by legitimate plodding; the miner's instinct of wealth acquired in a single night prevailed, in spite of all" (813).

This spirit, and the subjugation of the land that it licensed, was not without its racial element. Norris's impulse to situate different groups of people in their natural environments was guided not only by a sense of horizontal space but also by a strict vertical hierarchy, at the pinnacle of which resided the Anglo-Saxon. The "West," therefore, operates in couple of distinct ways in Norris's thought. On the one hand, his argument about fiction hinges on the assumption that the West "produced" this brave and vigorous new race of adventurers. Norris's westerner embodies the sublime, unconquerable brutality of the nature that forged him; he is the human equivalent of the unstoppable wheat. But at the same time, the idea of the "West" is not at all rooted in the mountains, prairies, redwood forests, or other landscape formations found on the American frontier; rather, the West refers to the ordained trajectory of the Anglo-Saxon people. When, at the end of *The Octopus*, the contested San Joaquin wheat is loaded onto the *Swanhilda*—the vessel that will convey it to "the hungry Hindoo"—Norris has the industrialist Cedarquist meditate on how the wheat is indicative of the direction of the much larger project of racial imperialism: "The Anglo-Saxon started from there at the beginning of everything and it's manifest destiny that he must circle the globe and fetch up where he began his march" (1094). The wheat, here, is allied with the spirit of Anglo-Saxon conquest: the passage of the wheat anticipates the continued westward march of the race and the eventual Anglo-Saxon conquest of the Orient. At the same time, of course, the very symbol of this imperial march is the wheat that will literally prevent the starvation of the Indians—sustaining the population that will later be subjugated. The *Swanhilda* operates as a kind of Trojan horse of charity. Part of what Norris is doing, then, in his endless description of the majestic and terrible wheat fields, is cultivating this landscape as a medium to naturalize the violence connected with the imperialist project. As W. J. T. Mitchell observes in *Landscape and Power* (1994), the landscape might be seen "as something like the 'dreamwork' of imperialism, unfolding its own movement in time and space from a central point or origin and folding back on itself to disclose both utopian fantasies of the perfected imperial prospect and fractured images of unresolved ambivalence and unsuppressed resistance" (10). Norris himself celebrated the imperialistic western march of the Anglo-Saxon in his 1898 reportage from Cuba during the Spanish-American War. "Santiago was ours," Norris wrote, "and the Anglo-Saxon blood of us, the blood of the race that has fought its way out of a swamp in Friesland, conquering and conquering and conquering, on to the eastward, the race whose blood instinct is the acquiring of land, went galloping through our veins to the beat of the horses hoofs" (*Surrender of Santiago* 19–20). The author's main goal in "The Literature of the West" was to defend the "adventurer," who was for Norris the primary representative of the indomitable spirit of Anglo-Saxon imperialism, as both a legitimate subject of fiction and as having a kind of natural priority over the landscape itself. In other words, Norris's argument seems to rest on the same principle of "natural right" that the Mussel Slough ranchers had invoked to legitimize their ownership of land itself and to authorize their violent response to the incursion of the railroad, which had the nation's laws on its side.

But Norris's conception of the "West" was perhaps not quite as firm as he initially lets on. Near the beginning of "The Literature of the West," Norris rationalizes the coexistence of his adventurers and Lighton's less-spirited, second-wave colonists by claiming that the West itself "is in a transitional period." That is, "there was a time when the wild life was the only life. There will come a time when the quiet life will be the only life. But as yet the West is midway of the two extremes" (*Criticism* 104). By the end of the essay, however, when Norris admits that "the great fight is almost over," and refers to the adventurous West as a "passing phase," it is clear that the transformation of the West is no longer at the "midway" point, and has in fact taken a considerable step in the direction of the "quiet" and away from the "wild." As this slippage suggests, the western landscape was already an object of profound nostalgia, suggestive of a past in which Norris's chosen people could figure their destiny as an unending march of conquest and occupation. Norris may have disagreed with Frederick Jackson Turner's thesis that the frontier had closed in 1893 (although he certainly believed that it was in the process of closing), but he would have readily agreed with Turner's notion that the frontier provided America with a unique set of experiences that had, in turn, produced a distinctively American type. As a corollary, Norris felt that American writers could achieve an authentic and powerfully nationalistic aesthetic by harboring the energies that were symbolically invested in the western landscape itself. But as we've seen, this nationalistic dream was infused with a strain of Anglo-Saxon chauvinism, in which the "West" was less a mappable landscape than it was a trajectory of racial dominance. The "West" referred to an immutable principle, but it also referred to a nostalgic, perhaps even melancholic, formulation of the land.

Like his creator, then, Presley's artistic aspirations are intimately connected to the western landscape and its hearty inhabitants. He regards himself as the bard of the San Joaquin Valley, and his poem as the epic of the founding of a great nation.[24] *The Octopus* begins (in epic fashion) with the statement of its argument, which is for an organic connection between place (the western landscape), race (the brave, vigorous Anglo-Saxon adventurer), and form (the epic, a story of the founding of the nation, involving great battles and acts of violence and so on.) The structure of this argument, however—the very insistence upon "unities"—is in some sense at odds with the official *content*, which is that "nature" is inexorable and all-consuming and impervious to human meddling. Presley's position seems to fall somewhere in between that of Vanamee—who has abandoned all aesthetic and cultural forms—and that of Mrs. Derrick—who has totally accepted and surrendered herself to them. Is there any way around this dilemma, for Presley and for us? Does nature finally "need" literature, in the way that one might say (much less controversially) that literature "needs" nature? Does nature depend upon literature for its naturalness? Or is reading itself "antienvironmental"?

Both positions are taken up and debated within contemporary ecocriticism. Vanamee's argument—that we should abandon our literary attachments for a relationship with "pure," revitalizing nature—is perhaps the default or at least the more traditional one. Indeed, the environmentalist impulse (in both its political and literary manifestations) frequently finds expression as part of a more general refusal to read. As Timothy Morton observes in *Ecology without Nature* (2007), literary attempts to evoke the "reality" of nature often involve a couple of assumptions, namely, "that (1) this reality is solid, veridical, and independent (notably of the writing process itself), and that (2) it would be better for the reader to experience it directly rather than just read about it" (30–31). As Morton suggests, there is a prominent attitude within ecocriticism (reflecting the widespread assumption in "nature writing" more generally) that views writing as a medium for transcribing an ontologically stable "environment," which is best experienced "directly." That is, we would be better off to close our books (with their narrow, anthropocentric interests) and turn our attention to the natural world, which at this moment is sustaining irreparable and catastrophic damage. Part of an ecological understanding of literature must include a sober consideration of the role played by literature *within* the ecology, and it is entirely possible, from a certain angle, to see that role as basically destructive: literature may be less an evolutionary adaptation than a shortcut to humanity's own extinction.[25] This was a principle concern for one of the earliest works of ecocriticism, Joseph W. Meeker's *The Comedy of Survival* (1972). Meeker wonders whether literature does more on balance for the continued survival of the human race than it did for our extinction. He therefore assessed the comic and tragic modes from an evolutionary perspective, arguing that comedy embodies the values of flexibility, diversity, and equilibrium, which are rewarded by nature, while tragedy valorizes inflexible codes of honor, monolithic passion, and a fatalistic worldview, all of which point in the direction of humanity's extinction.

If "tragedy" is a genre that must be outgrown for the sake of our continued evolution, "theory," for some ecocritics, is an even more dangerous atavism. One prominent faction within ecocriticism remains steadfastly opposed to all attempts at "theorizing" nature as an abstraction, a linguistic or cultural construct, as opposed to a knowable and objective reality. These critics worry that theory (especially in its Continental, poststructuralist incarnations) might quite literally represent a hazard to the health of our planet. For instance, in their volume *Reinventing Nature? Responses to Postmodern Deconstruction* (1995), Michael E. Soulé and Gary Lease argue that the "deconstructionist view"—which emphasizes our historical-cultural embeddedness and insists that our encounters with nature are also always mediated and conditioned by our cultural assumptions—ironically works to legitimate the most rapacious depredations of the "capitalist right," and they contend that "certain contemporary forms of intellectual and social relativism can be just as destructive to nature as bull-dozers and chain saws" (xv, xvi). Glen A. Love demonstrates a similar commitment to retrieving nature as an objective reality in *Practical Ecocriticism: Literature, Biology, and the Environment* (2003), where he argues that the defining quality of ecocriticism should be "ecological relevance. In a real world of increasing ecological crisis and political decision making, to exclude nature except for its cultural determination or linguistic construction is also to accept the continuing degradation of a natural world that is most in need of active human recognition and engagement" (8). Because "postmodern skeptics" deny the existence of a stable, essential nature, "there is no reason to consider nature as anything but another venue for doing what we do: control it, change it, use it up. Thus, a cultural-constructionist position—in addition to ignoring biology—plays into the hands of the destroyers" (Love 21).

In *The Octopus*, therefore, Norris has not only zeroed in on industrial agriculture as a locus of environmental debate that would become only more crucial over the next century, he has also provided us with a range of possibilities for making sense of literature's relationship to nature. Read against the grain, it is clear that the moral weight of the text is firmly behind Mrs. Derrick, despite the fact that she is marginalized for judging nature by aesthetic standards. Presley yearned to "to get back to that first, clear-eyed view of things"; he worried that "we are out of touch. We are out of tune." But Mrs. Derrick suggests that the best way to get back "in tune" with nature is to read it—to respond to it artistically, aesthetically, to refract it through all our cultural and artificial frames. That may seem hopelessly "culturally constructionist," or "presentist," but think again about the "environmentalism" as it was first practiced by George Perkins Marsh. A quick glance through *Man and Nature* reveals a few things about the origins of environmentalism. First, Marsh was not particularly Thoreauvian or "experiential" in his method; in fact, his thesis pretty much demanded that the author spend his time in the library, rather than out of doors. Second, he was emphatically *not* an antihumanist, as would suit Jackson Lears. Third, and just as firmly, he was not a scientist. He was, in fact, a well-traveled diplomat and amateur linguist who was supposed to have been fluent in twenty languages. But even if he had been scientifically inclined, antebellum-era science was, as Marsh readily concedes, incapable of quantifying ecological change through the centuries. Marsh's practice, instead, was akin to that of the environmental literary critic: he pores over texts by the Greeks, Raphael Holinshed, Edmund Spenser, and Thoreau (among others) in order to demonstrate the disappearance of certain species and the manifestation of other forms of environmental degradation.[26] Environmentalism has therefore always depended upon a close alliance between literature and nature, between fieldwork and deskwork, and its indispensible method has always been close reading. There is a danger, obviously, in forsaking nature for the pursuit of narrow anthropocentric interests; but, as *The Octopus* makes clear, there is also a danger in abandoning ourselves entirely to nature. To submerge oneself entirely in nature, to relinquish all aesthetic or interpretive distance, is not only a relinquishment of the self, it is also a relinquishment of nature. This absolute abandonment or "getting too close" to nature becomes a lurid parody of ecocritical practice, because it involves losing the capacity to appreciate and admire nature in the very act of being subsumed into it. As *The Octopus* draws to a close, Norris provides us with a vivid illustration of this anxiety.

The penultimate chapter of *The Octopus* finds the villainous S. Behrman on his long-awaited "day of triumph" (1088). By now, agents of the P&SW had successfully usurped the ranches of the San Joaquin from the surviving members of the settlers' league. S. Behrman had installed himself on Los Muertos, where he had supervised the harvesting of the wheat, as well as its delivery, via rail, to Port Costa, where it would be shipped overseas. Behrman has thoroughly relished every phase of his victory, and he therefore decides to oversee the final stage, the loading of the wheat onto the *Swanhilda*. As he watches the "cataract" of wheat cascading into the hold, Behrman catches his foot on an unseen rope and plunges headfirst into the wheat below.[27] The stunned railroad agent recovers the presence of mind to call for help, but it is no use; "the pouring wheat drowned out his voice" (1091).

In his first conversation with Vanamee hundreds of pages earlier, Presley had puzzled over how to maintain an authentic relationship with nature: he wanted to be intimate with nature, to feel and partake of its power, but he didn't want to fully lose himself in nature. He didn't want to "suffocate" in nature, to be "swallowed up" in it as Vanamee had been. In his representation of the demise of S. Behrman, who gradually drowns in a rising sea of wheat, Norris concretizes Presley's metaphorical concerns. The details of Berhman's demise reveal how the unstoppable flow of natural force works to strip him of his senses: quite literally, he loses himself in nature. The wheat—"persistent, steady, inevitable"—rains down upon him, *into* him: the grains pelt him "like wind-driven particles of ice" (1091), they transfix him like "needles" (1092). The wheat seems to want to force its way into Behrman, to undo the thin membrane separating him from the world: "the unnumbered multitude of hurtling grains flagellated and beat and tore his flesh. Blood streamed from his forehead and, thickening with the powder-like chaff-dust, blinded his eyes" (1092). Nearing the end now, bleeding profusely, Behrman "paused to collect his senses" (1093). But his senses are exactly what the wheat has stolen, and with them, his sense of himself: "Reason fled. Deafened with the roar of the grain, blinded and made dumb with its chaff, he threw himself forward with clutching fingers, rolling upon his back, and lay there, moving feebly, the head rolling from side to side. The Wheat, leaping continuously from the chute, poured around him. It filled the pockets of his coat, it crept up the sleeves and trouser legs, it covered the great, protuberant stomach, it ran at last in rivulets into the distended, gasping mouth. It covered the face" (1093).

In the final sentence, Berhman's face has become simply "the" face, another object in the world. "Behrman" has disappeared: having been completely filled up with nature, he has lost himself. Where Presley had insisted upon the importance of one's ability to "record his impressions," Behrman's demise envisions eco-writing in its nightmare incarnation: nature strips him of his senses, of his ability to record his impressions, before killing him and reducing him to sheer organic matter. Behrman has done what some first-wave ecocritics are always admonishing us to do: he has gone back to nature.[28]

This chapter began by observing some of the obvious ways in which Norris's naturalistic nature was different from our own. Contemporary climatologists emphasize the hazards of anthropogenic interference, the human-caused traumas that do not so much affect nature "directly" as they contribute to complicated feedback mechanisms that may erupt into any variety of catastrophic symptoms. "Nature" has become a terrifying and unpredictable monster that humanity has created and unleashed. And literature itself, some ecocritics warn, may even enable or contribute to such mechanisms by disseminating humanistic values that rely upon an anthropocentric conception of the universe, by privileging modernist "consciousness" as an ethically defensible mode of representation, and by distracting us from the urgent needs of our natural environment. At the same time, literature and reading have proven to be invaluable instruments for the "environmentalist" cause itself and for ecocritics who, at the end of the day, must accept the degraded condition of literacy in order to express their ideas.

At a glance, it would appear as though Norris would simply reject the vision of "nature" that underlies both sides of this argument. Nature, as he repeatedly and explicitly told us in *The Octopus*, was an immutable, inexorable FORCE. Nature, as embodied by the wheat, was not determined by our actions; nature was that which determined *us*. Norris had intended *The Octopus* to prove a couple of essential points, which he saw as interrelated. Nature, he believed, was an unstoppable but beneficent force, one that ultimately underwrote and justified his own literary practice, which grew out of a deep unity of place (the West), race (Anglo-Saxons), and genre (epic.) Norris would not have distinguished the two strands of this argument, but he would have seen the second as arising from the first: his "naturalism" was in profound accordance with the nature that produced it. He sought to demonstrate this relationship through the literary education of Presley, the poet who, over the course of the novel, would develop his aesthetic sensibility in close proximity to nature. Presley's education, however, makes us aware of certain paradoxes inherent to Norris's "official" understanding of nature. For one thing, that nature suffered from conspicuous gender trouble: it was an emphatically "male" space (opposed to female domesticity and actively repulsive to Mrs. Derrick), while at the same time nature was an earthy woman, one whose scent and feel betrayed a deep need to be plowed. For another, the novel was quick to qualify the naturalistic doctrine of "life, not literature." If one goes too deeply into life, if one abandons the literary entirely, one risks losing one's senses and self within the immensity of the flow. One needs to be inside and outside at the same time.

These two paradoxes, then, are the cracks through which we can glimpse a nature that looks very much like our own. The gender paradox speaks to the compensatory masculine logic that had brought Presley to the West in the first place. After his stretch at an eastern university had left him ill and frail, Presley needed some time in the country to buck up. But is it not possible that Norris's vision of nature (inexorable, resistless) was similarly ruled by a compensatory logic? Is it not conceivable that Norris's empurpled insistence on nature's immutability betrays a nagging suspicion of some underlying frailty? In short, is it not likely that Norris's genuflections to the colossus of nature stem from the same insecurity that caused him to make similar pronouncements concerning masculine dominance? In the end, it's obvious that *The Octopus* certainly does imagine a nature very much like our own—a nervous and delicate nature, one that will demand our respect and attention—although Norris tries to contain and marginalize that vision by situating it within a nervous and delicate woman. Mrs. Derrick herself constituted one side of the second paradox in which Presley found himself: the need to be both inside and outside of nature at the same time. And that is a paradox with which the contemporary ecocritical movement continues to grapple.

The official "argument" of *The Octopus*, I suggested in my introduction, is not dissimilar in structure to Milton's argument in *Paradise Lost*: Norris intends to demonstrate to his readers the presence of a divine beneficence in nature. In other words, *The Octopus* is a "naturalist" novel, but it is also explicitly intended as an exercise in naturalization. The object of naturalization is not only "the supernatural," Pauline attitude about the permanence of goodness, but it is also the myth of a national homeland, of a racial destiny, and of a literary praxis. At bottom, Norris's representational mode is nominally empiricist, as evidenced by his near-constant insistence upon the existence of a "life" and "nature" that existed "out there" and could be accurately represented. As Frederic Jameson observes of "the great realistic novelists," however, this empiricism is also necessarily a strategy of containment: "The evocation of the solidity of their object of representation—the social world grasped as an organic, natural, Burkean permanence—is necessarily threatened by any suggestion that the world is not natural, but historical, and subject to radical change" (193).[29] When read "against the grain," *The Octopus* reveals that nature, too, is "not natural" and "subject to radical change." Indeed, as Annie Derrick testifies, the natural world has already undergone one such radical change, although it will be up to readers to imagine others. Norris's naturalism positions itself as a celebration of unbridled force and naturalizes human technologies of rationalization as mere handmaidens of nature's business, but "The Epic of the Wheat" may also be a bridge to more ecological (and ecocritical) conceptions of our relationship to the natural world. Doubtless, *The Octopus* contains within it the seeds of our present ecological catastrophe. But it also contains other seeds, and whether those are allowed to grow and flourish will depend less upon any force of nature (colossal, neurotic, or otherwise) than on our own willingness to struggle against the current flow.

4

Crimes of Art and Nature

An American Tragedy and the Problem of Abortion

A Test Case

In April of 1927, Donald Friede, a senior vice president at Horace Liveright's publishing firm in New York, was dispatched to Boston on a polemical errand. Friede was going to have himself arrested for selling a costly, two-volume, thousand-page naturalistic novel to an officer of the law. Artistic repression and censorship—"Comstockery," as it was derisively known—was on the rise in Boston: the Vice Squad had recently suppressed nine books for their supposedly "obscene, indecent or impure language," and the list was rumored to expand.[1] Boni and Liveright was hospitable to Theodore Dreiser (and later to Hemingway, Faulkner, and Freud, among others) in no small measure due to the publisher's reputation for standing firm against what H. L. Mencken called the "fanatical moral tyranny" (qtd. in Gilmer 164–65) then brewing in the New England capital. In a matter that surely combined equal doses of "principal and publicity" (Gilmer 165), Liveright maneuvered to challenge the ban, using Dreiser's *An American Tragedy* (an enormous best seller for the firm) as a test case.

So, on April 16, Donald Friede arrived at police headquarters in Boston, looking for an officer willing to purchase his filthy wares. After several failed attempts, Friede found a buyer in Lieutenant Donald J. Hines of the vice squad, and a warrant was promptly issued for his arrest. The trial began within days, and Arthur Garfield Hays, the famous civil liberties lawyer, defended Friede with aplomb: "In a two-volume book of many hundreds of pages," Hays told the court, "none but a curious kind of human animal would thumb it through to find the few particular passages that would arouse sex impulse" (Hays, *Freedom* 191).[2] Hays lambasted the "reformers . . . responsible for a wave of repression sweeping the country," and he insisted that

Dreiser's novel "should not be judged by its effect on moronic minds" (qtd. in "Publisher"). But Judge Devlin was having none of it. He found that certain passages violated the law banning the sale of "literature manifestly tending to corrupt the morals of youth" and fined the publisher one hundred dollars ("Publisher").

Friede had to wait two years for his appeal to be heard, but he was nonetheless assured that the verdict would be reversed. Clarence Darrow, another leading attorney for the American Civil Liberties Union, would join Arthur Hays to manage the appeal, and Dreiser would be there in person to testify. When the trial opened on April 16, 1929, District Attorney Doyle took a straightforward approach: he simply read aloud various excerpts from Dreiser's novel that he considered offensive and entered them as evidence. Hays objected on the grounds that the jurors needed some semblance of context in order to understand the passages that they were expected to evaluate. Hays therefore tried to have the entire novel admitted as evidence, and when he was overruled, he asked Dreiser to take the stand to provide a synopsis of the narrative. If the jury couldn't know the whole tale, perhaps they could at least hear from the teller. But Dreiser was not permitted to discuss the novel apart from the supposedly objectionable passages isolated by the D.A., thus ensuring that the jury would have no sense of what the author had hoped to achieve.

That evening, Friede, Darrow, Hays, and Dreiser attended an anticensorship rally at Ford Hall. The two lawyers held forth on the issues of free speech and censorship, while Margaret Sanger, founder of the American Birth Control League, appeared on stage with her mouth taped shut (Boyer 193). That gathering, dubbed the "Ford Hall Frolic" by local reporters, served only to cement the relationship between the advocates for "indecent doctrines" and birth control activists in the minds of Friede's jury (Boyer 194). When the court reconvened, the district attorney further reinforced this association: "A story like this is indecent," he said of the *Tragedy*; "it's an invitation to young people to learn birth control" (Hays, *City Lawyer* 238). Darrow got in one last jab for the defense, insisting that "we cannot print all our literature for the weakminded and the very immature" (qtd. in Gilmer 171). But Hays knew the jig was up. He wired Liveright, predicting that the jury would "vote Catholic" (Lingeman, *Journey* 321). Friede was found guilty and fined, and the ban on *An American Tragedy*—which had "only served to stimulate sales" (Loving 335) over the previous two years—remained in place.

This notorious chapter in the annals of American censorship provides an occasion not only to reconsider the importance of abortion and birth control in *An American Tragedy* but also to understand the matrix of legal and socio-symbolic links between literary and biological reproduction—and between abortion and censorship—in Progressive Era American culture. In the following pages, I offer a critical look at a pair of Theodore Dreiser's polemical essays on birth control and infanticide before turning to *An American Tragedy*, a novel in which a woman's inability to procure an abortion leads directly to her death. By situating my discussion of the novel within the social and legal context of the abortion debate in America, I hope to highlight the ways in which Dreiser's reaction against the kinds of repressive legislation spearheaded by Anthony Comstock reveals a corresponding notion of the sacred at work in his own project. Dreiser may have objected to the anti-abortion rhetoric of sacred and inviolable human life, but his polemical stand against censorship reveals an investment in the sacred quality of art or creative life. Read in the context of Dreiser's polemical engagements with abortion and censorship, *An American Tragedy* pivots on what Ronald Dworkin calls the "twin bases of the sacred" (77) in art and nature. Far from simply announcing the social necessity of abortion on demand, Dreiser's novel raises questions about the importance of natural and creative dimensions of investment in human life, and it reinscribes the inviolability of life through a narrative that encourages us to understand its protagonist as a work of art.

Censorship/Abortion

In January of 1989, in an address to some 67,000 March for Life demonstrators in Washington, D.C., former president George H. W. Bush condemned abortion with a telling phrase. Bush told the crowd that abortion on demand was "an American tragedy," and he pledged to overturn *Roe v. Wade*, the 1973 Supreme Court decision legalizing it (Stepp and Devroy). The title of Dreiser's novel had come to name the very issue that the book had been banned for broaching six decades earlier.[3] While Bush's attitude toward abortion was vigorously conservative, his rhetoric was hardly exclusive to his side of the argument: to this day, "tragedy" remains the most politically palatable adjective to describe abortion for those on both sides of the issue. Thus, 2008 Republican presidential candidate John McCain declares, "at its core, abortion is a human tragedy," while Barack Obama prefers to call it a "personal tragedy" (Allott), and, for her part, Hillary Clinton sees it as "a tragic choice" (Allott).[4]

But abortion was not always a tragedy in America. While abortion had been on the books in some states since the 1820s, authorities in antebellum America were less than vigilant when it came to prosecuting the offenders. Most abortions were performed before "quickening," traditionally assumed to be the moment in fetal development when ensoulment took place and human life began (Davis 41–44). Abortion laws of the period reflected the quickened/unquickened distinction, stipulating that abortions procured before quickening were misdemeanors, while abortions performed later in pregnancy were felonies (Hull and Hoffer 22). But there were other, more pragmatic reasons why abortion was rarely prosecuted. Abortions had always been highly secretive events, in which the legal "victim," the pregnant mother, was also complicit with (and often quite grateful for) the assistance of the offender and unlikely to report it. Moreover, as N. E. H. Hull and Peter Charles Hoffer observe, "the manner of passage and the language of the first antiabortion provisions in the states indicated that there was no great swell of popular opposition to abortion. The laws were generated by an internal process of refinement of the criminal law" (22). For a variety of metaphysical, legal, and social reasons, then, antebellum-era Americans tended to treat abortion with a cautious pragmatism. To be sure, it was a shady, unpleasant business, one best kept safely out of public view. But every community had its abortion practitioners, and while it was officially illegal in most jurisdictions, abortion was certainly something less than the full-fledged national tragedy it would become.

By the middle of the nineteenth century, abortion laws in America were evolving quickly, increasing in specificity and severity. When New York revised its antiabortion statutes in 1845, lawmakers introduced a number of crucial distinctions: it was now the death of the fetus, rather than the death of the mother, that constituted a criminal offense. Moreover, the differentiation between quickened and unquickened ceased to be relevant: abortion attempted at any point during the pregnancy was now officially a crime.[5] And the mother herself, not just the abortionist, was now also subject to prosecution (Mohr 124). A decisive federal victory for antiabortion forces came in 1873, when, thanks to the vigorous lobbying of Anthony Comstock, Congress passed the first obscenity law, the Act for the Suppression of Trade in, and Circulation of, Obscene Literature and Articles for Immoral Use. Comstock, a middle-class morals reformer, would become the first official censor of the United States, and his bill "remains to this day the nation's most sweeping intrusion of government into private conduct, excepting the requirement of compulsory public school education for young children" (Hull and Hoffer 36).

Together with the state laws it encouraged, the Comstock Act outlawed abortion and all forms of contraception in sweeping, categorical terms: it was now illegal to "sell, or lend, or give away, or in any manner to exhibit . . . [or] otherwise publish or offer to publish in any manner . . . any obscene book, pamphlet, paper, writing, advertisement, circular, print, picture, drawing or other representation . . . or any drug or medicine, or any article whatever, for the prevention of conception, or for causing unlawful abortion" (Hull, Hoffer, and Hoffer 29).[6] As head of the New York Society for the Suppression of Vice, Comstock loved to burst into the dens of abortionists and birth control providers, gun drawn; he was paid for each arrest, and he was also fond of boasting about the number of "filth merchants" who had committed suicide as a consequence of his crusade (fifteen) (Lingeman, *Journey* 128). However, Comstock's 1873 legislation was, in some ways, a good deal more shrewd and artful than the man himself. Indeed, the Comstock Act owed its particular power to the fact that it did not go after the perpetrators of abortion or contraception directly. Rather, the act served to turn abortion and contraception into literature and then outlawed that literature as pornographic. As a result, Dreiser's novel, which was coincidentally an argument for the social necessity of information regarding birth control and abortion, would itself be banned under the same legal principles that had been used to ban abortion itself under Comstock. Comstock's innovation was not to outlaw abortion and contraception as such (although his bill managed to do that too), but to define all contraceptive information as "obscene" and thereby restrict the cultural transmission of those ideas. Comstock knew that he couldn't singlehandedly raid every abortion clinic, or punish every abortionist, so he instead enacted a much more audacious program of cultural erasure: if he could snuff out the literary expression of abortion, perhaps he could gradually erase the very *idea* of abortion. Already, we see a certain conflation of literary and biological reproduction—the policing of bodies through the policing of paper.

It should also be remembered that in the late nineteenth and early twentieth century, abortion was not only a so-called woman's issue—it was also explicitly connected to a host of race and class anxieties in America. Recall a memorable scene early in *The Great Gatsby*—published in 1925, the same year as *An American Tragedy*—in which Tom Buchanan suddenly erupts into a stilted jeremiad on the perilous condition of the Nordic races. "Civilization's going to pieces," he grumbles. "Have you read 'The Rise of the Colored Empires' by this man Goddard?" Nick hasn't. "Well, it's a fine book," Tom continues, "and everybody ought to read it. The idea is that if we don't look out the white race will be—will be utterly submerged. It's all scientific stuff; it's been proved" (Fitzgerald 14). Tom's book has a couple of real-world precedents; in Lothrop Stoddard's *The Rising Tide of Color against White World-Supremacy* (1920), the author considers the First World War as the "White Civil War." There was also a real Goddard, Henry Herbert Goddard, who argued for the hereditary nature of "mental deficiency" in *The Kallikak Family: A Study in the Heredity of Feeble-Mindedness* (1912).[7] But Tom's book could just as easily stand in for an entire genre of "scientific stuff" on race and breeding, in which highly educated authors worried that the cultural legacy of their Teutonic ancestors (democracy, literacy, progress, and so on) was in danger of being demographically overwhelmed, or else genetically diluted by an incoming torrent of inferior blood supplied by swarthy new immigrants.

Under these lights, antiabortion emerged as an issue of the highest national importance. Declining birthrates among college-educated women was particularly troubling. As the Boston physician Horatio Storer put it, "upon the loins . . . of our women . . . depends the future destiny of the nation" (qtd. in Hull and Hoffer 40). And Theodore Roosevelt, speaking to the National Congress of Mothers in 1905, framed the issue with characteristic bluntness: "the first and greatest duty of womanhood," he said, consisted of having children "numerous enough so that the race shall increase and not decrease" (41). As for the woman who "deliberately forgoes these blessings . . . why, such a creature merits [hearty] contempt" (42). In a political climate where the specter of "race suicide" loomed as a scientific reality, abortion had acquired a menacing new aspect.

Where "scientific" thinkers like Stoddard worried about the swelling tides of genetic pollution that threatened to sink the master race, Comstock betrayed a similar anxiety in the literary realm. Comstock sought to police sexuality and reproduction by managing literary expression; therefore, we might consider Comstock's campaign against foreign literature as ideologically contiguous with Stoddard's crusade for racial purity. Comstock had fought to ban works like *Arabian Nights*, the *Decameron*, and Rousseau's *Confessions* on the basis that foreign literature was "more harmful than the crudest pornography" (Lingeman, *Journey* 128). Indeed, the New York Society for the Suppression of Vice had begun keeping tabs on the nationality of everyone arrested on obscenity complaints in order to buttress immigration officials "in their efforts to keep undesirable classes from our shores" (qtd. in Lingeman, *Journey* 128). Comstock, whose legislation had always read sexual and literary reproduction in terms of one another, projected the theories and ideals of racialist purity into the literary marketplace.

In spite of the formidable political opposition and Comstockery, the bourgeois alarm over race suicide, the papal encyclicals and other forms of religious resistance that have persisted to this day, public opinion in parts of America slowly warmed to the idea of abortion, in no small part due to the eventual success of the birth control movement. The most important American birth control advocate in the era—the woman who coined the phrase itself in 1914—was Margaret Sanger, the activist who would rally with Dreiser and Friede in Boston. The success of the birth control movement can be attributed to a number of factors. For one, as the traumas associated with the First World War percolated deeper into the national psyche, the old arguments for population growth had begun to make some commentators queasy. Writing in a 1926 volume edited by Sanger, Norman Thomas lashed out at those who equated birth control with racial disarmament—a view that not only commodified procreation but turned motherhood into an arm of the military-industrial complex. Thomas asked, are we "to deny mothers knowledge of Birth Control in order that sons whom they have borne in pain and travail may perish in the horrible agony of trenches of battlefields by shells or poison gas" (48)? In the aftermath of the Great War, Roosevelt's martial metaphors for motherhood rang false.

But much of the movement's success came down to Sanger's own perseverance and devotion to the cause. Sanger had grown up in a large New York Irish Catholic family and saw her mother suffer heavily under the physical and psychological hardships of motherhood. She discovered Socialist politics in 1910 and developed relationships with prominent radicals, including John Reed and Emma Goldman. In 1914, she founded the *Woman Rebel*, a periodical dedicated to publishing articles on the perils of overpopulation and a grab bag of other radical causes. The journal was in clear violation of the Comstock statutes, and she fled to England, where she studied under Havelock Ellis, to avoid prosecution. Sanger returned to America to open the nation's first birth control clinic in Brooklyn in 1916, and she dedicated herself to disseminating information on birth control. In the watershed year of 1925, she organized a conference of scientists, economists, and medical professionals. This group of experts, which included the head of the American Medical Association, resolved that birth control was "completely within the realm of preventative medicine," thus endowing the movement with its first air of professional legitimacy. While Sanger would continue to be plagued by lawsuits and the depredations of Comstockery for the rest of her life, she had managed with her New York conference to fundamentally shift the coordinates of the debate.

Dreiser and Sanger had collaborated at least once prior to their "frolic" at Ford Hall in Boston. In 1921, Dreiser contributed an article to Sanger's *Birth Control Review*, which concluded by giving the movement his "unqualified endorsement" ("Word" 13). Dreiser's position on the issue is perhaps unsurprising given his political-cultural orientation, but the unconventional way in which he lays out that argument will prove significant for our consideration of *An American Tragedy*. Dreiser begins his "A Word Concerning Birth Control" by glossing over some of the points we have just considered. Exactly who, he asks, has something to gain from preventing the dissemination of birth control information? Dreiser identifies three types of organizations that thrive on excess human capital. For obvious reasons, a belligerent, militaristic state bent on "manifest destiny" requires vast demographic resources to fulfill its expansionist program. (A few paragraphs later, Dreiser will sneer at "Roosevelt and his race suicide mush" [12].) The same goes for large manufacturing interests, which require surplus labor to drive down production costs. And religions like Roman Catholicism, Islam, and certain sects of Evangelical Protestantism are deeply invested in demographic growth. Each of these national, corporate, and religious institutions had a great deal to lose from widespread acceptance of women's reproductive autonomy. But Dreiser insists that society would be better off if the poor would put their own economic interests before those of any religion or corporation. In what amounts to a socialistic appropriation of Adam Smith's "invisible hand," Dreiser argues that when the poor attend to their own economic self-interest ahead of any interests of the state, benefits accrue to the population as a whole. Dreiser then appeals to the natural order to explain why this is so.

When Dreiser looks at patterns of reproduction in nature, he finds an inverse relationship between levels of intelligence and numbers of offspring. His argument evolves through several categories of species, beginning in the sea. Examining the birthrates from seventy-five well-distributed species of fish, Dreiser tells us that the typical female fish spawns some 646,000 eggs per annum. Fish are not intelligent, Dreiser says, but they are "regulated by exact chemical and physical forces" ("Word" 5). He then moves up the evolutionary hierarchy to amphibians, who, he reports, lay 441 eggs per female per year. Reptiles are smarter than the average amphibian, and thus they have markedly fewer offspring: only seventeen per year. And birds, more clever yet, lay on average "a trifle over five" eggs for every female (6). As we progress through the mammals to the higher orders of apes the number continues to diminish, until we arrive at human beings, who "do not exceed one offspring every two years" (6). All of this, for Dreiser, can point to only one conclusion: "As the intelligent parental care increases, the number of offspring needed for the perpetuation of the species decreases" (11). This observation permits Dreiser to make a rather astonishing claim. It is natural for a woman to interfere with her own reproductive cycle, because to do so is to act in accordance with the procreative laws of nature itself. "Nature manifests a tendency to overcome useless waste with intelligent care," he says (6). Therefore, to reduce mechanically or chemically the amount of human waste is to act in harmony with nature and her forces. It's perfectly natural for a woman to use birth control.

The decision to have a child, therefore, should not be obfuscated by religious injunctions against birth control, or by Rooseveltean claptrap about "race suicide." The decision should be rooted in economics alone. No parent is ethically permitted to populate the planet with offspring he or she cannot afford. In fact, Dreiser claims, responsible members of society are by no means obliged to stand by while their precious resources are sucked dry by promiscuous wastrels. He recommends "reaching the evil at its source" with a policy of forced sterilization of the mentally incompetent. Would it not be perfectly reasonable to "compel even the ignorant and the criminal and the hopelessly incompetent of all walks to waste themselves in idle unproductive pleasuring, if such be their bent, rather than that they should be permitted to spawn a helpless or criminal brood afterward to be looked after by the police, the hospitals, the asylums and the homes for the defective" (6)?[8]

Despite the rather hardhearted, perhaps even callous position Dreiser seems to adopt in this essay, in which he meditates on the social benefits that would follow from a policy of involuntary sterilization of the mentally incompetent, Dreiser's argument and tone here come across as soft and temperate compared to the position he had advocated in "The Right to Kill," a polemic published some three years earlier in the New York *Call*. "The Right to Kill" sees Dreiser less concerned with preventing undesirable births than with canceling out those that have already occurred. He opens by introducing us to a terribly sick and malformed baby born in Chicago a few years before. Dreiser itemizes the unnamed baby's catalog of ailments: she was partially blind and deaf, had some kind of a growth on her shoulder, and suffered from various other physical deformities. It was clear to her doctors that the child was in for a very difficult, painful life, and so, Dreiser states approvingly, she was "allowed to die" (224). The public response, Dreiser recalls, was typically rancorous: "the discussion grew so furious, as it always does under such conditions—in the United States especially—that it threatened to result in the prosecution" of everyone involved (224).[9] But Dreiser has little patience for these moralists, newspaper editorialists, and "religionists," as he calls them. Not only were the parents of that unfortunate child justified in their decision to "allow" their child to die (although it is impossible to know precisely what actions were permissible by that "allow"), it is in fact incumbent upon society to actively destroy its weaker offspring.

It will come as no surprise that Dreiser supports his argument for infanticide with an appeal to nature. "Might is right," he says, "because, strangely enough, might is always involved with a form of outward racial, chemical or geological compulsion. . . . The strong do rule, superior brain controls inferior brain so long as brains are manufactured" (225). But rather than looking to nature for supporting examples, Dreiser looks to the distant past. In ancient Rome, "mothers exposed their children without, apparently, other than family consultation and decision," and "in Greece, under Spartan rule, defective children were exposed, but there was a tribunal which passed on those who were to live and those who were allowed to die" (225). There's that "allow" again, veiling the actual activity of infanticide, as though to suggest that death were the natural habitat of these children; they are "exposed" to an all-consuming nature (while Dreiser's nature is exposed as death itself). Yet in the "Christian Nation" of America, it is foolishly taken for granted "that life, however painful to the holder of it, is abnormally sacred and must be persisted in, though the holder of it himself object" (225). And because Christianity is so mistaken on this score, on its stubborn insistence on the sacrality of human life, Dreiser declares that Christianity "should be kicked out of doors and forgotten" (226). Dreiser's metaphor turns Christianity itself into the malformed baby, the defective child who should be exposed to terminating nature and allowed to die.

Aside from his sweeping declarations that "there are no invariable rules" and that "might is right," Dreiser offers two reasons why the killing of severely disabled babies is at least acceptable, if not morally necessary. First, he claims, it is in the interests of defective babies themselves to die, rather than having to endure a painful existence that "the child might curse its life after, if it could" (225). It is also better for society as a whole that such wretched lives should end quickly, for these unfortunate persons are necessarily "a helpless drain" on the rest of us (226). Institutions like jails, asylums, and long-term care facilities, which succor the "sick, halt, insane, degenerate, and criminally and congenitally deformed," serve only to "disarrange" or "clog" nature's designs (227). It's as though our social gardeners had rationed a generous supply of water and fertilizer only for the cultivation of weeds. But here, perhaps feeling a tug at his conscience, Dreiser feels an urge to clarify something: "I am not advocating that the sick and halt now grown to maturity be taken out and summarily murdered, but I do think that in infancy a greater selective judgment as to the character of babies worth rearing might be exercised" (227). There is nothing elsewhere in the essay to explain the creeping humanitarianism of this caveat: from the moral principles established thus far, there's no clear reason why a severely disabled adult should be more valuable than a severely disabled child. Surely nature, in her vast indifference, does not discriminate according to age. As Dreiser states in his conclusion, murder constitutes "the merest skin shrug" to the planet as a whole (229). Because life "is a grinding game," and because "the weak and defective *are* ground out after much suffering" (227) in any event, why not simply do away with them peremptorily? Dreiser favors the establishment of a "jury or a grand jury" to decide which children should be permitted to grow up, as well as to determine which people should be "prevented from rearing progeny in any form" (227).

In these two essays, then, Dreiser not only outlines a naturalistic justification for birth control and infanticide (and abortion, which falls somewhere between), he also emerges as a kind of inverted double for Anthony Comstock. Comstock believed in the innate sacrality of human life. To preserve as much of that sacred life as he could, he dedicated himself to destroying countless works of "obscene" art—art that, in his view, dishonored and threatened what ought to be honored and conserved. The 1906 annual report for the New York Society for the Suppression of Vice indicated that Comstock and his subordinates had destroyed one thousand pounds of obscene books that year alone (Lingeman, *Gates* 389). The society's measurement of their success in *pounds* is telling: Comstock did not consider the targeted works (*Leaves of Grass* among them) as distinct examples of human creative potential, and measuring them in terms of brute mass suggests a kind of mental flattening that had already occurred in the minds of the persecutors. This is not art, they seemed to be saying; it is just "stuff," a homogenous, decomposing load of obscenity, a quantifiable byproduct of man's sinful nature. But is there not, perhaps, a comparable mental flattening that has occurred in Dreiser's understanding of severely disabled children? When Dreiser states that decisions concerning human reproduction should be grounded not on religion or morality but on *economics*, is he not encouraging us to think of babies by the pound? Dreiser's argument is founded on particular calculations about the quantity of resources (pounds of grain, gallons of water) necessary to sustain flesh. Nowhere does that flesh seem to refer to a human individual; again, it is just "stuff."

Dreiser and Comstock seem to offer two competing conceptions of the sacred, and yet this apparent opposition can be used to illuminate their similarities.[10] Both perspectives seem to close off the category of the human to certain dimensions of investment. Comstock could not recognize the individual creative investment in art that he had deemed obscene. There was something almost alchemic in the way Comstock used the category of "obscenity" to reduce vastly different people and artworks (e.g., Walt Whitman and abortion pamphlets) to the same noxious substance. At the Friede trial, the district attorney ensured that the jury was literally blind to the novel as a unique whole: jurors were permitted to consider only the excerpted words and passages—the words and passages which were profanity a priori—thus turning *An American Tragedy* into a tract for birth control. Everything that made the *Tragedy* an individual work of art was amputated by the district attorney; all that remained were the profane words and concepts that the *Tragedy* shared with every other work of literature that was already profane. The profanity had come to stand in and speak for the work as a whole. But Dreiser seems to be equally blind to the individuality, the human potential, of those too young and disabled to express themselves. In "The Right to Kill," he introduces us to a disabled baby by producing a catalog of ailments and disfigurements, as if those particular profanities against nature stood in (and spoke for) for the disabled person herself. If there was anything human in that profoundly sick child, Dreiser was blind to it, and his very description of the child produces her as a subhuman subject fit for retroactive abortion. Dreiser could not (or would not) see past the deformities that, for him, were an obscenity against nature. He wouldn't let his readers see past them either, which is a violence comparable to the district attorney's radical abridgment of his own novel.

Both Dreiser and Comstock hold something sacred, and they defend it by railing against their textual and biological profanities. Dreiser finds his profanity in nature, while Comstock finds it on the page. To be more precise, Comstock uses profanity on the page in order to police crimes against nature. They both define and conserve the sacred through the profane, and they define the profane through the logic of synecdoche: individual words (for Comstock) and physical deformities (for Dreiser) are taken to substitute for the whole of the art and person. A text with a profane word is obscene; a child with a deformity is defective. These two apparently opposing poles of sacrality thus define themselves by what they are willing to abort.

The irony is that both Comstock and Dreiser had declared allegiance to the same thing: "life itself." Comstock saw that life in human reproduction and sought categorically to preserve human life by destroying certain kinds of art. Dreiser mocked the sacrality of human life as a despicable vanity of the "religionists," and his work produces a version of nature that justifies the destruction of certain kinds of lives in service of nature's higher laws. For Dreiser, art is sacred insofar as it is in fidelity with nature, which is why he didn't hate censorship in itself but hated the censorship of "true art" with a fervor comparable to Comstock's hatred of abortion.[11] Both men are crucially interested in human creativity, and their different conceptions of biological and artistic expressions of individuality reflect not only the double-sided nature of the Comstock Laws of their own age (which attempted to control bodies by censoring texts) but demarcate the parameters for the abortion debate in the so-called culture wars of our own time.

Dreiser's Mimetic Desire

Midway through book two of *An American Tragedy*, Clyde Griffiths, newly installed in a midlevel clerkship in the Lycurgus collar factory owned by his uncle, boards a train to Schenectady to perform an unenviable errand. Clyde heads to the nearby town, where he won't be recognized, in hopes of finding a less than scrupulous druggist willing to help him out of a delicate situation. At this point in the *Tragedy*, Clyde is already fully enamored with the resplendent Sondra Finchley, a society girl and daughter of a Lycurgus textile magnate, who exudes an aura of wealth, class, leisure, and luxury. Sondra is the woman of his dreams, and she is tantalizingly close. But Clyde, who had only recently gravitated to Sondra's social orbit, had also been dallying with Roberta Alden, a factory girl fresh from the farm. Now, of course, she was pregnant.

Critics like Bill Brown have perceptively identified the quintessentially Dreiserian subject in the figure of the Gilded Age flaneur, the infinitely restless and desiring subject who negotiates a city made of glass, searching for some missing aspect of herself in the eye-catching displays of shop windows. Clyde's arrival in Schenectady provides us with an interesting twist on this familiar conceit: "Walking up and down the one very long Main Street still brightly lighted at this hour, looking now in one drug-store window and another, he decided for different reasons that each particular one was not the one" (391). Moving from window to window, Clyde resembles an almost Carrie Meeber–like figure, except that instead of looking for just the right hat or pair of gloves, he's looking for pills to abort Roberta's fetus. For a time, Clyde cannot bring himself to enter any of these establishments. Peering into one, he decides that the "bespectacled eyes" and "iron gray hair" of the druggist were enough to indicate his upstanding moral character (391). In the next window, he is encouraged to find a "shrewd-looking man of perhaps thirty five" (391), but is put off by the appearance of a young female assistant.

Finally, after trolling up and down the block, Clyde meditates on all he has to lose and decides that he must enter one of the stores. It has often been suggested that Carrie Meeber was animated by an erotic yearning to fill a lack—a yearning that manifested itself physically in her compulsive rocking. Similarly, Clyde's desire—his yearning to rid himself of the baby, and his fear of losing Sondra should he fail—is enough to make him almost physically ill: "so disturbed was he by the panorama of the bright world of which Sondra was the center and which was now at stake, that he could scarcely think clearly. Should he lose all this for such a world as he and Roberta could provide themselves—a small home—a baby, such a routine work-a-day life as taking care of her and a baby on such a salary as he could earn, and from which most likely he would never again be freed! God! A sense of nausea seized him" (430). Clyde's sense of vertigo (a kind of male morning sickness?) results from a chiastic vision of two worlds: "the bright world of which Sondra was the center," and the dark world growing in the center of Roberta. Richard Poirier has said that "American writers are at some point always forced to return their characters to prison" (29), by which he meant that the subjects of American fiction are always eventually ensnared and encumbered by their own social and sexual natures; they are always (in Norman Mailer's phrase) the prisoners of sex.

Like his literary heirs Bigger Thomas and Gary Gilmore, Clyde will fulfill Poirier's dictum on a literal level when he is sent to prison at the end of the novel. But here, in his nauseating vision, Clyde prophesies another sort of prison, a prison growing in Roberta's womb. Poirier used "prison" to mean the death of style, but prison could just as easily represent the end of time, the death of the future. For Clyde, the place of the womb is this future-killing prison: the claustrophobic imagery of the "small home," the kind of deadening repetition implied in Clyde's "work-a-day life," along with the plaintive cry that "he would never again be freed," all work to suggest the prison house of Roberta's womb, a "life" sentence of forced labor that will preemptively terminate his future with Sondra. What Clyde hopes to abort, then, is not only the fetus in Roberta's womb but a future world defined by confinement and repetition and his own future self, which is in some sense constituted and contaminated by that world. Because Clyde has "no self to which he might be 'true,'" Philip Fisher argues that his character is almost totally defined by the various real and imaginary worlds he occupies in the course of the novel. He becomes different people as he looks in different windows; as he inhabits spaces, they inhabit him. In Fisher's memorable phrase, Clyde "is a blank center engulfed by worlds" (147). Roberta's womb represents one such engulfing world. If Lycurgus's Wykeygy Avenue is the great synecdoche for Clyde's social ambitions, a permanent relief from poverty, Schenectady is the synecdoche for a more urgent relief: it is freedom from the future-engulfing world growing inside of Roberta Alden. Success in Schenectady would mean a relief from this nauseating prophesy; it would mean the freedom to look in other windows and to find other selves.

After making overtures to a couple of pharmacists, Clyde returns to Lycurgus with a box of mystery pills. But their only effect is to make Roberta sick. The next step is to visit an abortion doctor, where the art of storytelling will be even more important. This particular story, however, must come from the mouth of Roberta. Clyde worries that he looks too much like his rich cousin Gilbert and his flashy clothes will tempt the doctor to charge an extortionate sum. Besides, the plight of a single, pregnant woman could inspire considerable pathos: "If only he could get her to say that she had been deserted by some young man, whose name she would refuse to divulge, of course, well, what physician seeing a girl like her alone and in such a state—no one to look after her—would refuse her? It might even be that he could help her out for nothing" (400). Clyde would provide Roberta with the outlines of the narrative, but "she must speak for herself" (400). Roberta is mortified by the idea that she should have to go alone ("how would I know what to say—how to begin?" [401]). However, Clyde insists that she adhere to the story: "just tell him how things are—and that you haven't got anything—if you'd only say I'd run away or something, see—" (402–3). This last suggestion strikes Roberta as entirely repellent, and her reluctance to participate in such a demeaning narrative registers in a "flicker of shame, contempt, despair at being connected with anything so cheap and shabby" (403). Clyde's story doesn't look good on her, doesn't fit her sense of self; it is "cheap and shabby" like an ill-fitting department store jacket. In the end, Roberta's sheer desperation trumps every other concern, and she agrees to Clyde's plan—on the condition that he find the doctor, and this shameful business be conducted somewhere far from home.

But for Clyde, finding an abortion doctor is easier said than done. Clyde's trajectory in the novel had brought him to a state with some of the most repressive abortion statutes in the country. Not only did New York's state law surpass the Comstock Laws by criminalizing the possession of instructions for birth control and abortion; the Empire state had even gone so far as to outlaw private conversations about such matters (Hull and Hoffer 36). In a jurisdiction where it was a criminal offense for a mother to have an honest conversation about contraception with her own daughter, how was an outsider like Clyde to find someone willing to abort Roberta's fetus? In another quintessentially Dreiserian scene, Clyde's instincts take him into a "gents' furnishing store" where, he hopes, the haberdasher will be able to direct him to an abortionist. After all, Orrin Short—the salesman whom Clyde has chosen to trust in this matter—had always "been useful to him in the matter of tips as to dress and style in general" (404). What greater qualification could be desired? In between examining Short's supply of ties (just in from New York!) and inquiring about a pair of socks, Clyde attires himself in another story. This time, he would be soliciting advice on behalf of a poor, newly married factory worker, who was threatened with an heir he could not yet afford. But Clyde has underestimated his audience: the worldly haberdasher sees straight through this hokum and leaps to the even more scandalous conclusion that Clyde has impregnated Sondra Finchley. Nonetheless, Short comes through with the name of a country doctor who was known to have assisted others in similar circumstances. Clyde counts this as a victory, but Dreiser is careful to depict Short's resentment at having been used for information by one of these "rich young bloods" (409). Short has mistaken Clyde for a real "swell," one of the local scamps who have nothing better to do than pursue their own idle, unproductive pleasuring. It is this mistaken assumption, and men like Short, that will send Clyde to the electric chair.

So, where the original scene of persuasion had been between father and pharmacist, Dreiser now provides a corresponding scene in which the mother must persuade the abortionist himself. But when she finds herself in the presence of the stolid, sober-looking Dr. Glenn, Roberta nearly collapses in shame and fear. Clyde had provided her with an alias—Mrs. Ruth Howard—and the broad outlines of her character—married just three months, financially strapped, desperate for medical help—but Roberta liked to think of herself as unfit for this kind of deception. "If only Clyde or some one were here to speak for her," she thought, "and yet she must speak now that she was here" (415). Again, women's reproductive autonomy is tied to another kind of creative power, an intimate kind of fiction making. But Roberta is choked with embarrassment: "I came . . . I came . . . that is . . . I don't know whether I can tell you about myself or not" (414). Before Roberta can bring herself to tell her story, Dr. Glenn arrives at some notion of her condition: "Roberta's charm and vigor, as well as her own thought waves attacking his cerebral receptive centers" (415), cause the doctor to ascertain the true source of her distress. Perhaps the most significant difference between this scene and Clyde's version of this exchange with the druggist is the fact that Dreiser's narration here takes us inside the mind of the doctor, whereas neither pharmacist was endowed with psychological interiority. Indeed, the thoughts and convictions held by Dr. Glenn are crucial to Dreiser's polemical thrust in the novel.

Partly due to his own recessive temperament, and partly because of the insular nature of his social world, Dr. Glenn "disliked and hesitated to even trifle with [abortions]. They were illegal, dangerous, involved little or no pay as a rule, and the sentiment of this local world was all against them as he knew" (415). Which isn't to say that these trepidations were insurmountable. But the country doctor was too shrewd an operator to undertake such a procedure without the explicit "sponsorship" of some esteemed family within the community. Of course, Glenn doesn't inform Roberta of this particular social prerequisite; indeed, he presents the situation to her under uncompromising moral lights: his "conscience," he claims, could never allow him to harm an unborn child, because "marriage is a very sacred thing—and children are a blessing, not a curse" (418). "And when you consider," he continues, "that you are actually planning to destroy a young life that has as good a right to exist as you have to yours"—he pauses for dramatic effect—"well, then I think you might feel called upon to stop and consider" (419). Here, Roberta breaks down—she discards her cheap and shabby pretense and appeals to Dr. Glenn with the naked truth. Not only is she unmarried, but she is virtually alone in the world. But this admission only further entrenches Glenn in his position. "I consider it wrong to interfere with nature in this way," he preaches, "a physician may not interfere in a case of this kind unless he is willing to spend ten years in prison, and I think that law is fair enough. . . . Don't forget that there is a life there—a human. . . . A human life which you are seeking to end and that I cannot help you to do. I really cannot" (422).

Dreiser makes Glenn the spokesman for the "moralists" and "religionists" whom he had excoriated in "The Right to Kill" and "A Word Concerning Birth Control"; this scene provides us with Dreiser's fullest exploration of social prohibitions against abortion (and their exceptions) from the perspective of the abortionist. In "I Find the Real American Tragedy," an essay he wrote for *Mystery Magazine* ten years after the publication of the *Tragedy*, Dreiser takes up the other side of the dilemma, considering the socially constituted nature of Clyde's desire. This essay finds Dreiser advancing a double-pronged thesis: that social conditions in Progressive Era America have produced a distinctively national "type" of murder (bearing in mind that "type," for the naturalists, connoted a quasi-scientific fixity), and that Clyde Griffiths (like Chester Gillette, the murderer upon whom he was based) wasn't so bad—in fact, he was basically a model citizen.

From his earliest days as a newspaperman in 1892, Dreiser recalls, he had observed "a certain type of crime in the United States" ("I Find" 291), which he saw as symptomatic of America's "national obsession" with wealth and social advancement. One feels the presence of both Marx and Veblen in passages that rail ferociously against those who impose "slave-like hour and wage terms" upon the poor, and who were more interested in "leisure and show—the fanfare and parade of wealth without any consideration for the workers from whom it was taken or the country as a whole" (292). "In fact, between 1875 and 1900," Dreiser says, the accumulation of wealth had become "an outstanding American madness" (292). (He also implies, but does not explain, that this American acquisitiveness somehow caused the First World War.) Regardless, "one of the quickest ways to get money was to marry it," he observes, rather than to "develop oneself and so have money come honestly. In short . . . Fortune hunting became a national disease" (292). One of the symptoms of this disease had been a rash of killings, in which a socially ambitious young man impregnated his sweetheart and then murdered her to clear the path for someone better. So he relates the murder of Grace "Billy" Brown by Chester Gillette in 1906—whose story was the basis for the *Tragedy* and "the OJ Simpson case of its day" (Lingeman, "Introduction" xiii)—as well as a score of others.

For instance, there was Carlyle Harris, "a young medical student, an interne [*sic*] in one of the leading New York hospitals, who seduced a young girl poorer and less distinguished than he was, or at least hoped to be" ("I Find" 293). Soon after, fate presented Carlyle with a beautiful woman "of a much higher station of his own," and so he set about poisoning the first girl with powders—"result: discovery, trial, and execution" (293). Dreiser blames Carlyle's mother for her obsession with her son's success, as well as America itself, for its own "craze for social and money success" (294). Clarence Richesen was undone by the same craze in 1911. A small-town preacher, who had "come up from nothing," Richesen fell in love with Avis Linnell, a young parishioner from similarly humble origins. Having impregnated Avis and moved to a much wealthier Boston parish, Richesen succumbed to the charms of another, richer young woman. From here, the preacher resorted to "poisoned powders and death. And at last [Richesen was] dragged from his grand pulpit to a prison cell. And then trial, and death in an electric chair" (295). Dreiser evidently kept a file of similar homicides. Shelly Fisher Fishkin speculates that Dreiser "probably knew at least ten such cases," although he had once "claimed that he knew of one crime of this nature that had taken place nearly every year between 1895 and 1935" (107).

The occasion for "I Find the Real American Tragedy" was the Robert Edwards case, a recent murder that fit the general pattern. Only this time, it was claimed in the press that Dreiser's novel itself had provided a blueprint for the crime.[12] The newspaper pundits who formulated this supposition didn't fully unfold their accusation, but what they were suggesting was that a real killer (Edwards) had patterned his murder on a literary source (Clyde Griffiths), who had patterned his killing on a literary source (a newspaper story in the *Times-Union*), within a novel by Theodore Dreiser, who had patterned his fictional killer on a real killer (Gillette), whom he had accessed through a literary source (the newspaper accounts of the Gillette crime from the New York *World*). Where the Comstock Laws formalized a legal relationship between literary and sexual reproduction, this murderous vortex suggests a corresponding relation between literary reproduction and homicide. The effect, here, is a *mise-en-abyme* in which killers within killers periodically break out of their representations to murder anew. But Dreiser resisted the connection between Clyde and Edwards—and not only because that line of influence seemed to implicate his novel in a murder. Dreiser's own beliefs led him to repress the elements of the literary, the imaginative and the fictive that haunt the possibility of "real" murder from its source. For Dreiser, people don't kill one another on account of books. Murder is not an imaginative act in any sense. Rather, people kill one another on account of the material forces operative in Progressive Era American society. Dreiser's need to believe that Clyde had not inspired Edwards was much deeper than a need to repress his personal culpability in a woman's death. The novel itself was at stake. For *An American Tragedy* to work, in Dreiser's mind—for it to *be a tragedy*—Clyde had to kill because his society prevented him from satisfying those desires it had itself inspired. Edwards may have read the *Tragedy*, but ultimately he was subject to the same oppressive social forces that had inspired Dreiser to write (and Clyde to kill) in the first place.

Dreiser sharpens this point later in the essay, when he argues that the Chester Gillette–Clyde Griffiths figure is not an exceptional "type" but entirely representative of his time and place: Clyde is not a monster; he is not radically outside the mainstream values of his society. He was not even "anti-social"; he was, in Dreiser's words, "*pro-social*": "*He was really doing the kind of thing which Americans should and would have said was the wise and moral thing for him to do, had he not committed a murder.* His would not ordinarily be called the instinct of a criminal; rather, it would be deemed the *instinct of a worthy and respected temperament*" ("I Find" 297; emphasis added). Dreiser intuitively understood Clyde to be performing a kind of deconstruction of American society from inside of it. Here, Dreiser states that Clyde was acting like a proper American up until the moment he committed the murder, which is when he did something wrong. But the entire sociophilosophical burden of the novel had been to situate the crime in a web of ideology so dense that it would be impossible to consider the murder as *separable* from the conditions that produced it. Clyde is never *more* American than when he kills Roberta, regardless of Dreiser's evasion of that point above.

Dreiser invokes the rhetoric of mental illness in a metaphorical way throughout the essay, referring to an "American madness" and a "national obsession" for wealth. But in the essay's final paragraphs, Dreiser literalizes these images in a meditation on Chester's homicidal mania: "he was confronted by a state to which he was socially and emotionally fearfully opposed, one which was sufficient, probably, to have affected his powers of reason. It could, and probably did, absolutely befuddle and finally emotionally derange a youth who because of his romantic dreams, and more, because when subject to them he was also subject to those dreadful economic, social, moral and conventional pressures about him, was finally driven romantically mad and brought to the point of committing a crime that was so terrible to the world" ("I Find" 298–99). The befuddling and deranging "state" to which he was so viscerally opposed is, of course, Billy Brown's state of pregnancy. This sense of derangement is what Dreiser manages to capture in the *Tragedy*'s famous murder sequence, in which Clyde is visited by a devilish Efrit who urges him to permanently rid himself of Roberta. In the end, it remains ambiguous (even to Clyde) whether the prospective father actually bludgeoned and murdered Roberta, or whether she flung herself upon him and was allowed to drown. But for all the murkiness of the events, there can be no such uncertainty as to their true causes: "those dreadful economic, social, moral and conventional pressures" that conflict with Clyde's desire and throw him into a state of bewilderment. Indeed, throughout the essay, Dreiser has repeatedly called attention to the formidable power of Clyde's desire, the relentless force of his ambition.

The true force of Clyde's desire is perhaps most evident in his outbursts of envy and jealousy. Clyde's most open display of passion in *An American Tradgedy* is provoked by neither Roberta nor Sondra but by Hortense Briggs, the promiscuous shopgirl from book one. In a telling scene, a few of the bellhops from the Green-Davidson Hotel take their sweethearts for an afternoon drive, and Hortense is rather forthcoming with her affection for Sparser, "the rakish, ne'er-do-well son of the superintendent" (121) Mr. Kimbark, whose car they have borrowed for the occasion. At one point in the afternoon, Clyde watches as Hortense and Sparser frolic together on a frozen creek, holding hands and collapsing into one another's arms. Clyde can only watch as "Hortense's skirts, becoming awry in some way, moved up to above her knees"; rather than demonstrating the slightest embarrassment, she simply sat there—"and Sparser with her and still holding her hand" (130). Smarting from his "fancied wounds," Clyde can scarcely suppress his rage: "he wanted to stop and quarrel with Sparser" (131). Instead, he saves his rancor for Hortense, who he starts in on "almost savagely" (135). At no other point in the novel, not even in the murder scene, does Dreiser use the word "savage" in connection with Clyde; that adjective is reserved for this particular burst of jealous rage. Quickly, however, the pair fall into an established social script: she tells him that a "girl can't do everything you want her to do just when you want her to do it," to which he offers a stock reply, "That's the old stuff they all pull. I know" (136). Here, Dreiser tells us, Clyde is "reciting almost verbatim the words and intonations even of the other boys at the hotel—Higby, Ratterer, Eddie Doyle—who, having narrated the nature of such situations to him, and how girls occasionally lied out of pressing dilemmas in this way, had made perfectly clear to him what was meant" (136). Moments later, Dreiser's plot externalizes Clyde's anger in the car crash, a narrative climax that operates as a kind of objective correlative to Clyde's savage mood. The accident kills a young girl, thus forcing Clyde to flee town, and throws the engine of the plot in motion. But what are we to make of these strangely twinned accidents—Clyde's jealous rage and the car crash? In what sense can anything that happens to Clyde be considered an accident?

As René Girard observes in *Deceit, Desire, and the Novel*, "it is always the same people who suffer from jealousy. Is it possible that they are all the victims of repeated accidents? Is it *fate* that creates for them so many rivals and throws so many obstacles in the way of their desires? We do not believe it ourselves, since we say that these chronic victims of jealousy or envy have a 'jealous temperament' or an 'envious nature.' What exactly then does such a 'temperament' or 'nature' imply if not an irresistible impulse to desire what Others desire, in other words to imitate the desires of others?" (12). Clyde is never free to choose the objects of his own desire, and perhaps nowhere is this more obvious than when he unleashes his "almost savage" passion for Hortense. Clyde's desire is not a spontaneous passion within himself, excited by some special quality inherent in the object. As Girard would put it, Clyde's desire is always mimetic and imitative, and one of Dreiser's great strengths in the novel was to expose the imitative nature of desire. This may contrast with our image of the typical "Dreiserian subject" as a self-perpetuating generator of desire. In an essay entitled "Dreiser and the History of American Longing," Jackson Lears captures much of what is commonly meant by that phrase, when he speaks of the "human longings" (63), "irrepressible yearning" (64), and "restless discontent" (77) of Dreiser's characters, and claims that "intimate feelings" are for Dreiser "the engine of social change" (64). But Clyde's desire is never "intimate" in the sense that it is something private or something shared between himself and another; that conception of the Dreiserian subject risks propagating the false notion of spontaneous desire, in that it seems to ascribe to individual characters those desires that, for them, are always located in the Other. Behind Clyde's desire there is always the intimation of another presence, whether that is an internal mediator (Ratterer, Higby, Gilbert, or even Samuel Griffiths) or an external mediator, a disembodied cultural idea that nonetheless occupies this third position in the triangulation of desire. Clyde's desire is always borrowed or imitated; it is never securely his own, which may be why his passionate imitations for Hortense increase in intensity when he is most intimate with the mediators of his desire. Dreiser tells us that he recites "almost verbatim the words and intonations even of the other boys at the hotel," but Clyde's imitation is not limited to these external properties (although his deep concern for the outer signifiers of social class manifests in his esteem for Orrin Short, the haberdasher);

he also imitates the desire itself, the passion of the Other that he imagines to emanate from within. This Other need not be an actual rival for the object of his affection, as it is here; more often, the mediator is external, and Clyde pursues objects that are determined for him by a sociomythic model of American cultural ascendance.

Clyde kills Roberta because his desires were frustrated by the "economic, social, moral, and conventional pressures" of American society, but his desires were never simply his own. Clyde's distinctive feature as a literary character is the incredible fecundity of his imagination, the uberousness of his ego. Throughout the text, Clyde is repeatedly impregnated by certain compelling ideas or memes that are swimming through the culture. Girard relates "desire according to the other" to the "seminal" function of literature, and it is immediately apparent how the character of Clyde is repeatedly inseminated by various external scripts that take up residence within his self. In the example above, we saw how the bellhops "narrated the nature" of certain kinds of sexual relationship to Clyde; Clyde then experiences these external narrations as desires originating as though spontaneously within himself. But there are many other examples: indeed, Dreiser is careful to show how every significant change in Clyde's character originates from outside of him. He is a kind of vessel for new selves, to be supplied by the culture. Thus, Clyde does not devise the murder; rather, the idea seems to take hold of him after he reads about a suggestive "accident" in the *Times-Union* newspaper. Clyde cannot conceive of a persuasive explanation for his own behavior, but he gladly accepts the "change of heart" defense authored by his lawyer, Jephson. This identity seems to collapse with his conviction, and Clyde is receptive to a new identity; this time, it will take the form of a religious conversion facilitated by Reverend McMillan, who will help compose Clyde's final "address to the world" (849). Clyde is a kind of vehicle for stories, a medium receptive to all of the seminal, textual memes that cross his path. Of course, it may appear anachronistic to apply Girard's notion of "seminal literature" to Dreiser's text. But the sense of anachronism fades when one recalls that the Comstock Laws had always sought to control human reproduction by managing the textual expression of sexual material. Comstock himself had been attuned to the seminal properties of literature all along.

Twin Bases of the Sacred

Dr. Glenn, who is Roberta's best hope for an abortion, denies her the procedure on the grounds that her fetus is "a young life that has as good a right to exist as you have to yours." Dreiser thought this was nonsense; for him, life was not a "right," it was a purposive but inscrutable constellation of forces, a "grinding game" in which individual lives were extinguished at every moment. Nonetheless, in his invocation of the fetus's "right to life," Glenn raises what would prove to be the most highly contested issue within the larger debate over women's reproductive autonomy in the twentieth century. At what point in its development does the fetus acquire rights and interests of its own? In *Life's Dominion*, Ronald Dworkin argues that it is the unanswerability of this question that has caused the abortion debate to descend into the present acrimonious quagmire. For Dworkin, the ethical permissibility of abortion will never be settled by determining, through scientific, legal, or metaphysical ratiocination, the exact point at which the fetus enters into humanity and acquires all of its rights and interests. The real issue, he says, hinges on the relative weight given to the natural and human investments that give life its value.

Crucial to Dworkin's analysis is the category of the sacred. Many of us, Dworkin observes, feel as though there is something sacred or inviolable about art: it is intrinsically regrettable, even tragic, when works of art are purposely destroyed. Dworkin notices a parallel attitude with regard to our natural environment. It is a kind of cosmic shame when humanity causes the extinction of a species by hunting it or destroying its habitat. And it is similarly tragic when our industrial processes level thousand-year-old rainforests, dump toxins into the ocean, release poisonous gas into our atmosphere, or otherwise permanently vandalize our natural environment. Having thus established what he calls the "twin bases of the sacred" in art and nature, Dworkin argues that each individual life contains both of these traditions. As he puts it, "each developed human being is the product not just of natural creation, but also of a kind of deliberative human creative force that we honor in honoring art" (82). This is a key point for understanding *An American Tragedy*. For it is everywhere apparent how Clyde is a natural creation, as Dreiser's narration draws our attention to the kinds of chemical and material processes at play in his body. But Clyde is also a work of art. In his ambitions, education, character, and worldview, Clyde represents an artistic creation of his family and society.

The fundamental schism in the abortion debate, for Dworkin, is not between those who are "pro-life" and those who are "pro-choice," but between those who privilege natural or human conceptions of the sacred. And this is precisely the tension dramatized at the center of Dreiser's novel. Insofar as he "consider[s] it wrong to interfere with nature" (422) by providing her with an abortion, Dr. Glenn assumes a stance familiar to many contemporary religious conservatives, for whom the natural investments in life are always transcendent. The abortion of Roberta's fetus (which he has every reason to believe will develop into a healthy baby) would be a waste of life, a desecration of nature. What Glenn cannot recognize is that for Roberta and Clyde, having a baby would amount to throwing away all of their ambitions, plans, projects, and emotional investments, which would be a different kind of waste. For Clyde (as for most of today's liberals), the squandering of one's creative potential, and the betrayal of one's desire, is an even more deplorable kind of waste than the biological variety involved in abortion. Clyde's aspiration for a life with Sondra is the perfect concision of his personally and culturally constituted desire. So the real ethical question raised by the novel is whether the abortion of Clyde and Roberta's baby, the waste of "life itself," is nevertheless justified in order to continue cultivating the emotional investments and creative activity of their own lives.

In one sense, Dreiser's *Tragedy* functions as a parable for the failures of Comstockery, in that the repressive tactics employed by the Griffiths cause at least two of their children to veer into sexual indiscretion. But if we can understand Clyde to represent the embodiment of the creative investments in human life, both personal and cultural, then Dreiser's novel is also about a kind of censorship. This becomes clearer when we try to isolate the source of tragedy in Clyde's narrative. By now it should be obvious, given what he wrote in "The Right to Kill" and elsewhere, that Dreiser would not have considered the death of a child or fetus to be a particularly tragic event. Nor is the murder of an adult, from Dreiser's perspective, necessarily worthy of that distinction. Murder, Dreiser said, was "the merest skin shrug" to the planet as a whole. From the standpoint of Dreiserian nature, events like abortion and murder are not exceptional or tragic, but expected outcomes in the "grinding game of life," in which the weak are inevitably crushed by the strong. This applies not only to Roberta's murder by Clyde but to Clyde's murder by the state.

The tragedy of Dreiser's novel emerges if we shift registers from the natural to the artistic—from seeing Dreiser as an advocate of abortion to Dreiser as an opponent of censorship. *An American Tragedy* becomes tragic if we see Clyde as a work of art. The tragedy, that is to say, is not the waste of biological life but the squandering of the creative energy, ambitions, emotional investments, and imaginative processes of communal and personal creation that (as Dworkin would suggest) constitute a powerful source of identification and communion with Dreiser's protagonist. To be sure, the novel's tragic sensibility is fired by the perversity of its central conceit, a scenario in which repressive state policies designed to safeguard prospective human life lead directly to the premature death of two adults. But a more profound perversion resides in the fact that "America," here, has come to play the twinned roles of artist and censor. In the broadest cultural-symbolic sense, America functions as the external mediator for Clyde's desire, providing him with a set of ambitions that it then destroys him for pursuing. Where Comstock wielded censorship ostensibly as a means of preventing death (destroying abortion literature to save lives), Dreiser's novel reveals censorship as a kind of death. The erasure of human creative potential is itself an abortive gesture.

An American Tragedy encourages us to see its protagonist as a work of art in a number of ways, although I will provide just two examples here. For one, consider how the novel begins and ends with scenes of artistic expression that are also scenes of parenting. The first, memorable lines of Dreiser's novel describe the ragtag band of Griffiths as they set up for a street performance of devotional music. Their audience, the procession of passers-by who catch a few seconds of the performance as they snake past, gives voice to a typically Dreiserian contempt for the "religionists." But the audience is less offended by the performance itself than by its perceived effect upon the performers. The Griffiths' recital is not creating the wrong kind of music; it is creating the wrong kind of people. "It ain't right to make a kid like that come out unless he wants to," says one observer (5). Another onlooker notices "the uneasy and self-conscious expression" on Clyde's face, and thought the parents "unkind" to "thus publicly force upon a temperament as yet unfitted to absorb their import, religious and psychic services best suited to reflective temperaments of maturer years" (5). The point of the scene isn't just that Clyde's mind is in danger of being warped by the excessive severity of his parents. In beginning and ending with scenes of parenting, the novel also emphasizes the deliberative creative processes at work in the invention of Clyde Griffiths. This point is underscored in the novel's closing pages, which duplicate the *Tragedy*'s opening scenario. Here, we see the same scraggly band of street performers setting up for another performance. The location has changed from Kansas to San Francisco, and there has been one change in the cast—Esta's illegitimate son Russell has stepped in to take the place of Clyde—but the scene is fundamentally unaltered, down to the attitudes of the onlookers: "Gee, it's pretty tough on the little kid," someone observes, "he's pretty small to be dragged around on the streets, don't you think?" (854).

Dreiser has taken us all the way around the compass of tragedy until we arrive back at the beginning. The mechanistic forces of the universe appear poised to unfurl another tragedy. But on the novel's final page, young Russell Griffiths asks his grandmother, Clyde's mother, for an ice cream cone, and Elvira obliges him with a dime. "She must be kind to him," she thought, "more liberal with him, not restrain him too much, as maybe, maybe, she had—She looked affectionately and yet a little vacantly after him as he ran. 'For *his* sake'" (856). In thinking about what kind of a person she hopes to create in Russell, Mrs. Griffiths reflects upon her role in the authorship of Clyde and his tragedy. Dreiser's novel does not end with the suggestion that this national tragedy is bound to repeat itself ad infinitum, but it ends with the recognition that the art of parenting (like other modes of social creation) reflects the deliberative human creative forces that make us the artists of life.

Mrs. Griffiths's function as Clyde's author is literalized when, in the novel's waning pages, she accepts the role of correspondent for a Denver newspaper. Too destitute even to afford the price of a train ticket, Mrs. Griffiths travels to Bridgeburg, New York, as a representative of the paper, where she will interview her son and cover his sentencing. Dreiser describes Mrs. Griffiths "seeking, paper and pencil in hand, to make notes of, for her, an unutterable scene, while a large crowd surrounded her. His own mother! And acting as a reporter! Something absurd, grotesque, insensitive, even ludicrous, about such a family and such a scene" (791). This grotesqueness is only heightened by Mrs. Griffith's realization at the end of the novel; she is employed to cover an execution that she had a hand in authoring. The moment when Clyde is sentenced to death is also, then, a scene of writing about censorship, and Dreiser focuses on the activity of another author as she attempts to capture the same scene from inside the text. Mrs. Griffiths not only channels the indomitable spirit of Dreiser's own mother (with whom the author was famously obsessed—and whom, in a sense, authored him), she is also perhaps a representative for the artist himself, for she is employed to turn Clyde's death sentence into a literary creation. This aspect of the plot was, of course, pure fiction: Chester Gillette's mother did not cover the trial and sentencing of her son. Dreiser added this narrative element to underscore the creative dimension of investment in Clyde's life. His death is a tragic waste of art.

A Postscript on Abortion as Art

On April 17, 2008, a news item appeared in the *Yale Daily News* about a provocative senior art project by undergraduate Aliza Shvarts. The project would document "a nine-month process during which [Shvarts] artificially inseminated herself 'as often as possible' while periodically taking abortifacient drugs to induce miscarriages" (Powers). Shvarts described her project as a large cube hanging from the ceiling, sheathed in plastic wrapping that was slathered with blood from the abortions. As the controversy intensified, Shvarts tried to clarify her intentions with her own article in the *Yale Daily News*, claiming that the piece was "meant to call into question the relationship between form and function as they converge on the body. . . . It creates an ambiguity that isolates the locus of ontology to an act of readership" (Shvarts). Shvarts seemed to be saying that her project was about removing things like fetuses and menstrual blood from their thoroughly naturalized contexts: she hoped to challenge the essentialized notion that these raw materials of the female body were necessarily "for" human reproduction, and that, when liberated from their place in heteronormative structures, the material remainders of abortion could be viewed aesthetically. Dreiser's art had been banned in part because it represented abortion as a viable option for its characters; in Shvarts's case, the abortion *was* the art.

The uproar incited by Shvarts's project was brief but intense. "It's clearly depraved," said National Right to Life Committee president Wanda Franz, "I think the poor woman has got some major mental problems. . . . She's a serial killer" (Donaldson-Evans). Others lauded the undergraduate as a genius, an heir to the spirit of Marcel Duchamp and Damien Hirst, two great innovators of the twentieth-century avant-garde. For her defenders, Shvarts's creation was not an abject exhibition of bodily waste; it was a precious—perhaps even sacred—work of art. But why did Shvarts's piece incite such controversy? When was the last time that an undergraduate art project found itself at the center of a heated national debate?

Shvarts's piece provoked such a passionate response because it seemed to put the natural and artistic poles of sacrality in direct competition with one another. It's not, as the artist herself claimed, that the project was an innocent reframing of the natural *as* the artistic. It's that the piece seemed to achieve artistic status at the *expense* of the natural. Shvarts confronted us with an object in which (sacred) art had been made possible by the destruction of (sacred) life. For many commentators, the most important question about Shvarts's piece was not whether it was good art, but whether it was art at all. To contemplate Shvarts's piece aesthetically, it seemed, was to take a politicized position that privileged artistic over natural dimensions of creative investment in human life. But I would suggest that those who reject Shvarts's claims are not necessarily in favor of heterosexist hegemony. One could reject the piece's artistic claims on the grounds that the destruction of human life is always an intrinsic shame—that the deliberate waste of human life necessarily demeans not just the human but also the *creative* dimensions of investment that are always involved in human life. In other words, Shvarts's project is not only art at the expense of life—which is what so infuriated the pro-life commentators at Fox News. If human life is always *already* artistic—one of the points, I've been arguing, of *An American Tragedy*—then Shvarts's project is also art that comes at the expense of *art itself*.

Whether its creator was a serial killer or an artistic genius, Shvarts's bloody cube was never exhibited. Yale officials attempted to abort the entire concept, claiming that Shvarts was a performance artist and that her piece was a work of "creative fiction": the idea of the piece, they claimed, along with the media's response to it, *was* the art. Shvarts herself maintained the "reality" of the art object, although she did retreat, slightly, from her original claims. Because of how she used the abortifacients in her menstrual cycle, there could be no proof that she was ever actually pregnant. Even Shvarts's version of events, then, was haunted by a certain possibility of "intimate storytelling"—a fictive core that similarly haunts Dreiser's *Tragedy*. In the Gillette murder trial, the prosecutors admitted as evidence a covered jar that purportedly contained Billy Brown's fetus as evidence of her pregnancy. Regardless of the dramatic (and artistic!) potential presented by such a scenario (what were the contents of that jar, and were they art?), Dreiser chose to eliminate the scene entirely. In his version of events, the reader is never confronted with this physical evidence of Roberta's pregnancy, leaving open the possibility that the pregnancy itself was fiction. A prospect that, if entertained, renders the story of Clyde and Roberta no less a tragedy.

5
"What I Killed for, I *Am*"
Domestic Terror in Richard Wright's America

Natural Disasters

In 1937, as Richard Wright was undertaking what would become his first published novel, a highly polemical fiction about a black boy driven to murder by the profoundly oppressive social conditions in the slums of Chicago, the international community was coming to terms with a new menace. Following the assassination of Yugoslavian King Alexander I and a French foreign minister by Croatian separatists in 1934, the League of Nations initiated the "the most significant early modern attempt to define terrorism" in the context of international law (Saul 79). While the word "terrorism" had, to that point, been in use for nearly a century and a half—referring, in the first instance, to Saint-Just's "Reign of Terror" and violence committed by the state, before abruptly shifting direction to describe all manner of violence directed *against* the state—there remained considerable dissent between nations on the meaning of "terrorism" as a genre of crime. However, given the increasing prominence of politically motivated violence, and in particular the ongoing string of assassinations, which extended back to include the shooting of Archduke Franz Ferdinand in 1914, the League of Nations sought to clarify the nature of the threat with the 1937 Convention for the Prevention and Punishment of Terrorism. This initial attempt to define terrorism in a global context, in the words of one legal scholar, "prefigured many of the legal, political, ideological and rhetorical disputes which plagued the international community's attempts to define terrorism in the 50 years after the Second World War" (Saul 78).

The legal invention and institutionalization of "terrorism," then, coincided with Richard Wright's invention of Bigger Thomas, perhaps the most terrifying figure in twentieth-century American literature. This was not merely an accident of history. Wright was a keen observer of international affairs, and he certainly understood his protagonist to be trafficking in the same chaotic political energies that were sweeping through 1930s Europe. More disturbing, today, are the prophetic flashes of terroristic violence that punctuate the text, nightmarish scenes that seem to speak directly to our own so-called age of terror. Consider the words of Boris Max, Bigger's Communist defense lawyer, when he warns the judge that his client is merely a single representative among armies of the disaffected. "There are others," he tells the court, "millions of others, Negro and white, and that is what makes the future seem a looming image of violence." Max's prophesy suddenly assumes an apocalyptic complexion: "The consciousness of Bigger Thomas, and millions of others more or less like him, white and black, according to the weight of the pressure we have put upon them, form the quicksands upon which the foundations of our civilization rest. Who knows when some slight shock, disturbing the delicate balance between social order and thirsty aspiration, shall send the skyscrapers in our cities toppling?" (*Native Son* 402). In wondering when some shock will send our skyscrapers toppling, Max anticipates what has become, for many, the defining image of terror in America. In Wright's prophesy, however, the towers are not brought down by some outward, external violence, but by a compromised foundation. Wright imagines this terrifying event as a kind of social earthquake—a "natural" disaster—in which our celebrated symbols of modernity are flattened by a force that is simultaneously beyond our control and somehow self-induced.

Many of Wright's contemporaries were plainly shocked by *Native Son* (1940). They were appalled by the text's matter-of-fact portrayal of brutal violence, daunted by a protagonist whose behavior and motivation seemed beyond comprehension, and offended by the suggestion that American society was to blame for the pathological nihilism bodied forth in Bigger Thomas. Much scholarly writing on the novel has sought to contextualize and reckon with the kinds of collective fear engendered by the work. But to speak of the "fear" produced by *Native Son* is to stop somewhere short of the truth. At the bloody crossroads of violence and politics is not fear alone but also "terror," that elusive political entity that, in the late-1930s, suddenly called out for definition on a global scale. Today, in light of the text's prophetic tremors—its predictions of urban apocalypse, its visions of looming violence and toppling skyscrapers, to say nothing of the horrors wrought at the hands of Bigger himself—it is clear that *Native Son* anticipates some millennial terror, a civilizational clash between "us" and "millions" of Bigger Thomases. But *Native Son* also challenges readers to risk grappling with a *domestic* cultural etymology of terror, to hazard the unsettling notion that terror has long resided within a system that, more recently, it appears to have attacked from without.

If "terrorism" carries with it a semantic memory, its most vivid recollections are decidedly short-term: as Alain Badiou has argued, it is now impossible to invoke the word without referring to the War on Terror, a sequence of events beginning on September 11, 2001, which must include the twin military reprisals in Iraq and Afghanistan and their attendant horrors, the rapid erosion of habeas corpus and other civil liberties under the Patriot Act, the human rights violations perpetrated at Camp X-Ray at Guantanamo Bay, the scenes of theatricalized abjection nauseatingly staged-managed by American soldiers at Abu Ghraib, and the rest.[1] If the word "terrorism" ever had any objective meaning (which is, of course, doubtful), it has been thoroughly overwhelmed by the sheer affective force that these recent events exert within the American political mind.

But if "terrorism" can be admitted to have something like a long-term memory, a cultural history that extends beyond the recent politicization and propagandization of the term, one can begin to trace the workings of a parallel terror narrative, one native to the American imagination. In this chapter, I examine the definition outlined in the Convention for the Prevention and Punishment of Terrorism before taking up a contemporaneous fictional representation of terror in Richard Wright's *Native Son*. By framing the novel within two discourses of domestic terror—the extralegal, community-sanctioned racial violence against African Americans in the post-Reconstruction South and the radical violence of the so-called Red Scares of 1885 and 1919—I hope to show not only how these terrorisms converge in Bigger Thomas but also how Bigger represents a distinctly modern figure for terror. Wright's early experience of dehumanizing racial violence under Jim Crow provided him with a unique insight into the operation of terroristic violence: as he would exemplify in Bigger Thomas, terror emerges not as a radical gesture performed by a profoundly alienated self—the Romantic notion of terror as the passionate expression of disaffected individuality—but as a political effect, where "terror" is the result of ingrained patterns of structural violence in a system in which the perpetrators are often least "themselves" in their moments of terror. In the courtroom drama with which the novel concludes, the narrative folds back on itself to interpret the manufacture of terror; here, Wright charts the basic rhetorical coordinates of an "America under attack," before raising the specter of lynching as the inevitable conclusion to the terror narrative. In the end, *Native Son* calls for a reexamination of our presuppositions about the relationship between terror and the social body, and intervenes today by confronting readers with a terror that is native to America itself.[2]

States of Terror

One point of agreement among observers is that the phenomenon of "terrorism" existed long before it was officially recognized as such. While "terrorism" gradually entered the U.S. legal and legislative discourses in the 1970s and 1980s, few would deny that America had already been grappling with domestic manifestations of terroristic violence for at least a century.[3] In 1912, Congress approved a commission on violence and industrial relations after two leaders of the Structural Ironworks Union were convicted of dynamiting the *Los Angeles Times* building, an attack that had killed some twenty-one nonunionized employees (Kaufman 8). There had been the case of Leon Czolgosz, the anarchist who assassinated President McKinley in Buffalo, New York, in 1901. Czolgosz's imagination had been inflamed by a speech delivered by Emma Goldman, a central figure in the American anarchist movement, who had inspired her lover, Alexander Berkman, to commit his own "propaganda of the deed" a decade earlier. In 1892, the industrialist Henry Clay Frick had employed the Pinkerton Detective Agency to suppress a strike at the Homestead Works Carnegie Steel Company, which resulted in the death of nine striking workers. Berkman, who had been captivated by the virulent revolutionary preaching of Johann Most before taking up with Goldman, saw in these events an opportunity for his attentat: he would kill Frick and then himself, while Emma Goldman would explain his glorious sacrifice to the American workers, inciting widespread revolution against their capitalist oppressors. Berkman succeeded in shooting Frick, but his larger scheme backfired: not only was Frick back at work within a week of the bungled assassination, Berkman had also effectively driven public support from the steel workers to the industrialists, and the strike was quickly suppressed.[4] If anything, Berkman had helped solidify a link between terrorism and the radical Left in the popular imagination, an association that proved to be "a powerful weapon in the hands of those prepared to use under-handed tactics in the struggle against unions" (Law 121).

For Richard Wright, however, domestic terror undoubtedly referred to something rather distinct from the popular conception of the terrorist "as a wild-eyed, foreign-looking maniac, with a bomb in one hand and a pistol in the other" (Avrich, *Sacco* 173). Indeed, for Wright, as for so many African Americans living in the South, extralegal state-sanctioned mob violence—not only lynching, as it is narrowly defined, but also rape, beating, arson, threats, and the like—completed what Cedric J. Robinson calls "the circle of horror drawn around black men, women, and children" (*Movements* 105). *Black Boy (American Hunger)*, Wright's autobiography, is punctuated with scenes of terror arising from the threat of white racist violence. Wright remembers waking up one day to learn that his uncle Hoskins, who had taken in Wright's family after they were deserted by his father, had been lynched by whites "who had long coveted his flourishing liquor business." Fear overwhelmed his family's grief as they immediately "packed up clothes and dishes and loaded them into a farmer's wagon. Before dawn we were rolling away, fleeing for our lives" (*Black Boy* 53). Later, Wright learns that a similar fate had befallen another acquaintance, this time for sleeping with a white prostitute. "Bob had been caught by the white death," Wright reflects, "the threat of which hung over every male black in the South" (164).

As with many forms of terror, the threat of racially motivated mob violence could exist quite independent from its "actual" occurrence. As Wright points out, in no way diminishing the real carnage inflicted upon black bodies, the terror of lynching was experienced primarily in the minds of those who were, like himself, not its direct targets: "I had never in my life been abused by whites, but I had already become conditioned to their existence as through I had been the victim of a thousand lynchings" (*Black Boy* 72). "Indeed," he later says, "the white brutality that I had not seen was a more effective control of my behavior than that which I knew" (165). Even if he was not the direct victim of lynching, Wright understood the prospect of lynching to operate as an "effective control" of his behavior. The "news" of lynching, disseminated by an expanding print media industry hungry for sensational copy, terrified black communities across the nation.[5] As an instrument of repression and control—and thus a form of "politically motivated violence," one perpetrated by "subnational groups or clandestine agents, usually intended to influence an audience"—lynching clearly constitutes a species of violence that the U.S. Department of State would today label "terrorism."[6]

Of course, no such formal definition existed prior to 1937. Even today, according to the United Nations Office on Drugs and Crime, UN member states have yet to achieve definitional consensus[7]—which is perhaps less than surprising, given the fact that, as Walter Laqueur observes, "there is no universally accepted definition as to what fascism or communism is or democracy and nationalism or virtually any other political phenomenon" (232). Of course, every terrorist also understands himself or herself as responding to a prior act of terrorism on the part of the state or some other group (the "real" terrorists), which is what makes the term doubly contentious. Nevertheless, much of what we mean by the term today, along with its incipient ambiguities, is suggested by the League of Nations 1937 Convention for the Prevention and Punishment of Terrorism, which defines terrorism in article 1, paragraph 2, as "all criminal acts directed against a State and intended or calculated to create a state of terror in the minds of particular persons or a group of persons or the general public" (qtd. in Saul 90). The ambiguities of the league's definition are readily apparent, beginning with its tautological structure: "terrorism," according to the convention, involves the creation of a *state of terror*, while "terror" itself remains undefined. The definition's use of the word "State" is also potentially fraught, since the contours and boundaries of "the State" are often precisely what are at issue. According to the civil rights laws of Bigger Thomas's time, his legal status as a member of the "state" was tenuous indeed. But all states can be permeable, fluctuating bodies rather than stable entities against which "terror" becomes intelligible; and as Richard Wright was well aware, states have not only been the passive recipients of terror; they have also proven capable of producing it.

But the most profound ambiguities about what constitutes an act of terrorism relate to the ways in which the concept requires us to make certain kinds of judgments about what is going on in the minds of the terrorists and their victims. "Terrorism," in the league's definition, is discernable not in any external, formal properties of the act in question but in the presence of an "intention" or "calculation" in the minds of the terrorists, and by a corresponding "state of terror" in the minds of the "general public." Because an act that terrorizes one population might be considered a mere crime (and thus manageable, routine) by another, "terrorism" emerges as the product of a kind of pathological psychic collaboration between the terrorist and the terrorized. Terror exists when we think it does. Of course, this is in no way to dispute the "reality" of terror—to mollify its actual, physical consequences, or to dissolve the mass murder of innocents into a postmodern haze of linguistic undecidability. But one of the unintended consequences of this definition of terror was to remove it from the sphere of objective criminal action and lodge it within the minds of particular individuals: terrorism here describes particular psychic effects and is thus highly subjective, phantasmatic, and contingent. It is also worth pointing out that the intentions of terrorists, in this definition, emerge as contiguous with the goals of certain kinds of culturally transgressive artists, who may be equally dedicated to producing particular effects "in the minds" of their audience.[8] Many of Richard Wright's critics, in fact, saw him as just such a literary terrorist.

Gothicism, Radicalism, and Wright's University

Published in 1940, *Native Son* was written in the wake of a massive influx of Southern blacks to northern cities, in an environment of institutionalized racism and simmering class conflict. The story relates a few days in the life of Bigger Thomas, a twenty-year-old black boy already reduced to a quasi-automaton by forms of systematic human persecution. In order to retain his family's meager public assistance income, Bigger reluctantly takes a chauffeur's position with Mr. Dalton, a wealthy real-estate magnate. One of Bigger's first tasks is to drive Dalton's daughter Mary to the university; en route, she orders him to pick up her boyfriend, the Communist organizer Jan Erlone, and the three of them head out for a drunken night on the town. At the end of the evening, Mary is too intoxicated to make it upstairs on her own, so Bigger—who had also been imbibing—must haul her up to her bedroom. Bigger lays her in bed and lingers there awhile, excited by the knowledge that his very presence in the white girl's room constitutes the violation of a powerful taboo. Suddenly, the blind Mrs. Dalton appears in the entrance of her daughter's room. Bigger panics. He smothers Mary's face with a pillow in order to keep her quiet, inadvertently killing her. Bigger flees the scene, but not before beheading Mary in his brutal attempt to cremate the corpse in the family's basement furnace. Things will not end well for Bigger. But before he is inevitably caught, sentenced, and electrocuted, Bigger composes a ransom note, hoping to capitalize on the accidental murder.

Bigger's ransom note has attracted the critical eye of more than one scholar. As a scene of writing, the ransom note might represent an instance of literary self-fashioning, a rare moment of agency in a plot governed by racist overdetermination. The murder itself may have been accidental, but Bigger's extortion plot represents a deliberate, premeditated effort to take ownership of his crime. Barbara Johnson, focusing on the line "*Do what this letter say*," argues that the letter "stands in some sense in the place of black vernacular literature," but she finds that the blackness of the ransom note is concealed beneath a more glaring redness (67). For when it comes to signing the letter, which Bigger has artfully composed in the first-person plural, the author signs "Red" and makes "one of those signs, like the one he had seen on Communist pamphlets" (177). The contextual function of this signature is obvious enough: Bigger wants a name "that would throw them off the trail" (177). In order to deflect attention from himself, the African American male attempts to dredge up another signifier of prejudice and paranoia.

But in having Bigger sign "Red," Wright also taps into a history of domestic terror in the United States (and in Chicago, in particular), of which Bigger is an unlikely heir. Red, in the decades prior to the novel's publication, was not only the color of communism and socialism, but it was also the color of revolution. It was the moniker of an amorphous and yet unified revolutionary force. "The Red Movement," Attorney General A. Mitchell Palmer had warned of this apparently singular entity, "is not a righteous or honest protest . . . [but] a distinctly criminal and dishonest movement in the desire to obtain possession of other people's property by violence and robbery" (qtd. in Avrich, *Sacco* 173). After a series of bombs exploded in seven American cities in June 1919—events that signaled the start of "a reign of terror in the United States," according to at least one official—the American public, inflamed by the nativist discourse surging in the press and in a Congress that had just passed the Immigration and Sedition Acts, sensed a vast, anti-American conspiracy threatening to undermine the nation from within: as Paul Avrich writes, "citizens and congressmen alike lumped all radicals—anarchists, communists, IWWs—into a single 'red menace' and demanded appropriate action" (175). In the Great Red Hunt following the June bombings, thousands of aliens were subjected to deportation proceedings; in December, 249 suspected "Reds" were shipped off to Russia aboard the "Soviet Ark" (Kennedy 290). At the same time, when James Weldon Johnson needed a shorthand for the bloody race riots that had erupted in more than two dozen American cities, he coined the phrase "Red Summer." In Chicago, the violence of the Red Summer displaced one thousand black families and defined the South Side Ghetto—the very neighborhood that would in turn "produce" Bigger Thomas and the crime he would attribute to "Red." Indeed, "Red" was so menacing that, during an earlier period of tumult, Chicago officials had gone so far as to ban the color itself. In the wake of the Haymarket Affair of 1885, red was expressly forbidden in all public circulars and advertisements (Law 119).

When Bigger signs his crime "Red," then, Wright manages to recall both the racial violence of 1919 and a history of domestic terror inclusive of anarchism, syndicalism, and Galleanism, those several radical and leftist movements that constituted the Red Scares of 1885 and 1918–19. Of course, Bigger also looks forward to the campaigns of liquidation that would ravage Europe in the very near future. But if Bigger authors "Red" as the fictional kidnapper of Mary Dalton, Bigger is also in some sense authored *by* this Red history. Surveying the world events of 1939, the twenty-year-old Bigger is quite literally a child of the Red Summer.

Bigger Thomas, then, embodies two streams of domestic terrorism, the radical and the racial. But it would seem controversial to suggest that Bigger's violence is itself terroristic, or that Bigger Thomas is in fact a kind of terrorist. After all, Bigger's actions lack the essential element of intentionality: far from an act "intended or calculated to create a state of terror" (in the League of Nations phrase), Bigger's murder of Mary is plainly an accident, a tragic consequence of the racist myth of the sexually rapacious black male. Indeed, it was Bigger's awareness of this myth that caused him to respond with such hysteria when confronted by Mrs. Dalton. Bigger might even be understood to fit in with the tradition of naturalist and existentialist characters forced to suffer through the vicissitudes of an overly intrusive hand of fate: figures like Dreiser's Hurstwood, who is made a thief by a safe door that slams shut as though of its own accord, or Camus's Meursault, who becomes a murderer when he finds himself suddenly blinded by the sun at the most inopportune moment. Situated within the context of Wright's novel, however, the political accents of Bigger's crime become more obvious. Mr. Dalton fancies himself a great philanthropist and friend of the black community—"Why, only today I sent a dozen ping-pong tables to the South Side Boys' Club" (294)—while reaping vast earnings from the slum tenements that he rents out to black families (including Bigger's) at extortionate prices. Mary's murder, therefore, while unpremeditated, also manages to enact a retributive logic: because Dalton's riches are directly tied to the economic exploitation of African Americans, Dalton himself actively perpetuates the conditions of possibility for his daughter's murder. Bigger's actions were accidental, but that "accident" was permitted by the forms of structural violence that had brought Bigger into the Dalton home as a charity case and then determined by Bigger's awareness of engrained cultural stereotypes. Indeed, it is in the very "accidental" nature of Bigger's violence, in its very *unintentionality*, that Wright locates the essence of modern terror.

Michael Ignatieff provides us with what may be the world's most concise definition of terrorism when he writes that it is "a violent form of politics" (82). Such a definition would exclude Mary's murder, a crime that quite obviously was not perpetrated to forward any political agenda. The question, however, is whether the agent of violence must always be cognizant of his own politics, or whether there are not certain situations in which a thoroughly politicized, "terroristic" violence may emerge as though from the political unconscious. Are there not circumstances in which consciously adopted political relations can seem to produce violent counterreactions that are in no sense "conscious" (but are also in no sense "apolitical")? Wright presents us with a scenario that seems to demand the reverse of Ignatieff's definition, where terrorism is a political—or politicized—form of violence. The point is not that Bigger was acting out some unconsciously held political conviction when he forced the pillow over Mary's mouth. Bigger's violence was determined by his own instinct to survive, not by a nascent politics. But we must also recognize how the "situation" of Bigger's crime is obviously triggered by a confluence of forces that are nothing if not political: it was the consciously adopted legislation of Jim Crow America that deposited Bigger on the Dalton doorstep; it was Bigger's fear of being lynched that made him suffocate Mary.

Bigger becomes the unconscious agent of political vengeance, regardless of his cognizance of that role.

Understood as part of the larger fabric of grievances and sociological convictions that constitutes the novel's own politics, then, the murder of Mary Dalton may be seen to represent a vicious reprisal against a racist social order that had it coming: "Say to yourself, Mr. Dalton," thunders Boris Max during the trial, "'I offered my daughter as a burnt sacrifice and it was not enough to push back into its grave this thing that haunts me'" (393). In Max's bloody Communist fantasy, the daughters of rich real-estate moguls are immolated in propitiation for the sins of their capitalist society. Wright's insight, which is quite separate from Max's, was that the most "terrifying" terrorism can occur without the conscious participation of any terrorist whatsoever. Terrorism can and does occur precisely because the terrorist himself has been radically evacuated of any agency of his own, where he is reduced to a pure relation of force. Bigger is least "himself" at the moment of his committing murder; he is simply a black male in a white woman's bedroom. His crime is nothing if not political.

Max uses the word "haunt" in his peroration above, which is suggestive in the context of terror—particularly given the novel's debt to gothic conventions. Critics have long noted how *Native Son* is overflowing with what James Smethurst calls the "topoi" of the gothic: "premonitions, curses, prophesies, spells, the subterranean, paintings, veils, trapdoors, demonic possession, graves, returns from the dead, ghosts, confinement, doubles, gothic mansions, visions, conspiracies, premature burial, and so on" (33). But Wright's text is also "gothic" in Teresa Goddu's more expansive sense of the term, in that it is both haunted by history and "haunts back" from history (4). Goddu argues that the American gothic articulates abjection and exposes the cultural contradictions inherent to America's national myth of New World innocence; it is, she says, "the primary means of speaking the unspeakable in American literature" (132). For Goddu, as for Wright, the gothic refers back to the unspeakable event of slavery—"that thing," as Max calls it above, that continues to haunt us from the past. The gothic, therefore, reminds us that the institution of slavery operated through violent, terroristic control of the African people: the American gothic is always soaked through with politics, even if that politics is submerged, unconscious, subterranean. Similarly, the fact that Bigger is the unconscious and involuntary agent of retribution in no way negates the crime's political content. Wright's insistence on Bigger's subjective inanition, his complete lack of personal agency, is the essence of the author's polemical thesis. In short, while Bigger's strangulation of Mary is politically neutral as far as its perpetrator is consciously aware, Wright's representation of Bigger's violence is overtly political and intended to create a "state of terror" in the minds of white readers.

At least, that is what he was understood to have achieved by many in the literary establishment of his age. Some midcentury American critics evidently felt that Wright's patent desire to intimidate his readership overstepped the boundaries of acceptable protest fiction and constituted an act of literary terrorism. "Richard Wright is playing with dynamite," Charles Glicksburg warned in the *South Atlantic Quarterly*: "he is holding a loaded pistol at the head of the white world while he mutters between clenched teeth: 'Either you grant us equal rights as human beings, or else this is what will happen'" (106). In Glicksburg's rabid formulation, Wright himself emerges as the unhinged radical of the popular imagination—the "Red menace" with dynamite in one hand and a pistol in the other. Writing in the *Atlantic* in 1940, David L. Cohn worried that Wright was trafficking in "the preaching of hatred, and incitement to violence," and Cohn issued a blunt reply: "the whites of America simply will not grant to Negroes at this time those things that Mr. Wright demands."[9] In speaking of Wright's "demands," and interpreting the text as a call to arms, Cohn obviously understands Wright's political project to be underwritten by the threat of actual violence. Even Ralph Ellison, once Wright's disciple, repudiated this aspect of his work in "The World and the Jug," wherein he wrote, "Wright believed in the much abused idea that novels are 'weapons,'—the counterpart of the dreary notion, common among most minority groups, that novels are instruments of good public relations" (161).

Ellison's charge that his former mentor conceived of novels as "weapons" for use in a culture war is indicative of Wright's commitment to a strand of 1930s political radicalism. Wright had established himself in Chicago at a time when the Communist movement was becoming increasingly involved in racial matters, following the Sixth Congress of the Comintern's "resolution on the Negro Question" in 1928 and the Scottsboro trials in 1931, among other interventions.[10] Wright's exposure to the movement came via his participation in the Chicago branch of the John Reed Club, which provided an informal venue for young, left-leaning artists and thinkers.[11] "The club," Wright explains in *Black Boy*, "was demanding that the government create jobs for unemployed artists; it planned and organized art exhibits; it raised funds for the publication of *Left Front*"—the club's literary magazine, to which Wright contributed—"and it sent scores of speakers to trade-union meetings" (306). But perhaps more importantly, the club provided Wright with a sense of communal intimacy—he described it as "my first contact with the modern world" (308). The first best-selling black writer in American history had never finished high school, but the John Reed Club became what biographer Hazel Rowley calls "Wright's university" (78). Wright was to form an equally intense attachment with the Communist Party itself, which he joined in 1934; he later called his relationship with the party "the first total emotional experience of my life" (qtd. in Crossman 117). The word "total" is apt in this context: the vast appeal of communism, for Wright, resided in its promise of a systematic solution to the profound racial, economic, and political problems that plagued America in that bleak moment. It promised a total solution.

If Wright's commitment to communism "approached the level and intensity of a religious experience," (518) as Werner Sollors put it, his devotion was not especially long in duration. Wright officially parted with the Communists in 1942, although his disenchantment with the party had been simmering for years.[12] As Cedric Robinson describes in *Black Marxism*, Wright's 1930s attachment to the party was to evolve, in the forties and fifties, into a distinctive black revolutionary praxis, one that retained certain key aspects of Marxism while emphasizing the unique role of black experience as the negation of Western capitalism. Robinson accords Wright a unique place in the black revolutionary tradition: unlike the movement's other leading thinkers, such as W. E. B. DuBois and C. L. R. James, Wright's personal background was relatively unmarked by the cultural assumptions of the petit bourgeoisie, meaning that he had not "directly profited from the 'cultural advantages' of the system" against which he would later mount his attack (*Black Marxism* 416). The circumstances of his upbringing allowed Wright to perceive black degradation as more profound than the standard Eurocentric conception of proletarian alienation, and as a more potent source of sweeping revolutionary potential. Bigger Thomas, then, constitutes an individual case study of this brute force of history. Bigger is a great distance from the progressive agent of proletarian revolution that Marx had envisioned; his revolutionary potential has less to do with the establishment of a dictatorship of the proletariat than it does with the creation of pure chaos. In contrast to Marx, at the end of capitalism, "Wright anticipated barbarism *and* socialism" (Robinson, *Black Marxism* 428).

The Fire This Time

To suggest that this background of radical politics "produced" the imaginative consciousness that authored *Native Son* would be to replicate precisely the style of materialist analysis Wright's novel uses to account for the monstrosity of his protagonist. What that approach omits is Wright's own genius, which he did not acquire over cups of coffee at the Chicago John Reed Club. This was the essence of Ralph Ellison's critique: in his most famous essay, "The World and the Jug," Ellison blasted Wright for his environmental determinism, noting how "environment is all" in *Native Son*—"and interestingly enough, environment conceived solely in terms of the physical, the non-conscious. Well, cut off my legs and call me Shorty!" (162). Ellison had "read most of *Native Son* as it came off the typewriter," but he was never smitten with communism as Wright had been ("Territory" 674). From Ellison's liberal perspective, Wright's apparent equation of material with intellectual and spiritual forms of poverty was grossly reductive and betrayed a lack of self-awareness. Bigger may be poor, but why should that deprive him of a life of the mind? "Wright could imagine Bigger, but Bigger could not possibly imagine Richard Wright," Ellison wrote, as "Wright saw to that" ("Jug" 162).

Ellison's critique, while severe, came off as positively temperate in comparison with a series of attacks launched by James Baldwin—another onetime disciple and friend of Wright's, who had followed him to Paris in 1948. Where Ellison's critique focused on Wright's philosophy of environmental determinism, Baldwin's criticism centered on the literary packaging of those ideas in the genre he sneeringly referred to as the "protest novel." "Below the surface of the novel there lies," Baldwin wrote, "a continuation, a compliment of that monstrous legend it was written to destroy. Bigger is Uncle Tom's descendent, flesh of his flesh, so exactly opposite a portrait that, when the books are placed together, it seems that the contemporary Negro novelist and the dead New England woman are locked together in a deadly, timeless battle" ("Protest" 17). In writing against the demeaning and sentimentalized constructions of blackness personified in Harriet Beecher Stowe, Wright had, in Baldwin's view, inadvertently accepted and propagated the fundamental terms of black oppression. Wright's protagonist may have been truculent and lethal (qualities that would lead some critics in the 1960s to see him as a proto-black nationalist) where Stowe's had been servile and ingratiating, but he had similarly "accepted a theology that denies him life" (Baldwin, "Protest" 17).[13] For Baldwin, Bigger Thomas was just Uncle Tom on steroids. But even more devastating, as Baldwin would charge in a later essay, "Many Thousands Gone," was that Wright's creation had served only to reinforce all of the most deplorable white stereotypes about the black "native son": "it is he whom we would rather our sisters did not marry; he is banished into the vast and wailing outer darkness whenever we speak of the 'purity' of our woman, of the 'sanctity' of our homes, of 'American' ideals" (29). Did such a wretched creature even exist? It didn't matter. In fashioning his morally vitiated, sexually depraved black protagonist, Wright had already validated the primary fears of white racists. If novels were weapons, Baldwin was convinced that Wright had shot himself in the foot.

These commentaries by Baldwin and Ellison, it should be said, were not spontaneous, gut reactions to *Native Son*. The essays I've quoted from were the products of some years' reflection and emerged from a postwar cultural environment that was markedly different from the one in which the novel was written. As Julia Foulkes warns, the "war often serves as a facile way for historians to mark significant social and cultural changes, and the decline of radicalism in the face of impending war is a primary example of this tendency" (226). Nevertheless, by the time Baldwin collected his polemics in *Notes of a Native Son* in 1955, the social geography of American life had changed in some appreciable ways. Federal reform initiatives like the Works Progress Administration—which had included the Federal Writers Project, a program that had employed thousands of artists, including Wright—had been dissolved.[14] The enormous economic growth following the war showed no sign of abating: capitalism appeared to have vindicated itself in the eyes of some of its critics, and labor radicalism was on the decline. Just as crucially, the war had sparked important demographic shifts: more than two million African Americans moved from the South to the North in the 1940s.[15] This combination of factors, Alan Brinkley has argued, incited a reorientation of liberal politics away from the reform agenda of the New Deal years. In Brinkley's phrase, the Second World War "began the process by which race would increase its claim on American consciousness and, ultimately, transform American liberalism" ("World War II" 315).[16] Not everyone accepts Brinkley's progressive account of this transition in liberal politics; Michael Denning, for instance, argues that issues of social struggle and class consciousness persisted but were increasingly coded in racial terms in the period following the war.[17] But while it had been written under the sign of a radical politics, Wright's novel was generally taken up as a "race novel" following the war.

In due course, however, as hope turned into exasperation for civil rights advocates of the 1950s and early 1960s, and as the explosive anger that had once made *Native Son* seem so extreme gradually percolated into the mainstream of black American political thought, Wright's analysis gradually acquired an air of inevitability. The violence and rage that Wright had construed as endemic to the black experience continued to receive literary exploration in the novels of Chester Himes (in Bob Jones, the "insanely belligerent" protagonist of *If He Hollers Let Him Go* [1945], Himes fashioned a highly self-conscious version of Bigger Thomas, whose self-awareness does not allow him to transcend the anxiety and panic that had caused Bigger to explode [88]). Wright's work had also inflamed the ethos of a younger generation of militant black writers and activists, including John A. Williams, Ishmael Reed, and Melvin Van Peebles. By 1963, no less a critic of Wright's than James Baldwin would issue a blistering prophesy of his own in *The Fire Next Time*, one in which he envisioned a racial apocalypse in tones not at all dissimilar to those Wright had invoked in the more sweeping passages of *Native Son*. While he would never accept Wright's sociological methodology, or the "negative theology" that he had discerned beneath the surface of Bigger's characterization, Baldwin's highly personal path to racial enlightenment seems to have brought him back around to the point where he had so vociferously parted with his former mentor. In the opening letter to his nephew, Baldwin puts matters bluntly: "This innocent country set you down in a ghetto in which, in fact, it intended that you should perish" (7). Of course, Baldwin's overt message to his nephew is one of transracial harmony; he must set white Americans free by loving them as his (younger) brothers. And yet it is impossible to ignore the element of threat and menace that underlies Baldwin's call for brotherly love. "The Negroes of this country may never be able to rise to power," Baldwin observes, "but they are very well placed indeed to precipitate chaos and bring down the curtain on the American dream" (88).

By 1963, the notion that blacks, if pushed, might very well "bring down the curtain" on America had been entrenched in the black nationalism and black power movements that would soon dominate the race issue. If the political establishment deferred racial justice any longer, warned Malcolm X in 1963, it "will be responsible for letting a condition develop in this country which will create a climate that will bring seeds up out of the ground with vegetation on the end of them looking like something these people have never dreamed of. In 1964, it's the ballot or the bullet" (405). The aggression intrinsic to much of the era's black nationalist rhetoric reached a crescendo in Amiri Baraka's "Revolutionary Theatre," written the same year. Baraka (then LeRoi Jones), cried out for a theater that "must show horrible coming attractions of *The Crumbling of the West* . . . and show the missionaries and wiggly Liberals dying under blasts of concrete" (211). Where an earlier generation of critics had disparaged Wright as a kind of lunatic anarchist holding a gun to the head of white society, younger artists like Baraka would quite openly frame their own aesthetic agendas in similar language. For Baraka, the sole purpose of art was to attack white society, to "crack their faces open to the mad cries of the poor" (213).

Baldwin, for his part, was every bit as critical of these more militant voices as he had been of Richard Wright. Baldwin's sense of racial dignity would not permit the thesis that any amount of white brutality could reduce the black subject to a mere mechanism of retributive violence. He would never concede that the impulse to violent revolution was a contingency of particular sociological indices or legislative reforms. But Baldwin imagined vengeance just the same—only a larger, disembodied, almost biblical vengeance, "a vengeance that does not really depend on, and cannot really be executed by, any person or organization, and that cannot be prevented by any police force or army: historical vengeance, a cosmic vengeance" (*Fire* 105). While Baldwin was highly skeptical of Wright's attempts to imagine an individual agent of historical vengeance, his own writing on race in America was, in the end, no less invested in apocalyptic rhetoric. Indeed, Baldwin's contention that "time catches up with kingdoms and crushes them," that "time reveals the foundations on which any kingdom rests, and eats at those foundations" (105), very nearly echoes the lines Richard Wright had given to Bigger's defense lawyer in *Native Son*, for whom the fragile "foundations of our civilization" would soon "send our skyscrapers toppling."

Legalizing Extralegal Responses to Terror

Since its publication, much of the critical reaction to Wright's novel has attempted to make sense of the terror embodied in Bigger Thomas. For some, the proper response was alarm: Bigger, for these readers, represented a senseless blast of hatred and resentment. How can we rationally account for Bigger's terror (these critics seem to ask) when it is Bigger's very *irrationality* that is so terrifying? Others, notably Irving Howe, sought to locate Bigger within a particular national and racial context, to consider how Bigger might be the symptom of a terror that has long resided within the system. One of the fascinating things about Wright's novel is the way it folds back on itself to consider precisely these issues. In "Fate," the last of its three parts, *Native Son* becomes a novel about making sense of terror, and Wright maps out two basic, opposing strategies for comprehending his terrifying protagonist. The first of these is adumbrated by Buckley, the state's attorney. From his perspective, the threat of terror represents a metaphysical evil: terror is senseless and incommunicable, and the only effective answer to terror is to respond in kind, by bringing the full capacity of state violence to bear on the perceived source. Boris Max, Bigger's defense lawyer, insists to the contrary that terror is indeed comprehensible and that future incidents of terror can be prevented only by grappling with their root causes, which are always economic and sociopolitical. The poles of this debate—in which the effects of terror are either dismissed as the irrational spasms of an unknowable and barbarous other or are construed as the logical (and perhaps inevitable) consequences of America's own political behavior—continue to structure contemporary conversations about terrorism. If Wright's novel gave the world a figure for the terror registered by the League of Nations' 1937 convention, it also imagines contrasting interpretations of that terror in ways that seem surprisingly contemporary.

Buckley's theory of terror evolves from a position of complete moral and metaphysical certainty. Bigger Thomas, in his assessment, represents the embodiment of pure anarchy: he is among those who "know no law, no self-control, no sense of reason" (408). The state's case is designed to reveal the "unnatural aspect" of Bigger's crime, which is, Buckley tells us, a "vile offense against God and man" (372). Buckley insists that his case is built on "concrete evidence" (372) as opposed to legal or theoretical interpretation; as he puts it: "There is no room here for evasive, theoretical, or fanciful interpretations of the law" (373). For Buckley, "theoretical interpretation" is just another phrase for the mush-headed, relativistic apology for self-evident evil. By their nature, theories are provisional and malleable, and inevitably expressed in the soggy medium of language; his position, by contrast, presents itself in terms of "concrete evidence" rather than in words—for instance, he painstakingly reconstructs the Dalton's furnace in the courtroom, in order to physically demonstrate how Bigger incinerated Mary's corpse. He presents sixty witnesses, as though the persuasiveness of his case resides in its sheer bulk. Indeed, Buckley emphasizes that language itself is not an adequate medium to communicate the true significance of Bigger's transgression. "Some of the facts of this evil crime are so fantastic," Buckley says, so "unbelievable, so utterly beastlike and foreign to our whole concept of life, that I feel incapable of communicating them to this court" (373). Buckley's case, in short, is rooted in metaphysical concepts that are beyond scrutiny; he emphasizes the alien nature of Bigger's offense, its "foreignness" to a society it attacks from without; he stresses the irrationality and incomprehensibility of Bigger's sins; and makes his case through feelings rather than "theories." Nothing short of the death penalty will be sufficient to exterminate the evil embodied by Bigger.

Max's case proceeds according to a very different set of assumptions. While Buckley continually emphasized the "foreignness," the alien nature of Bigger and his transgressions, Max insists that they emerge from within a distinctly national experience. For Max, the necessary background for understanding Bigger Thomas is not only his personal history, as it unfolded in the slums of Chicago, but the history of slavery, and thus the history of America itself. At one point in elucidating this background, Max draws Bigger into relation with America's founding colonists: "In him and men like him is what was in our forefathers when they first came to these strange shores hundreds of years ago" (393). Max does not elaborate on the nature of this connection, but the answer is implied. By setting Bigger up as an heir of the *Mayflower*, Max suggests that Bigger's yearning for freedom is a latter-day expression of a distinctly American revolutionary subjectivity. For Max, Bigger's appeals for liberty fit in with the long national struggle against diverse forms of human persecution: as a figure of political and economic disempowerment, Bigger's rebellion carries forth the ideals embodied in the Declaration of Independence.

Max's determinism finds a couple of sources in Wright's thought, the first of which we considered in his interest in radical politics throughout the 1930s. Another important influence for Wright was the Chicago School of Sociology, which was established by Robert Park—who apparently asked Wright, "How the hell did you happen?" (Rowley 250)—and included figures like John Dewey, Thorstein Veblen, and George Herbert Mead. Wright developed strong friendships with Horace Cayton and St. Clair Drake and wrote the introduction to *Black Metropolis*, their influential 1945 study of African American ghetto life in Chicago's South Side. Wright was impressed by the "huge mountains of fact" with which the Chicago sociologists demonstrated the impact of modern urban life on black familial existence, and he understood his own novelistic efforts as the fictional counterparts to their scientific approach ("Introduction" xviii). If "you doubted the reality of Bigger Thomas," he wrote in his introduction, "then examine the delinquency rates cited in this book; if, in reading my autobiography, *Black Boy*, you doubted the picture of family life shown there, then study the figures on family disorganization given here. . . . To expect the contrary would be like expecting to see Rolls-Royces coming off the assembly lines at Ford's River Rouge plant! The imposed conditions under which Negroes live detail the structure of their lives like an engineer outlining the blue-prints for the production of machines" (xx).

In Max's sociologically tinged assessment, Bigger's crime is not irrational and incomprehensible, but rather it is the natural, predictable—almost mechanical—outcome of his sociopolitical heritage. If neighborhoods were like factories, Bigger was the signature model of Chicago's South Side. But the terror of Bigger Thomas runs both wider and deeper than the particular ghetto that produced him; as Max suggests, Bigger's terror is endemic to the American revolutionary subjectivity, and the execution of Bigger Thomas does nothing to eradicate that terror. In fact, Max argues, the state's violence serves only to exacerbate the conditions of social injustice that produced

Bigger's crime. Contemplating Bigger's execution, Max states, "The wheel of blood continues to turn!" (392), suggesting that the state's murder of Bigger Thomas turns on the same axis of evil that wrought Mary's death in the first place.

Max disagrees with Buckley not only on the origins of the crime but on the origins of the law itself. Where Buckley's arguments stem from the belief that "the law is holy" and "the foundation of all our cherished values" (408), Max asserts that the law is a man-made instrument used by the "mob-masters" and "wire-pullers" (386) in order to exploit and oppress the masses. Buckley operates as though legal concepts are self-evident, transcendent categories, and he denigrates "theoretical" interpretations of the law as quibbling prevarications. Max, by contrast, attempts to radically subjectivize legal concepts in order to emphasize their limitations in this context: Bigger may have committed "an act which we call a crime" (391), a murder that "*we* claimed warrants the death penalty" (400), but that's "only *one* side of it!" (401). Max's case involves redefining some of the key concepts in play: he reminds the judge that not every homicide is considered "murder" and insists that the difference between legitimate and illegitimate killing is a function of the context in which the act is situated. "Do men regret when they kill in war?" he asks. "No," Max states, "you kill to keep from being killed! And after a victorious war you return to a free country, just as this boy, with his hands stained with the blood of Mary Dalton, felt that he was free for the first time in his life" (396).

When Max likens Bigger to a freedom fighter—when he asks if "men regret when they kill in war" and imagines Bigger taking up arms for the creation of a "free country"—he seems to suggest that Bigger is something more than an ordinary criminal, that the limited scope and procedural conventions of criminal court simply aren't designed to accommodate crimes like Bigger's. And at times, Buckley seems similarly skeptical of the court's ability to dispense justice. If the court spares Bigger's life, Buckley says, "I shall resign my office and tell [the electorate] that our courts, swamped with mawkish sentimentality, are no longer fit instruments to safeguard the public peace!" Buckley transparently draws upon the power of the mob in order to ensure a guilty verdict and to underscore the mob itself as the source of the court's authority:

> "It is not often . . . that a representative of the people finds the masses of the citizens who elected him to office standing literally at his back, waiting for him to enforce the law." The room was quiet as a tomb. Buckley strode to the window and with one motion of his hand hoisted it up. The rumbling mutter of the vast mob swept in. The court room stirred.

"Kill 'im now!"
"Lynch 'im!"
The judge rapped for order. (373)

If the court fails to execute Bigger Thomas, Buckley implies, it will lose its legitimacy in the eyes of the people. In essence, the court must lynch Bigger Thomas so that the mob doesn't have to. As Christopher Waldrep has shown, one historically pervasive interpretation of lynching emphasizes the breakdown of structures of criminal law to justify forms of community-endorsed, extralegal violence: "When people judged their courts inadequate," Waldrep writes, "they [claimed] the right, in the face of horrible crime, to act outside the law" (61). This raises an obvious problem for the law itself. With Bigger's "horrible crime" on one side and the angry mob on the other, the court seems to be caught in a double bind: the sole way for the court to retain its legitimacy and its monopoly on violence—to prove to the people that the system is functioning, and that there is no cause for lynching—is to perform the very action demanded by the lynch mob itself. But if, as Buckley seems to threaten above, the court can prove its efficacy and legitimacy only by performing the execution demanded by (and essentially, acting in the place of) the lawless, illegitimate, extralegal mob, Wright's scenario blurs any clear distinction between legal and extralegal violence. When the judge inevitably sentences Bigger to death, reconsolidating the legitimacy of legal institutions and apparently reasserting the difference between the legitimate execution of Bigger and the lynching that has been avoided, Wright shows that the court has simultaneously erased any distinction between legal and extralegal violence—that it has effectively lynched Bigger Thomas for its own purposes.[18]

Wright's implication—that the justice system has in this case simply imbued a semblance of legitimacy and legality to what was in effect a lynching—is not only a critique of the racism endemic to the criminal justice system but also constitutes a necessary final element to Wright's narrative of terror. In sentencing Bigger to death, the judge clarifies the exact nature of the threat posed by the defendant: "In light of the unprecedented disturbance of the public mind," the judge states, "you, Bigger Thomas, shall die . . . in a manner prescribed by the laws of the state" (417). What makes Bigger exceptional is not his murder, which hardly presents a unique challenge to the legal institution; what makes Bigger exceptional is his "unprecedented disturbance of the public mind"—his creation, to quote the 1937 League of Nations convention, of a "state of terror in the mind . . . of the general public." In implying that Bigger's transgression represents something more insidious than an ordinary murder, the judge tacitly accepts Buckley's claim about the exceptional significance of the case, that it represents "a fight for civilization" (374).

Wright's point is that when crimes are reframed as fights for civilization, when transgressions become terrorism, lynching returns as a viable response of a terrorized community. In making the case about the whole of civilization, in questioning the legitimacy and efficacy of legal institutions themselves, Buckley successfully argues for an interpretation of Bigger as a menace capable not only of breaking laws but of radically undermining the institutional framework of the "law" itself. In turning Bigger's murder into a case of civilization against barbarism, Buckley anticipates a rhetorical turn, in our age, toward what is sometimes called the "lesser evil" approach—claims that extraordinary (and often unconstitutional) measures such as coercive interrogation, unwarranted or indefinite detention of suspects, and targeted assassinations are defensible if deemed necessary for defeating the greater evil of terrorism.[19] Advocates of the lesser evil approach ask whether the law must not under extraordinary conditions be prepared to sacrifice its own rules in order to conserve the larger ideals of the law itself. Civilization may behave barbarically, in other words, when barbarism is necessary to conserve civilization itself. Wright shows how Buckley, in advancing a parallel argument, unleashes a logic whereby the law is provoked into undoing itself: in order to contain the "unprecedented disturbance of the public mind" the law takes on the role of a state-sanctioned lynch mob—a legalized "extralegal" violence.

In the end, then, Bigger's lynching constitutes the unavoidable conclusion to Wright's prophesy. Terrorism is a crime unlike other crimes, a way of breaking the law that cannot be made to fit intelligibly within the structure of the law itself. But if terror is crime that exists outside the law, then the mob, in *Native Son*—the cry of "lynch 'im!" issued from just beyond the courthouse walls—serves to remind us of the punishment that similarly exists outside the law. Just as terrorism resists formal incorporation into our legal institutions, the persistence and adaptability of lynching suggests a punishment for crimes that defy legal reckoning. In Bigger Thomas, therefore, Wright not only prophesied the embodiment of modern terror and provided contrasting paradigms for interpreting the menace he represents, but he also supplied the terror narrative with its inevitable conclusion.

Greeley, Colorado

At a glance, one would be hard-pressed to imagine a world further removed from the ghetto of Chicago's South Side—and the deforming influences of poverty and institutionalized racism documented by Drake and Cayton—than the small liberal enclave of Greeley, Colorado. Greeley was founded by the Union Colony of Colorado in 1870 as a self-proclaimed utopian community (of "high moral standards") and was named for its original benefactor—Horace Greeley, the *New York Tribune* editor who is said to have coined the phrase, "Go West, young man!"[20] Even in the 1940s, Greeley had happily maintained "the moral rigor, temperance and civic-mindedness that were the hallmarks of its founding fathers" (Calvert 95). It was a dry town—until the 1970s, alcohol and its attendant vices had been relegated to nearby Garden City—and each street seemed to have its own church. But in the eyes of at least one notable visitor, even Greeley was not immune to what Howe had dubbed "the disease of our culture" (102).

In November of 1948, little more than a year after Wright had permanently given up on living in America and relocated to Paris, an Egyptian writer named Sayyid Qutb sailed from Alexandria to New York. Qutb, a delicate forty-two-year-old who would soon become "the single most influential writer in the Islamist tradition," ended up in Greeley, where he enrolled in the Colorado State College of Education (Berman 60). The timing of this venture was not accidental: Qutb's "campaigns against the socioeconomic situation and his demand for social justice" in various Egyptian magazines had brought him the wrong kind of attention from authorities, and certain well-placed friends had thought it advisable for Qutb to take an extended vacation (Musallam 111). The ostensible purpose of Qutb's trip was a vaguely defined "educational mission," and he would indeed find an education in America—though perhaps not exactly the one his Egyptian friends had hoped for. Qutb's journey to America was meant to have been a liberalizing experience for the author, but it ended up having the opposite effect (L. Wright 23). Of course, it is impossible to gauge, from this distance, the depth of Qutb's radicalism at the time he arrived in America. He later claimed that "he was not even a very religious man" before coming to the country—despite the fact that he had memorized the Qu'ran by the age of ten (L. Wright 8; Berman 61). It may be going too far to suggest, with Emmanuel Sivan, that Qutb's American journey "was indeed the formative experience that converted him . . . to fundamentalism" (22). Some of Qutb's negative attitudes and prejudices about American culture must have been formed prior to his arrival. Nonetheless, as John Calvert argues, Qutb's stay in the United States "did at least contribute to his sense of national exceptionalism by generating experiences which confirmed and honed the distinctions which he had long supposed separated the West, including America, from the East" (89).

Qutb's American experience also "made him sharply aware of himself as a man of color." Lawrence Wright describes a telling episode that took place in Greeley in 1949, when Qutb and several friends were turned away from a movie theater because the proprietor had mistaken them for African Americans. "But we're Egyptians," one of the group protested. "The owner," Wright says, "apologized and offered to let them in, but Qutb refused, galled by the prospect that black Egyptians could be admitted but black Americans could not" (19). Some time later, Qutb would write (in a tone not unfamiliar to readers of James Baldwin) that "racism had brought America down from the summit to the foot of the mountain—taking the rest of humanity with it" (qtd. in L. Wright 19).[21] When Qutb returned to Egypt in 1951, he dedicated himself even more thoroughly to the Islamist movement, and by 1953, he "had become a leading ideologue of the Muslim Brothers" (Musallam 121). His writing was now more militant: his time in America "strengthened his conviction that writing is not worthwhile unless it has practical application. The articulation of an idea is not enough by itself; it must have deep conviction behind it, and must be expressed in action" (Musallam 119). He had become convinced, in other words, that writing should function as a weapon. Qutb's American experience had also convinced him that the distinction between capitalism and communism was superficial compared to the rift between Islam and the West. In Qutb's theology, Islam was more than a religion—his brand of Islamism called for qu'ranically inspired answers to all political, economic, and legal questions (Calvert 91).[22] Islam, for Qutb, was the total solution.

In his introduction to Cayton and Drake's *Black Metropolis*, Wright had warned that America's ghettos were producing precisely the kind of desperate subjects that Hitler had so recently exploited; he even intimated that these ghettos were capable of producing a Hitler of their own (xxiv-xxv). Years before, in *Native Son*, Wright had written that Bigger liked to hear about "how Hitler was running the Jews to the ground; of how Mussolini was invading Spain" (115). Wright felt that the materially and spiritually oppressive conditions of the ghetto were forming exactly the kind of vitiated subjectivity that was most susceptible to the pathological mass movements that had seized Europe. But the symptoms of what Max had deemed America's originary terror were not confined to the ghetto. The disease had metastasized; even faraway "utopian communities" like Greeley, Colorado, were not free of contamination. In 1989, Chicago's National Civic League named Greeley as one of ten "All-American Cities" (Calvert 95). To contemplate the role that the racism of this "All-American" city may have played in helping to radicalize Sayyid Qutb is to enter into the logic of the American gothic. Leslie Fiedler thought that the gothic provided a route into "certain areas of our social lives where nightmare violence and guilt actually exist. To discuss, for instance, in the light of pure reason the Negro problem in the United States is to falsify its essential mystery and unreality; it is a gothic horror of our daily lives" (493). For Fiedler, what is most terrifying about the gothic is the fact that it is already a part of our "daily lives": the gothic refers to a terror that will not be segregated and contained in ghettos; it seeps up from our utopias and our "All-American" cities. As Jacques Derrida put it shortly after 9/11, the most "terrifying" terrorism "always has something 'domestic,' if not national, about it" (qtd. in Borradori 188).[23] Bigger's ambiguous, death-row confession—"what I killed for, I am!" (429)—reflects, on a personal level, the way in which terror is always internal and constitutive of the identity it appears to undo from without.

It will come as no surprise that of the two paradigms for conceiving terror outlined in the final part of *Native Son*, modern critics have almost unanimously accepted Max's reading of Bigger's crime. Partly because Max's analysis (which underscores Bigger's historical and geographic particularity and sees his murders as emerging from a confluence of social forces that are context bound) is ideologically contiguous with the priorities of contemporary literary scholarship, critics have been less than willing to explore the notion that both Buckley and Max stand in as misreaders of Wright's text. In "How 'Bigger' Was Born," the 1940 essay in which Wright attempted to grapple with the various ideas and personages from his past that had converged in Bigger Thomas, the author appears to trouble the idea that there is anything essentially American—or even essentially African—about Bigger Thomas. Instead, Wright's reflections reveal a Bigger who was animated by the same terrifying political forces that were then surging overseas: "I was fascinated by the similarity of the emotional tensions of Bigger in America and Bigger in Nazi Germany and Bigger in old Russia. All Bigger Thomases, white and black, felt tense, afraid, nervous, hysterical, and restless. From far away Nazi Germany and old Russia had come to me items of knowledge that told me that certain modern experiences were creating types of personalities whose existence ignored racial and national lines of demarcation, that these personalities carried with them a more universal drama-element than anything I'd ever encountered before" (*Native Son* 446). "Bigger Thomas," here, is identified less with a particular environment to which he is "native" than he is with a web of feelings ("tense, afraid, nervous, hysterical and restless"), a "universal drama-element" that renders subjects susceptible to the various forms of totalitarianism then ascendant in Europe. "Bigger Thomas" now refers less to a specific black boy in the slums of Chicago than to a potentially global psychological pathology, an inclination to revolutionary violence springing up in conditions of extreme desperation. Bigger's predilection for violence—his overwhelming urge to "blot out" those around him, to view violence as a cleansing force—brings him into alignment with Frantz Fanon's meaning of "native" when he writes, in *The Wretched of the Earth*, that only violence "frees the native from his inferiority complex and from his despair and inactivity: It makes him fearless and restores his self-respect" (94).

Native Son is not only a searing critique of the systemic racial persecution engrained in American economic and legal institutions or just an exposé of the appalling social conditions endured by African Americans in Chicago's South Side. Wright's narrative is also propelled by a prophetic conception of how the racial state produces its response in terrorism. In the government's continual failure to enact meaningful legislative reform—in America's failure to live up to its officially endorsed ideals of universal liberty—and in the larger cultural failure to uproot prejudices and dispel stereotypes of black inferiority and sexual degeneracy, Wright was convinced that American society was breeding an increasingly desperate underclass immanently capable of erupting into terroristic violence. Most obviously, Wright's prophesy came to fruition in the widespread rioting and the entrenchment of militant black separatist and nationalist parties in the decades following the novel's publication.[24] But the novel's most pressing intervention today lies in its imagining of a distinctly modern kind of terror, a profoundly selfless, seemingly automatic form of terror that takes place more because of the existing relations of force than because of the conscious intent of any terrorist. And a conspicuous element of this modern terror will reside in the interpretive breakdown that Wright painstakingly fleshes out in the final third of the novel. Neither Buckley's metaphysical certainty nor Max's rudimentary dialectical materialism are sufficient to explain Bigger's crimes or what they mean. Buckley fits into an ancient pattern when he calls for a glorified lynching; Max's interpretive failure, while perhaps more sympathetic (or at least sentimental), is no less conspicuous in his final meeting with Bigger:

> "I didn't want to kill!" Bigger shouted. "But what I killed for, I *am*! . . . What I killed for must've been good! . . . When a man kills, it's for something . . . I didn't know I was really alive in this world until I felt things hard enough to kill for 'em."
>
> Max's eyes were full of terror. (429)

The "terror" in Max's eyes is the terror that attends the realization that one's interpretive paradigms have failed, that one is finally at a loss. Max has completely misunderstood Bigger, and if we are duped into thinking that Bigger has killed "for something," so have we. For Bigger Thomas is not a freedom fighter; he's not a revolutionary warrior—and to see him as such is to posit both a political agenda and an autonomous self that were radically absent from the moment of Mary's murder. That slaying was an automatic response to Bigger's desperation, a desperation that was in turn produced by ingrained patterns of structural oppression. "In the end," as Fanon put it, "Bigger Thomas acts. To put an end to his tension, he responds to the world's anticipation" (*Black Skin* 139). In conjuring a situation in which a black male's fear of being lynched produces the violence that will then necessitate the lynching, Wright prophesied the ways that white racial terror effectively "anticipates" into existence the terror it most fears. But to allow, as Wright clearly did in his essay, that Bigger Thomas was not confined to a particular geographical or temporal locality—that he was not acting on the basis of a particular intention or looking to redress a specific catalog of grievances—but that he was, in effect, acting out a script as infinitely renewable as our own terrifying "anticipations," is to be open to the fact that Bigger haunts us still. In Bigger Thomas, Wright gave America a figure for the terror that, he was convinced, would cast a long shadow over the nation's future. Bigger could be Communist or Fascist, white or black (or "Red"), seemingly alien or wholly native. *Native Son* forces us to confront the necessity of our own cultural investments in the production of terror—the ways in which our own institutions, cultural forms, attitudes, and anticipations have made Bigger an endlessly readable and misreadable figure for the terror within.

Epilogue

Why Norman Mailer Hates Plastic

Midway through a 2001 French television documentary on Norman Mailer, an unseen interviewer pushes the author to elaborate on the 1960 incident in which he stabbed his second wife, Adele Morales.[1] The seventy-eight-year-old Mailer, squirming perceptibly in his seat, says something about how the incident revealed to him that he lacked a "clear path through to philosophy." Then he taps on a piece of plastic and says, ponderously, "This is *worse* than individual violence."

Stabbing one's wife was bad, surely, but plastic—now there was an evil worth getting worked up about. "Children grow up *sucking* on this stuff," Mailer had growled earlier in the interview, holding up a piece of Tupperware, "they finger it. But there's nothing. Your fingers feel nothing. You touch a glass, you feel a little bit. You touch wood, you get quite a bit. But you touch this, nothing comes back. And you've had now for four decades more and more infants live with this stuff and play with it, and you cannot possibly feel any affection for it." To this point, you might think that Mailer's problem with plastic is that it is too hygienic, too sanitized, too far removed from the grit and grain of organic reality. But, as is often the case, Mailer's mind is headed in the opposite direction. "After all," he goes on, "what is plastic, when you stop to think about it? Plastic is the excrement of oil. That's how it started. What happened is all these people who were making their billions, their early billions on oil, were throwing away the waste product of oil when they refined it . . . and suddenly someone said, 'look, we're throwing away a fortune.' And so now we're surrounded by the excrement of oil." Mailer's problem with plastic is not that it is too clean but that it's inherently dirty. Humanity's relentless drive toward efficiency—to make even our byproducts productive, to make our waste do some kind of work for us—has led to the metastasization of a kind of shitty totalitarianism, a hyperrational world in which everything now comes packaged in a film of excrement.

Of course, when one really "stops to think about it," plastic is not the "excrement" of oil in any scientific sense: the industrial production of synthetic amorphous polymers does not involve anal excretion in the sense suggested by Mailer. But then science, for Mailer, was a very large part of the problem, part of the larger system of rationalization that had reduced postwar American life to an inauthentic shadow of genuine experience. Mailer was not responding scientifically to these deadening phenomena but religiously. "One's teeth when they're repaired," he went on, "are now filled with plastic. Once upon a time you had mercury in there. You had gold. You had silver, you had various metals. You could have a certain companionship with the Devil. Mercury gave you God knows what. . . . It poisoned you on one hand; on the other hand it put you in contact with occult forces! Now what do you have in your teeth? Plastic. Your mouth feels numb. You kiss less well." In this brief tirade against plastic, Mailer makes a miniature version of the move he made in almost all of his fiction and "nonfiction" prose: a naturalization of the conflict between "authenticity" and "plasticity," which itself stood in for a battle between God and the devil. In Mailer's cosmology, a metaphysical struggle was playing itself out in the physical substances of our bodies and the materials surrounding us. When one touches a piece of plastic, one doesn't "feel" anything—one is less in contact with the primal and authentic energies in the universe. Plastic, Mailer thought, had a numbing effect on human lives, and one of the ways we try to overcome that desensitization is through more extreme violence: hence his claim that plastic was worse than "individual" acts of violence. The most potent force opposing plasticity was not violence but sexual pleasure, the orgasm (which was one of the reasons why Mailer disapproved of condoms, which introduced plastic into the moment of sexual contact). Plastic, as a literal product of and a metaphor for "technology," was an instrument of the Evil One. Plastic was also "excrement," which, for Mailer, was always the devil's medium. The devil, therefore, was capable of ruining our lives from without, by using technology to desensitize us or to give us cancer ("modern disease and modern technology are inseparably connected," Mailer said ["Vices" 43]). But the devil was also always within, lurking within close proximity to the anus.[2] This system, or rather these convictions, could lead Mailer into some unfortunate logical tangles, particularly in relation to homosexuality. Reporting on the 1992 Republican National Convention, Mailer ruminates on the deeper significance of AIDS:

> Was excrement a side-product of nature, offensive to some, as the Democrats would doubtless have argued, or was Satan in everyone's shit? Which, in turn, was a way of saying that the devil was present more of-

> ten in homosexual than in heterosexual encounters—exactly the question that blazed in the divide. We are dying, said the victims of AIDS, and you have no mercy. Are you cold to our pain because we are the devil's spawn?—beware, then, for we will haunt you. That was the question. Was the gay nation guilty or innocent, victims of devils, damned by Jehovah or to be comforted by Christ? ("By Heaven Inspired" 1104)

There is an understandable temptation, for those who would seek to sanitize Mailer or make his views more safely consumable today, to reduce all of this to the level of metaphor. Mailer can't "seriously" be suggesting that there's something devilish about gay sex; he must be speaking figuratively. But there's little to suggest that Mailer wasn't completely earnest in making these solemn pronouncements. Mailer really did feel that there was something quite literally deadening and desensitizing and cancerous in the nature of plastic; he believed that excrement was quite literally the habitat or medium of the devil. The question of AIDS seems to push Mailer's cosmology to its breaking point: it's one thing to associate the devil with "shit" in an abstract sense, but it's quite another to suggest that homosexual encounters are invigilated by Beelzebub, and that the ravages of AIDs may therefore be the natural price of these filthy and Satanic practices. Unpleasant as such sentiments now sound, it would nonetheless be a serious interpretive misstep to read the above statements as in any sense "metaphorical," as representative of substances, concepts, and conflicts "other" than the ones he's describing. Mailer thought that one's very soul hung in the balance of how one came down on these questions.

Norman Mailer, perhaps more than any other postwar American author, is widely considered to be an heir to the naturalistic tradition. But what makes us want to call Norman Mailer a "naturalist" author? In what sense are these and Mailer's other ideas "naturalistic"? There have been a variety of answers. For Donald Pizer, Mailer's work "express[es] the naturalistic theme of the hidden recesses of value in man's nature despite his tragic fate in a closely conditioned and controlled world" (*Twentieth-Century* 92). For Richard Lehan, Mailer's naturalism resides in a Nietzschean conception of power and morality—a belief that men are "driven by a lust for power in a world that is ferocious as the jungle" (*Realism* 221)—an idea that is "a legacy of naturalism" (222) and one he would go on to develop in *The Naked and the Dead* (1948), *The Presidential Papers* (1963), *Cannibals and Christians* (1966), *Why Are We in Vietnam*? (1967), and *The Armies of the Night* (1968). Mailer scholar Andrew Wilson locates Mailer's naturalism in his "biological/social determinism," his belief in "the predetermined dictates of nature" (29).

Mailer could be a naturalist in other ways, too. His novels and essays (some more explicitly than others) work to naturalize his distinctive cosmology, in much the same way that Norris's *The Octopus* was framed as an attempt to naturalize the supernatural. The journalistic techniques that Dreiser employed in *An American Tragedy*, moreover, are more than a little redolent of the techniques Mailer would take up (and extend) in *The Executioner's Song*. In "The White Negro," Mailer connected primitivist black sexuality with a capacity for sudden violence that he found to be spiritually liberating—sentiments that Wright was flirting with in his representation of Bigger Thomas, and ones he would expand upon later in his career.

Mailer might be termed a "naturalistic" author for all of these reasons: his tragic view of human worth struggling against external forces, his Nietzschean understanding of power, his "social determinism," his naturalizing of the supernatural, his use of journalistic techniques. The problem is that while each of these definitions seem to describe a single work or two of Mailer's, or capture a single dimension of many works, all of them manage to miss whatever quality makes Norman Mailer "Norman Mailer." They are not adequate in describing what makes Mailer valuable or interesting or fun to read; they somehow sidestep Mailer's essential "Mailerness." But at the same time, the above definitions similarly miss whatever quality makes naturalism "naturalism"; they sidestep the crucial quality that differentiates naturalism from all other genres. That quality is polemicism.

It's no coincidence that Norman Mailer, the quintessential twentieth-century naturalist, was also an inveterate, lifelong polemicist. Naturalism, I have been arguing, has always been animated by polemicism, and no single twentieth-century figure on the American literary landscape was able to wield polemic more consistently or effectively (or for greater personal gain) than the author of "The White Negro." But if Norman Mailer is the twentieth-century naturalist par excellence, he also constitutes a useful example of how *not* to approach naturalism. Let us momentarily return to the question Mailer poses above: "Was excrement a side-product of nature, offensive to some, or was Satan in everyone's shit?" Confronted with such a question (and this is the kind of deliberately provocative, self-consciously offensive question about some pressing new issue of public life that has been a speciality of the naturalists), the critic has a choice to make. One could, of course, attempt to extract from this a naturalistic system of thought—one that relies, perhaps, on Darwinian or Nietzschean concepts, or emphasizes the compensatory humanism that emerges from the tragic acceptance of the inevitability of cruel biology, or whatnot—and then pull back to use that system to explicate one or more of Mailer's texts. But my suggestion about Mailer—and my suggestion about the naturalists more generally—is that such a question is already its own answer. The best response will therefore come in the form of additional questions, questions pertaining to Mailer's use of polemicism. Who has the most to gain from polemic of this sort? Does this polemic serve to lay the foundations for a new fictional, cultural, or social edifice, or is it destructive for its own sake? If Mailer's words are weapons, who is on the receiving end, and in whose name will the cleansing violence be performed? Naturalism has been confronting us with questions of this sort since the turn of the last century. And we have been answering them, in one way or another.

Notes

Introduction

1. Donald Pizer is a notable exception (see, for instance, *Naturalism and the Jews*). While other critics certainly register some of the moral haze that surrounds the naturalists' politics, we await a relatively frank assessment of literary naturalism's relationship to democracy, human rights, individualism, and other fundamental values of Western liberalism.

2. Louis Menand's essay on Wright in *American Studies* traces the author's enduring fascination with totalitarian power.

3. None of this is to minimize Dreiser's significant charitable work. During his tenure at the *Delineator*, for instance, Dreiser devoted himself to child rescue efforts; he was associated with various other laudable causes over the course of his life. We can recognize and applaud those efforts while appreciating the gravity of his political shortcomings.

Chapter 1

1. My understanding of Mencken draws on Teachout and Hobson.

2. On Wright's discovery of Mencken, see Rowley, *Richard Wright* 44–47.

3. In "Memories of My Grandmother," an unpublished essay in the Wright Collection at the Beinecke Library at Yale, Wright meditates on how his attitudes were inevitably shaped by Margaret Bolden's powerful influence.

4. On the role of the virtuous young woman as the ideal consumer of literature, see Douglas, as well as Campbell, especially her chapter "The Iron Madonna."

5. Some historians have seen Jackson's populism as a direct precursor to that of Franklin Roosevelt—another great antagonist of Mencken's. See Wilentz and Brand.

6. The most influential accounts of Puritanism in America are P. Miller *The New England Mind: The Seventeenth Century* (and *The New England Mind: From Colony to Province*, and Bercovitch *Puritan Origins* and *American Jeremiad*.

7. Indeed, it may have been the arbitrary and inexact nature of Mencken's reading of Puritanism that made his reading of the naturalist rebellion so durable. That is, the place of the "Puritans" in Mencken's analysis could be occupied by any number of other forms of cultural authority against which the naturalists were rebelling.

8. These statistics are quoted in "The Hypocrites Club," *Economist*, March 13, 2008.

9. On naturalism's relationship to anti-Semitism, see Pizer *American Naturalism and the Jews*.

10. The naturalists were "proto" social Darwinists only because that term wasn't coined until the 1930s.

11. Dreiser always kept two sets of books, but it was not until his last years that he publicly embraced his contradictions, joining the Communist Party *and* finding God.

12. See Lears, *No Place of Grace* 117–24.

13. Norris did spend a short amount of time in the Uitlander's militia in South Africa, although the evidence suggests that this was more of a personal adventure for Norris than "war" as it was experienced by the generation that came before and after his own.

14. Of course, the United States did participate in various military adventures over this time, but in all cases the action was so far away that it was evidently possible to retain an attitude of "innocent" jingoism.

15. Nonetheless, the most successful scholars in the humanities routinely indulge in polemic: Stanley Fish, Martha Nussbaum, Harold Bloom, Susan Gubar, Camille Paglia, Slavoj Zizek, Jacques Derrida, and Noam Chomsky are just a few of the scholars who leap to mind in this regard. Polemic, then, is institutionally frowned upon but paradoxically excusable or perhaps even necessary for admittance into the upper echelons of the profession.

16. See Hobson 341.

17. Zola's impact on Norris, and on the American naturalists more generally, has been discussed at length by a number of critics, including Link 16–20, and Lehan "European Background" (among other places). See also Ahnerbrink 21–29.

Chapter 2

1. See Link 10–20.

2. "Consider," Mencken wrote, "[the pedagogue] in his highest incarnation:

the university professor. What is his function? Simply to pass on to fresh generations of numbskulls a body of so-called knowledge that is fragmentary, unimportant and, for the most part, untrue. His whole professional activity is circumscribed by the prejudices, vanities and avarices of his university trustees, that is, a committee of soap-boilers, nail-manufacturers, bank-directors and politicians. The moment he offends these vermin he is undone. He cannot so much as think aloud without running a risk of having them fan his pantaloons" (*Gist* 102).

3. See McElrath and Crisler 188–198.

4. See Dudley 11–12, 100–102.

5. Like Dreiser, Crane, and London, Norris would acquire some postsecondary education but never obtain his degree. Richard Wright did not complete high school.

6. Some insight into the nature of the naturalists's polemicism may be gleaned from Norris's great disdain for Howells, which he assumed often and loudly in print, while enjoying the advice and company of the established writer in his private life. Indeed, Howells read and had approved of *McTeague* before its publication; as Malcolm Cowley writes, "Howells was the real patron and precursor of naturalism in America" ("Naturalism" 56). Attacking Howells was a way of clearing a space for Norris's own writing in the literary marketplace.

7. The full text of Lewis's address is available at http://nobelprize.org/nobel_prizes/literature/laureates/1930/lewis-lecture.html.

8. Wright added that "only enemies of peace and Russia can see it as anything else" (Kinnamon and Fabre 25).

9. Norris's first novel, *Vandover and the Brute* (1914), was first released more than a decade after the author's death, while his *McTeague* was subjected to deep cuts for a variety of offenses, most memorably its depiction of a small boy micturating in his pants. All of Theodore Dreiser's novels drew the censoriousness of morally upstanding critics, and many were cut by editors. *Sister Carrie* was suppressed entirely after an extremely limited print run, which biographers have suggested may have led to the psychological collapse of the author in 1902. Dreiser's *The "Genius"* was also suppressed; even *An American Tragedy*—his greatest critical success, which very nearly won him a Nobel Prize—was banned in some jurisdictions because of its supposed endorsement of birth control. Richard Wright's *Native Son* was subjected to severe cuts before the material was restored by the Library of America in the 1990s. The entire second half of *Black Boy* (the section dealing with communism) was cut by Wright's editors, while approximately one quarter of *The Outsider* was cut out before it was allowed to be published.

10. Geroge J. Becker first used the phrase "pessimistic materialistic determinism" (35) in connection with the naturalists in "Modern Realism as a Literary Movement." Philip Rahv and Malcolm Cowley similarly endorse the idea.

11. See D. Bell and Schlesinger.

12. For a helpful account of the journalistic profession, see C. Wilson, as well as Mott.

13. On the spirit of the age, see Whyte.

14. The single Library of America volume of Stephen Crane's "works" clocks in at 1,351 pages of small-type print published by Crane before his death at the age of twenty-eight. Just how quickly did the naturalists work? Jack London is perhaps representative in this respect. He wrote 1,000 words a day, six days per week, fifty-two weeks per year, with no extra time allowed for planning or revision. The result was fifty books in seventeen years. Dreiser must have worked at a similar pace in order to produce the millions of words of prose he generated in addition to his novels. Harold Frederic is said to have written 4,000 words a day, while Upton Sinclair is supposed to have written 18,000 in one day. As Malcolm Cowley quipped, this immense productivity is one reason that almost all the American naturalists read better in translation ("Not Men" 424).

15. In *A Man's Game*, John Dudley nicely fleshes out the gendered implications of this tension between effeminate "observing" and masculine "doing." See especially his chapter on sports writing and boxing, "Inside and Outside the Ring: The Establishment of a Masculinist Aesthetic Sensibility" (19–54).

Chapter 3

1. In works such as "The Neuro-Psychoses of Defence," and "Neurosis and Psychosis," Freud develops the idea of neurosis to refer to nervous conditions in which the patients' bodily symptoms were unrelated to perceptible anatomical factors.

2. Theodore Dreiser conceived of humanity's relationship to nature in similar terms: "Man dreams of what he would like to do, and builds up paper defenses, ways and means. But nature knows, apparently what she must, or wishes—and, alas, sweeps his feeble defenses all away" (*Prose* 229).

3. Neurasthenia was very much "the disease of the age," as Lears puts it (49). The malady was common among the male artists, scholars, clergymen, and businessmen in a middle class increasingly vulnerable to nervous prostration or (as it was popularly known) "brain sprain." Norris's fellow neurasthenics included the artists Owen Wister and Frederic Remington, writers like Dreiser, Howells, Henry and William James, and at least two presidents, Woodrow Wilson and Theodore Roosevelt (Rotundo 186). Both Charlotte Perkins Gilman and Edith Wharton were forced to endure S. Weir Mitchell's "rest cure" for the same ailment. According to the influential New York neurologist George M. Beard, who popularized the diagnosis in his books *American Nervousness* (1881) and *Sexual*

Neurasthenia (1884), the causes of neurasthenia were as diverse as its symptoms, which included insomnia, blurred vision, indigestion, asthma, headache, hypochondria, baldness, and—menacingly—"brain collapse." The physician cautioned readers that the malady was exacerbated by indulgence in "evil habits" and "special excitements," among other euphemisms for self-abuse, but felt that onanism was ultimately secondary to the "one great predisposing cause—civilization" (*American Nervousness* 15). On Norris's own bout with the disorder, see McElrath and Crisler 232.

4. This compromise, as Pizer (*Novels of Frank Norris* 116) and others have noticed, is likely influenced by the evolutionary theism of Le Conte.

5. While McElrath denies that Vanamee functions as an authorial spokesman, he goes on to argue that Norris's novel appeals to the ethic expressed in the Sermon on the Mount, and that Norris "show[s] the potential and real value of an experiment in Judaeo-Christian living" ("Frank Norris's *The Octopus*" 143).

6. Both Mark Seltzer and Walter Benn Michaels touch on issues of environmentality in their important discussions of *The Octopus*, although neither is explicitly interested in the "environment" as that category would be theorized by "ecocriticism." As for ecocriticism itself, the school has had surprisingly little to say about naturalism, and nothing at all to say about *The Octopus*.

7. Of course, "ecocriticism," like any approach to reading, has been formulated in many different ways; see for instance, Glotfelty xv-xxiv, as well as Buell *Future*, and Rosendale. One of the foundational questions for all ecocritics is whether early writers on nature like Emerson or Thoreau count as "ecocritics," or whether that term should be reserved for more recent academic criticism. Glotfelty, coeditor of *The Ecocriticism Reader* (1996), a first attempt to consolidate a school of ecocriticism, supplies us with one answer. Her introduction to the reader implicitly excludes earlier nature writers and advocates of environmental conservation, writers like Aldo Leopold, who did not live in an age of "environmental crisis." Other scholars are more invested in locating ecocriticism within an extended tradition of environmentally oriented writing. Mazel advocates the long view of ecocriticism, which is intended to provide the movement with "a usable past." Mazel contests the standard history of ecocriticism, which sees environmental literary studies primarily as an academic offshoot of the modern environmentalist movement that underwent a slow process of institutionalization beginning in the 1970s. In Mazel's alternative history, environmentalism and ecocriticism were interconnected from the start.

8. For a clever dissection of Norris's stylistic idiosyncrasies, see M. Bell, "The Revolt Against Style: Frank Norris" in *The Problem of American Realism*.

9. Perhaps even more insidious (for these critics) than modernism's insistence that all is consciousness are academic formulations of "linguistic deter-

mination," as Love writes, "although I recognize that our perceptions of nature are necessarily human constructed, these constructions are also, necessarily, the product of a brain and a physiology that have evolved in close relationship to nature" (8).

10. This understanding of the symbolic function of the wheat has been around at least since Walker's *Frank Norris*.

11. Norris's "cosmic optimism" is in accordance with what Lears calls the "cosmic harmony" of the early scientific naturalist John Muir. "When we try to pick out anything by itself," Muir wrote, "we find it hitched to everything else in the universe" (qtd. in Lears, "Cranks" 40).

12. See Lears, "Cranks."

13. Michaels argues that instead of "dramatizing the customary [that is, Populist] agrarian fear of the middleman, the novel here transforms distribution into consumption. . . . The railroad that distributes the wheat turns out to be imagined as consuming it" (195).

14. Naturalism reveals "the romance of the commonplace," as Norris put it. For a succinct definition of what Norris means by the terms, see "A Plea for Romantic Fiction" (*Novels and Essays* 1165–69).

15. On the gunfight at Mussel Slough, see McElrath and Crisler 347–50, R. Brown, *No Duty to Retreat* 87–115, and Pizer, *Novels of Frank Norris* 118–21. Josiah Royce's novel *The Feud at Oakfield Creek* (1887) is another novel based on events related to the massacre.

16. See McElrath and Crisler 347–48.

17. Muir is also remembered for his close friendship with Teddy Roosevelt, and in 1903 he convinced the president to enclose Yosemite Valley within the natural park. On Muir's life and accomplishments, see Worster.

18. Folson considers the novel's treatment of the railroad trust in relation to its official "cosmic optimism." Folson argues that the real argument in the novel "is not over Force at all, or public service, or private property, but rather over what is a fair profit" (137).

19. For a lively account of the rise of industrial agriculture in America, see Pollan 72–84.

20. In *The Fiction of Frank Norris*, Graham associates Mrs. Derrick's taste with the "New York literary cultists" and their values of "idealism, spirituality, refinement, and soft optimism" (102). "Her favourite books are," Graham says, "an index of overrefined, escapist art" (103). Such was certainly Norris's intention. But we should also recognize the ways in which Mrs. Derrick functions as a figure of survival at the end of the narrative, and that her very aesthetic refinement and softness is part of what makes her point of view ecologically defensible today.

21. "Damn the 'style' of a story," Norris himself had barked in "An Opening for Novelists." While the aesthete busies him- or herself "rounding a phrase" or "sus-

taining a metaphor" or "composing a villanelle" or "niggling a couplet," men are getting "shanghaied," "hatcheted," "stabbed," and otherwise dispatched (*Novels and Essays* 1114). How could mere literature compete with such excitement?

22. For a consideration of Vanamee as a "poet by nature," see Graham 105–6.

23. There is no debating that the official line of the novel (and the imagined trilogy of which it was supposed to be the first part) is that the wheat is symbolic of nature's sublime inexorability. It is only when we "read against the grain," so to speak, that we can also recognize how the novel undercuts its own thesis by demonstrating the artificiality of its central symbol.

24. As Schama puts it, national identity "would lose much of its ferocious enchantment without the mystique of a particular landscape tradition: its topography mapped, elaborated, and enriched as a homeland . . . landscapes can be self-consciously designed to express the virtues of a particular political or social community" (15).

25. As Kern writes, ecocriticism is "designed to expose and facilitate analysis of a text's orientation both to the world it imagines and to the world in which it takes shape, along with the conditions and contexts that affect that orientation, whatever it might be" (260).

26. Mazel highlights Marsh's practice of close reading and makes the claim that writers as diverse as Robert Lowell, D. H. Lawrence, Perry Miller, and Leo Marx should also be included in the school.

27. I should perhaps clarify that the "wheat," in this scene, is also the WHEAT: despite the fact that Mrs. Derrick has already focused our attention on the ways in which the wheat is a profoundly unnatural human creation, the conclusion of Norris's novel encourages us once again to read the wheat as a signifier for nature's ultimate beneficence.

28. Michaels sees this moment as a failure of Behrman's appetite. "Even the gluttonous Behrman isn't hungry enough to eat his way out of the wheat," Michaels writes, and his death, too, is imagined as a moment in which appetite fails" (184).

29. This strategic concealment is perhaps akin to the ideologized construction of the "the landscape" itself. As Mitchell observes, our insistence upon the purity of nature is in some sense intended "to erase the signs of our own constructive activity in the formation of landscape as meaning or value, to produce an art that conceals its own artifice, to imagine a representation that 'breaks through' representation into the realm of the nonhuman" (16–17).

Chapter 4

1. Gilmer reports that by January of 1928 "there were approximately seventy modern books banned in Boston, although by this time no single group [the

Watch and Ward Society, the District Attorney, or the Police Department] wished to claim credit for the wholesale suppression" (167).

2. Amusingly, Dreiser himself would admit an affinity with these "curious animals." "For several years," he wrote in *Dawn*, "my main concern with old or famous books was to find the portions that dealt with sex, though the merit of a conservative book was by no means beyond me" (270).

3. This coincidence would not have been possible had Dreiser followed the advice of his publisher. Liveright had encouraged him to name the book "Ewing" or "Warner" (Lingeman, *Journey* 235). This was one occasion on which Dreiser's aesthetic sensibility prevailed.

4. The McCain quote comes from his presidential campaign website, available at http://www.johnmccain.com/Informing/Issues/95b18512-d5b6-456e-90a2-12028d71df58.htm (accessed March 5, 2009).

5. As Mohr points out, "quickening" was still essential for pregnancy to be proved, and "consequently, even though pre-quickened abortions were theoretically illegal in New York after 1945, in practice the quickening doctrine remained very much a part of New York juridical interpretation into the 1880s" (124).

6. George Bernard Shaw, whose *Mrs. Warren's Profession* was persecuted by Comstock, once stated that "Comstockery is the world's standing joke at the expense of the United States. Europe likes to hear of such things. It confirms the deep-seated conviction of the Old World that America is a provincial place, a second-rate country-town civilization after all" (qtd. in Schlosser 120).

7. The full text of Goddard's work is available online at http://psychclassics.asu.edu/Goddard/index.htm.

8. Of course, the pursuit of "idle unproductive pleasuring" is an adequate enough description of Dreiser's own activities during certain periods of his life. As biographer Richard Lingeman observes of one particularly salacious stretch of Dreiser's diary, "he felt the same documentary urge to record that a day ended with lovemaking that he did to describe the weather, or the name of a caller, or the price of a purchase at the store" (*Journey* 154). Sometimes, "his promiscuity resembled an addiction." He worried about the toll that his voracious appetites would exact upon his health, writing, "I must give up so much screwing or I will break down"; at other times, according to Lingeman, he "seemed to fancy—and sometimes seriously advocate—polygamy" (*Journey* 154, 153). Helen Richardson Dreiser—who would eventually marry Dreiser, and who had been one of his lovers since showing up at his door in 1919, claiming to be one of his relatives—believed that he was infertile. As Jerome Loving speculates, "had he been fertile there no doubt would have been a tribe of illicit Dreisers running around" ("Re: Dreiser"). Dreiser's reading of zoological demographics, then, which found an inverse relationship between intelligence and offspring, also happened to cast the

naturalist himself in a rather flattering light: the infertile brainiac was perched comfortably atop his own natural hierarchy.

9. Dreiser would probably not be surprised to learn that this debate over the sacrality of human life—all human life—has not abated over the past century. Consider the public outcry surrounding the Terry Schiavo case, in which her husband Michael fought a seven-year legal battle to have his wife (who had been in a persistent vegetative state since 1990) disconnected from her feeding tube. He was eventually successful, and Terry Schiavo died from dehydration in 2005.

10. Dreiser does not resort to religious rhetoric in his fight against censorship—partly, no doubt, due to his unceasing belligerence toward the purveyors of organized religion. But he clearly thought there was something inviolable about a work of art, that the wanton destruction or censorship of a work of art was a kind of *intrinsic* shame. Dreiser's arguments against censorship therefore tend to hinge less upon the benefits of unfettered speech than on the rank immorality of violence against art. In other words, Dreiser's anticensorship position is structured by a conception of the sacred, despite his "official" atheism.

11. In "True Art Speaks Plainly," Dreiser inveighs against art "that bears no honest relationship to either the whole of nature or to man." Art that honors this relationship, with honesty and without subterfuge, "this is morality as well as art" (*Uncollected Prose* 481).

12. Interestingly, Clarence Darrow—who defended Dreiser's novel in Donald Friede's 1929 appeal—once made a similar argument about Nietzsche, to whom Dreiser had an acknowledged debt. In perhaps his most famous case, *The State of Illinois v. Nathan Leopold and Richard Loeb* in 1924, Darrow argued that Leopold had become "obsessed" with Nietzsche's doctrines. "There isn't any question about the facts," Darrow told the judge. "He believed in a superman. He and Dickie Loeb were the supermen. The ordinary commands of society were not for him. Is there any question about what was responsible for him?" (Darrow). Darrow's argument here is not explicitly pro-censorship. But he did manage to spare the lives of his clients by transferring true guilt back to their primary sources. When he asks whether there is "any question about what was responsible," the implication is that Nietzsche is at least partially responsible for authoring the acts inspired by his text.

Chapter 5

1. In *Polemics*, Badiou highlights the ways in which "terrorism" exacts a semantic and analytic toll along with its more obvious physical ravages.

2. The body of writing on terrorism in America is truly vast. On the anarchist movement, see Avrich *Haymarket Tragedy* and *Sacco and Vanzetti*, as well

as Temkin; for more general accounts of America's relationship with terrorism, see Hewitt, as well as the work of Philip Bobbitt, Walter Laqueur, and Bruce Hoffman.

3. It is less than clear when "terrorism" entered the official discourse in America: Bruce Hoffman estimates in an email to the author that the Munich attacks of 1972 may have occasioned its first official use, but he hastens to add that 1972 "is just a guess."

4. On Berkman and Goldman, see Wexler 61–65, and Avrich, *Anarchist Portraits* 21–4.

5. See Robinson, *Black Movements in America* 151.

6. "Introduction: Patterns of Global Terrorism," U.S. Department of State, April 30, 2001, http://www.state.gov/s/ct/rls/crt/2000/2419.htm (accessed March 2, 2010).

7. "Definitions of Terrorism," United Nations Office on Drugs and Crime, http://web.archive.org/web/20070129121539/http://www.unodc.org/unodc/terrorism_definitions.html (accessed March 20, 2009).

8. In *Crimes of Art and Terror*, Lentricchia and McAuliffe explore the "twin motivations" of some artists and terrorists, both of whom would "undo," by their different means, "the West's economic and cultural order" (2).

9. Cohn's essay, "The Negro Novel: Richard Wright," originally appeared in the May 1940 *Atlantic* and is reprinted in *Native Son*.

10. On the Communist Party and African Americans, see Mullen and Smethurst, and Solomon.

11. On the John Reed Clubs, see Cowley, *Dream of the Golden Mountains*, as well as Denning 205–11.

12. In 1949, he contributed an essay to Crossman, the watershed volume in which six prominent ex-Communists detailed their disillusionment with the party.

13. For interpretations of Bigger as a black militant, see Cleaver and Margolies.

14. See Aaron. On Wright's involvement in the WPA, see Rowley 108–9, 119.

15. See Lemann and Arnesen.

16. See also Brinkley, *Liberalism and its Discontents*.

17. Denning considers Wright to be an important author of the "ghetto pastoral" (253), a critically marginalized form of modernism that was nonetheless influential to the culture of the Popular Front.

18. We should also recognize in Bigger's lynching what Hazel Carby has called "the ever-present underside of artistic or philosophical imaginings of black masculinity as tropes of utopian possibility." Lynching, Carby writes, may represent a "search to expose, and perhaps even an attempt to claim, an essence of manhood that is both feared and desired" (47).

19. See Ignatieff, as well as Yoo.

20. A detailed history of Greeley is recorded in Willard.

21. Qutb wrote prolifically both before and after he was imprisoned by the Egyptian government in 1954. His most-cited writing appears in *Milestones* (1964) and *In the Shade of the Qu'ran*, the thirty-volume exegesis of the Qu'ran he began in 1954, which has slowly been translated into English. Much of Qutb's work is available piecemeal from various online sources.

22. On Qutb's Islamism, see Khatab.

23. In a post–9/11 interview with Giovanna Borradori, Derrida argued that the "worst, most effective 'terrorism,' even if it seems external and 'international,' is one that installs or recalls an interior threat, at home—and recalls that the enemy is *also always* lodged on the inside of the system it violates and terrorizes" (qtd. in Borradori 188).

24. See Canot and Abu-Lughod.

Epilogue

1. Parts of the interview with Mailer are available online at http://www.youtube.com/watch?v=gnMMccvV5Dw.

2. Nowhere is this more explicit than in Mailer's final novel, *The Castle in the Forest* (2007), where the Evil One presides over the decidedly dirty coupling of Alois and his niece Klara, the product of which was Adolf Hitler. Mailer suggests that Hitler's malevolence may have been further stoked by his mother's over-attention to his "pip-squeak of an anus," which she was continually polishing and "kept as immaculate as an opal" (84).

Works Consulted

Aaron, Daniel. *Writers on the Left*. New York: Oxford UP, 1977.

Abu-Lughod, Janet L. *Race, Space, and Riots in Chicago, New York, and Los Angeles*. New York: Oxford UP, 2007.

Ahnebrink, Lars. *The Beginnings of Naturalism in American Fiction: A Study of the Works of Hamlin Garland, Stephen Crane, and Frank Norris, with special reference to Some European Influences*. Cambridge: Harvard UP, 1950.

Allott, Daniel. "The Fallacy of 'Personally Opposed, But . . .'" *American Spectator*. 30 April, 2007. Available online at http://spectator.org/archives/2007/04/30/the-fallacy-of-personally-oppo. (Accessed March 2, 2009.)

Arnesen, Eric. *Black Protest and the Great Migration: A Brief History with Documents*. Bedford: St. Martin's P, 2002.

Atkins, John. George Orwell. London: Calder & Boyars, 1954.

Avrich, Paul. *Anarchist Portraits*. Princeton: Princeton UP, 1988.

———. *The Haymarket Tragedy*. Princeton: Princeton UP, 1984.

———. *Sacco and Vanzetti: The Anarchist Background*. Princeton: Princeton UP, 1991.

Badiou, Alain. *Polemics*. New York: Verso, 2006.

Baguley, David. *Naturalist Fiction: The Entropic Vision*. Cambridge: Cambridge UP, 1990.

Baker, Houston. *Blues, Ideology, and Afro-American Literature: A Vernacular Theory*. Chicago: U of Chicago P, 1984.

Bakhtin, Mikhail. *The Dialogic Imagination*. Ed. Michael Holquist. Trans. Caryl Emerson and Michael Holquist. Austin: U of Texas P, 1981.

Baldwin, James. "Everybody's Protest Novel." *Notes of a Native Son*. New York: Bantam Books, 1955. 9–17.

———. *The Fire Next Time*. New York: Vintage International, 1993.

———. "Many Thousands Gone." *Notes of a Native Son*. New York: Bantam Books, 1955. 18–36.

Bannister, Robert. *Social Darwinism: Science and Myth in Anglo-American Thought*. Philadelphia: Temple UP, 1979.

Barker-Benfield, G. J. *The Horrors of the Half-Known Life*. New York: Routledge, 2000.

Beard, George M. *American Nervousness: Its Causes and Consequences, a Supplement to Nervous Exhaustion (Neurasthenia)*. 1881. New York: Arno, 1972.

Becker, George. *Documents of Modern Literary Realism*. Princeton: Princeton UP, 1963.

Bederman, Gail. *Manliness and Civilization: A Cultural History of Gender and Race in the United States*. Chicago: U of Chicago P, 1995.

Beer, Gillian. *Darwin's Plots: Evolutionary Narrative in Darwin, George Eliot, and Nineteenth-Century Fiction*. London: Ark, 1983.

Beer, Thomas. *The Mauve Decade: American Life at the End of the Nineteenth Century*. New York: Knopf, 1926.

Bell, Daniel. *The End of Ideology: On the Exhaustion of Political Ideas in the Fifties*. Glencoe: Free Press, 1960.

Bell, Michael Davitt. *Culture, Genre, and Literary Vocation: Selected Essays on American Literature*. Chicago: U of Chicago P, 1993.

———. *The Problem of American Realism*. Chicago: U of Chicago P, 1993.

Benjamin, Walter. *Illuminations*. Trans. Harry Zohn. New York: Schocken, 1968.

Bentley, Eric. *The Cult of the Superman: A Study in the Idea of Heroism in Carlyle and Nietzsche*. Goucester: Peter Smith, 1969.

Bercovitch, Sacvan. *American Jeremiad*. Madison: U of Wisconsin P, 1978.

———. "Introduction." *Cambridge History of American Literature*. Vol. 3. *Prose Writing 1860–1920*. Cambridge: Cambridge UP, 2005.

———. *The Puritan Origins of the American Self*. New Haven: Yale UP, 1975.

Berman, Paul. *Terror and Liberalism*. New York: Norton, 2003.

Berthoff, Warner. *The Ferment of Realism: American Literature, 1884–1919*. New York: Free Press, 1965.

Bloom, Harold, ed. *American Naturalism*. Philadelphia: Chelsea, 2004.

Bontemps, Arna. "Three Portraits of the Negro." *Saturday Review* 28 March 1953, 15–16.

Borradori, Giovanna, ed. *Philosophy in a Time of Terror*. Chicago: U of Chicago P, 2003.

Bowlby, Rachel. *Just Looking: Consumer Culture in Dreiser, Gissing, and Zola*. London: Methuen, 1985.

Boyer, Paul S. *Purity in Print: The Vice-Society Movement and Book Censorship in America*. New York: Scribner, 1968.

Brand, H. W. *Andrew Jackson: His Life and Times*. New York: Doubleday, 2005.

Brinkley, Alan. *Liberalism and Its Discontents*. Cambridge: Harvard UP, 1998.

———. "World War II and American Liberalism." *The War in American Culture: Society and Consciousness During World War II*. Eds. Lewis A. Erenberg and Susan E. Hirsch. Chicago: U of Chicago P, 1996. 313–30.

Broadhead, Richard. *Cultures of Letters: Scenes of Reading and Writing in Nineteenth-Century America*. Chicago: U of Chicago P, 1993.

Brown, Bill. *The Material Unconscious: American Amusement, Stephen Crane, and the Economics of Play*. Cambridge: Harvard UP, 1996.

Brown, Richard Maxwell. "Back Country Rebellions and the Homestead Ethic in America, 1740–1799." Brown and Fehrenbacher 73–99.

———. *No Duty to Retreat: Violence and Values in American History and Society*. New York: Oxford UP, 1991.

Brown, Richard Maxwell, and Don E. Fehrenbacher, eds. *Tradition, Conflict, Modernization: Perspectives on the American Revolution*. New York: Academic, 1977.

Buell, Lawrence. *The Environmental Imagination: Thoreau, Nature Writing, and the Formation of American Culture*. Cambridge: Belknap, 1995.

———. *The Future of Environmental Criticism: Environmental Crisis and Literary Imagination*. Malden: Blackwell, 2005.

Butler, Robert. *The Critical Response to Richard Wright*. Westport: Greenwood, 1995.

Cain, William E. "Presence and Power in McTeague." Sundquist 199–214.

Calvert, John. "'The World is an Undutiful Boy!': Sayyid Qutb's American Experience." *Islam and Christian-Muslim Relations* 11.1 (2000): 87–103.

Campbell, Donna M. *Resisting Regionalism: Gender and Naturalism in American Fiction, 1885–1915*. Athens: Ohio UP, 1997.

Canot, Robert. *Rivers of Blood, Years of Darkness*. New York: Morrow, 1968.

Capetti, Carla. "Sociology of Existence: Richard Wright and the Chicago School." *MELUS* 12 (Summer 1985): 25–43.

Carby, Hazel V. *Race Men*. Cambridge: Harvard UP, 1998.

Cassuto, Leonard, and Clare Virginia Eby. "Introduction." *Cambridge Companion to Theodore Dreiser*. Ed. Cassuto and Eby. Cambridge: Cambridge UP, 2004. 1–14.

Chamberlin, Edward J., and Sander L. Gilman, eds. *Degeneration: The Dark Side of Paradise*. New York: Columbia UP, 1985.

Chase, Richard. *The American Novel and Its Tradition*. Garden City: Doubleday Anchor, 1957.

Civello, Paul. *American Literary Naturalism and Its Twentieth-Century Transformations*. Athens: U of Georgia P, 1994.

Cleaver, Eldridge. *Soul on Ice*. New York: Dell, 1968

Cowley, Malcolm. *The Dream of the Golden Mountains: Remembering the 1930s*. New York: Penguin, 1981.

———. "Naturalism in American Literature." *Evolutionary Thought in America*. Ed. Stow Persons. New Haven: Yale UP, 1950. 300–333.

———. "'Not Men': A Natural History of American Naturalism." *Kenyon Review* 9 (1947): 414–35.

Cowley, Malcolm, ed. *After the Genteel Tradition: American Writers since 1910*. Carbondale: Southern Illinois UP, 1964.

Crane, Stephen. *Maggie: A Girl of the Streets*. 1893. Ed. Thomas Gullason. New York: Norton, 1979.

———. *The Red Badge of Courage*. 1895. Ed. Donald Pizer. New York: Norton, 2008.

Crewe, Jonathan. "Can Polemic Be Ethical? A Response to Michel Foucault." *Polemic: Critical or Uncritical*. Ed. Jane Gallop. New York: Routledge, 2004. 135–52.

Crossman, R. H. S., ed. *The God that Failed*. New York: Harper & Row, 1965.

Darrow, Clarence. "Closing Argument: The State of Illinois v. Nathan Leopold & Richard Loeb." UMKC School of Law. http://law2.umkc.edu/faculty/projects/ftrials/leoploeb/darrowclosing.html. (Accessed March 8, 2009.)

Darwin, Charles. *Darwin: A Norton Critical Edition*. New York: W. W. Norton, 1979.

Davis, Nanette J. *From Crime to Choice: The Transformation of Abortion in America*. Westport: Greenwood, 1985.

"Definitions of Terrorism." United Nations Office on Drugs and Crime. 20 March 2009. http://web.archive.org/web/20070129121539/http://www.unodc.org/unodc/terrorism_definition s.html.

Denning, Michael. *The Cultural Front: The Laboring of American Culture in the Twentieth Century*. New York: Verso, 1996.

Derrida, Jacques. "The Law of Genre." Trans. Avital Ronell. *Critical Inquiry* 7.1 (1980): 55–81.

Dimock, Wai-Chee. "World History According to Katrina." *differences* 19.2 (2008): 35–50.

Dimock, Wai-Chee, and Lawrence Buell, eds. *Shades of the Planet: American Literature as World Literature*. Princeton: Princeton UP, 2007.

Donaldson-Evans, Catherine. "Yale Officials Conclude Student's Shocking Claim of 'Abortion Art' Was 'Creative Fiction.'" Foxnews.com 17 April 2008. http://www.foxnews.com/story/0,2933,351608,00.html. (Accessed March 3, 2009.)

Douglas, Ann. *The Feminization of American Culture*. New York: Knopf, 1977.

Dreiser, Theodore. *America Is Worth Saving*. New York: Modern Age, 1941.

———. *An American Tragedy*. 1925. New York: Signet Classic, 2000.

———. *A Book about Myself.* New York: Boni and Liveright, 1922.

———. *Dawn: An Autobiography of Early Youth.* Ed. T. D. Nostwich. Santa Rosa: Black Sparrow Press, 1998.

———. *The "Genius."* Ed. Clare Virginia Eby. Urbana: U of Illinois P, 2008.

———. "I Find the Real American Tragedy." Dreiser, *Theodore Dreiser: A Selection of Uncollected Prose* 291–99.

———. "The Right to Kill." Dreiser, *Theodore Dreiser: A Selection of Uncollected Prose* 224–29.

———. *Sister Carrie.* 1900. Ed. Donald Pizer. New York: Norton, 2006.

———. *Theodore Dreiser: A Selection of Uncollected Prose.* Ed. Donald Pizer. Detroit: Wayne State UP, 1977.

———. "A Word Concerning Birth Control." *Birth Control Review* 5.4 (April 1921): 5–13.

Dudley, John. *A Man's Game: Masculinity and the Anti-Aesthetics of American Literary Naturalism.* Tuscaloosa: U of Alabama P, 2004.

Dworkin, Ronald. *Life's Dominion.* New York: Knopf, 1993.

Ellis, Havelock. *Man and Woman: A Study of Human Secondary Sexual Characteristics.* 1894. New York: Scribner's, 1908.

Ellison, Ralph. "Going to the Territory." *The Collected Essays of Ralph Ellison.* Ed. John F. Callahan. New York: Modern Library, 2003. 493–785.

———. "The World and the Jug." *The Collected Essays of Ralph Ellison.* Ed. John F. Callahan. New York: Modern Library, 2003. 155–88.

Emery, Edwin. *The Press and America: An Interpretive History of Journalism.* Endlgewood Cliffs: Prentice, 1962.

Erenberg, Lewis A., and Susan E. Hirsch. "Introduction." *The War in American Culture: Society and Consciousness During World War II.* Eds. Erenberg and Hirsch. Chicago: U of Chicago P, 1996. 1–16.

Fabre, Michel. *Richard Wright: Books and Writers.* Jackson: UP of Mississippi, 1990.

———. *The Unfinished Quest of Richard Wright.* New York: William Morrow, 1973.

———. *The World of Richard Wright.* Jackson: UP of Mississippi, 1985.

Fanon, Frantz. *Black Skin, White Masks.* New York: Grove, 1967.

———. *The Wretched of the Earth.* New York: Grove, 1961.

Fiedler, Leslie. *Love and Death in the American Novel.* New York: Dell, 1966.

Fisher, Philip. *Hard Facts: Setting and Form in the American Novel.* New York: Oxford UP, 1985.

Fishkin, Shelly Fisher. *From Fact to Fiction: Journalism and Imaginative Writing in America.* Baltimore: Johns Hopkins UP, 1985.

Fitzgerald, F. Scott. *The Great Gatsby.* Ed. Ruth Prigozy. New York: Oxford UP, 1998.

Fleissner, Jennifer L. *Women, Compulsion, Modernity: The Moment of American Naturalism*. Chicago: U of Chicago P, 2004.

Folson, James K. "Social Darwinism or Social Protest? The 'Philosophy' of *The Octopus*." *The Merrill Studies in The Octopus*. Ed. Richard Allan Davison. Columbus: Charles E. Merrill, 1969. 132–40.

Foucault, Michel, "An Interview with Michel Foucault." *Foucault: A Reader*. Ed. Paul Rabinow. New York: Pantheon, 1984. 381–90.

Foulkes, Julia L. "Politics and Culture in the 1930s and 1940s." *A Companion to American Cultural History*. Ed. Karen Halttunen Malden: Blackwell, 2008. 214–29.

Freud, Sigmund. *Civilization and Its Discontents*. Trans. David McLintock. New York: Penguin, 2002.

———. "The Neuro-Psychoses of Defence." *The Standard Edition of the Complete Psychological Works of Sigmund Freud*. Vol. 3. Trans. James Strachey. London: Hogarth P, 1975. 41–61.

———. "Neurosis and Psychosis." *The Standard Edition of the Complete Psychological Works of Sigmund Freud*. Vol. 19. Trans. James Strachey. London: Hogarth P, 1971. 149–153.

Fried, Michael. *Realism, Writing, Disfiguration*. Chicago: U of Chicago P, 1987.

Gallop, Jane. "Introduction." *Polemic: Critical or Uncritical*. Ed. Gallop. New York: Routledge, 2004. 1–12.

Geismar, Maxwell. *Rebels and Ancestors: The American Novel, 1890–1915*. Boston: Houghton Mifflin, 1953.

Giles, James R. *The Naturalistic Inner-City Novel in America: Encounters with the Fat Man*. Columbia: U of South Carolina P, 1995.

Gilmer, Walker. *Horace Liveright: Publisher of the Twenties*. New York: David Lewis, 1970.

Girard, Rene. *Deceit, Desire, and the Novel*. Trans. Yvonne Freccero. Baltimore: Johns Hopkins UP, 1965.

Glotfelty, Cheryll. "Introduction: Literary Studies in an Age of Environmental Crisis." *The Ecocriticism Reader*. Ed. Cheryll Glotfelty and Harold Fromm. Athens: U of Georgia P, 1996. xv–xxiv.

Goddu, Teresa. *Gothic America*. New York: Columbia UP, 1997.

Gogol, Miriam, ed. *Theodore Dreiser: Beyond Naturalism*. New York: New York UP, 1995.

Gosling, F. G. *Before Freud: Neurasthenia and the American Medical Community, 1870–1910*. Urbana: U of Illinois P, 1987.

Gossett, Thomas F. *Race: The History of an Idea in America*. New York: Oxford UP, 1997.

Gould, Stephen Jay. *The Mismeasure of Man*. New York: Norton, 1981.

Graham, Don, ed. *Critical Essays on Frank Norris*. Boston: G. K. Hall, 1980.

———. *The Fiction of Frank Norris: The Aesthetic Context*. Columbia: U of Missouri P, 1978.

Guest, David. *Sentenced to Death: The American Novel and Capital Punishment*. Jackson: UP of Mississippi, 1997.

Hakutani, Yoshinobu. *Richard Wright and Racial Discourse*. Columbia: U of Missouri P, 1996.

Hakutani, Yoshinobu, and Lewis Fried, eds. *American Literary Naturalism: A Reassessment*. Heidelberg: Carl Winter, 1975.

Halttunen, Karen. *Murder Most Foul: The Killer and the American Imagination*. Cambridge: Harvard UP, 1998.

Harper, Phillip Brian. *Are We Not Men: Masculine Anxiety and the Problem of African-American Identity*. New York: Oxford UP, 1996.

Hayles, N. Katherine. *Chaos Bound: Orderly Disorder in Contemporary Literature and Science*. Ithaca: Cornell UP, 1990.

Hays, Arthur Garfield. *City Lawyer*. New York: Simon and Schuster, 1942.

———. *Let Freedom Ring*. New York: Da Capo Press, 1972.

Hewitt, Christopher. *Understanding Terrorism in America: From the Klan to Al Qaeda*. New York: Routledge, 2003.

Hicks, Granville. *The Great Tradition: An Interpretation of American Literature Since the Civil War*. New York: Macmillan, 1933.

Himes, Chester. *If He Hollers Let Him Go*. London: Sphere, 1967.

Himmelfarb, Gertrude. *Darwin and the Darwinian Revolution*. New York: W. W. Norton, 1962.

Hobson, Fred. *Mencken: A Life*. New York: Random, 1994.

Hochman, Barbara. *The Art of Frank Norris, Storyteller*. Columbia: U of Missouri P, 1988.

Hofstadter, Richard. *Social Darwinism in American Thought*. New York: W. W. Norton, 1962.

Howard, June. *Form and History in American Literary Naturalism*. Chapel Hill: U of North Carolina P, 1985.

———. "Sand in Your Mouth: Naturalism and Other Genres." Newlin, *The Oxford Handbook of American Literary Naturalism* 92–103.

Howe, Irving. *A World More Attractive: A View of Modern Literature and Politics*. New York: Horizon P, 1963.

Hull, N. E. H., and Peter Charles Hoffer. *Roe. v. Wade: The Abortion Rights Controversy in American History*. Lawrence: UP of Kansas, 2001.

Hull, N. E. H., William James Hoffer, and Peter Charles Hoffer, eds. *The Abortion Rights Controversy in America: A Legal Reader*. Chapel Hill: U of North Carolina P, 2004.

Ignatieff, Michael. *The Lesser Evil*. Princeton: Princeton UP, 2004

James, Henry. *The Art of Fiction and Other Essays*. New York: Oxford UP, 1948.

Jameson, Fredric. *The Political Unconscious: Narrative as a Socially Symbolic Act*. Ithaca: Cornell UP, 1981.

Jan Mohamed, Abdul R. *The Death-Bound Subject: Richard Wright's Archeology of Death*. Durham: Duke UP, 2005.

Johanningsmeier, Charles. "Naturalist Authors and the American Literary Marketplace." Newlin, *The Oxford Handbook of American Literary Naturalism* 357–72.

Johnson, Barbara. *The Feminist Difference: Literature, Psychoanalysis, Race, and Gender* Cambridge: Harvard UP, 1998.

Jones, LeRoi [Amiri Baraka]. "The Revolutionary Theatre." *Liberator* 5 July 1965, 4–6. Republished in LeRoi Jones, *Home: Social Essays*. New York: William Morrow, 1966. 210–15.

Joyce, Joyce Ann. *Richard Wright's Art of Tragedy*. Iowa City: U of Iowa P, 1986.

Kaplan, Amy. *The Social Construction of American Realism*. Chicago: U of Chicago P, 1988.

Kaplan, Harold. *Power and Order: Henry Adams and the Naturalist Tradition in American Fiction*. Chicago: U of Chicago P, 1981.

Kaufman, Bruce. *The Origins and Evolution of Industrial Relations in the United States*. Ithaca: Cornell UP, 1992.

Kazin, Alfred. *On Native Grounds: An Interpretation of Modern American Prose Literature*. New York: Doubleday, 1956.

Kennedy, David M. *Over Here: The First World War and American Society*. New York: Oxford UP, 1980.

Kern, Robert, "Ecocriticism: What Is It Good For?" *The ISLE Reader: Ecocriticism, 1993–2003*. Ed. Michael P. Branch and Scott Slovic. Athens: U of Georgia P, 2003. 258–81.

Khatab, Sayed. *The Political Thought of Sayyid Qutb: The Theory of Jahiliyyah*. New York: Routledge, 2008.

Kinnamon, Keneth. *The Emergence of Richard Wright: A Study in Literature and Society*. Urbana: U of Illinois P, 1972.

———. *Richard Wright: An Annotated Bibliography of Criticism and Commentary, 1983–2003*. Jefferson: McFarland, 2006.

Kinnamon, Keneth, and Michel Fabre, eds. *Conversations with Richard Wright*. Jackson: UP of Mississippi, 1993.

Kolbert, Elizabeth. *Field Notes from a Catastrophe*. New York: Bloomsbury, 2006.

Laqueur, Walter. *No End to War: Terrorism in the Twenty-First Century*. New York: Continuum, 2003.

Law, Randall D. *Terrorism: A History*. Malden: Polity, 2009.

Lears, Jackson. "Dreiser and the History of American Longing." *The Cambridge*

Companion to Theodore Dreiser. Ed. Leonard Cassuto and Clare Virginia Eby. Cambridge: Cambridge UP, 2004. 63–82.

———. *No Place of Grace*. New York: Pantheon, 1981.

———. "The Usefulness of Cranks: Nature as a Standpoint for Social Criticism." *New Republic* 7 October 2009, 32–43.

Lehan, Richard. "American Literary Naturalism: The French Connection." *Nineteenth-Century Fiction* 38 (1984): 529–57.

———. *The City in Literature: An Intellectual and Cultural History*. Berkeley: U of California P, 1998.

———. "The European Background." Pizer, *The Cambridge Companion to American Realism and Naturalism: Howells to London* 47–74.

———. *Realism and Naturalism: The Novel in an Age of Transition*. Madison: U of Wisconsin P, 2005.

———. *Theodore Dreiser: His World and His Novels*. Carbondale: Southern Illinois UP, 1969.

Lemann, Nicholas. *The Promised Land: The Great Black Migration and How It Changed America*. New York: A. A. Knopf, 1991.

Lentricchia, Frank, and Jody McAuliffe. *Crimes of Art and Terror*. Chicago: U of Chicago P, 2003.

Lingeman, Richard. *Double Lives: American Writers' Friendships*. New York: Random, 2006.

———. Introduction. *An American Tragedy*. By Theodore Dreiser. New York: Signet Classic, 2000.

———. *Theodore Dreiser: An American Journey*. New York: G. P. Putnam's Sons, 1990.

———. *Theodore Dreiser: At the Gates of the City*. New York: G. P. Putnam's Sons, 1986.

Link, Eric Carl. *The Vast and Terrible Drama*. Tuscaloosa: U of Alabama P, 2004.

London, Jack. "The Yellow Peril." *Jack London Reports*. Eds. King Hendricks and Irving Shepard. New York: Doubleday, 1970. 370.

Long, Lisa. "Genre Matters: Embodying American Literary Naturalism." *American Literary History* 19 (2007): 160–73.

Love, Glen A. *Practical Ecocriticism: Literature, Biology, and the Environment*. Charlottesville: U of Virginia P, 2003.

Loving, Jerome. *The Last Titan*. Berkeley: U of California P, 2005.

———. "Re: Dreiser." E-mail to the author. 19 March 2009.

Lucács, Georg. "Narrate or Describe? A Preliminary Discussion of Naturalism and Formalism." *Writer and Critic and Other Essays*. Ed. Arthur D. Kahn. London: Martin Press, 1970. 110–48.

Lutz, Tom. *American Nervousness, 1903: An Anecdotal History*. Ithaca: Cornell UP, 1991.

Lynn, Kenneth. *The Dream of Success: A Study of the Modern American Imagination*. Boston: Little, Brown, 1955.

MacKinnon, Catherine A. *Women's Lives, Men's Laws*. Cambridge: Belknap, 2005.

Mailer, Norman. "By Heaven Inspired." *The Time of Our Time*. New York: Random House, 1998. 1092–113.

——. *The Castle in the Forest*. New York: Random House, 2007

——. "An Impolite Interview with Paul Krassner." *Pontifications*. Ed. Michael Lennon. Boston: Little, Brown: 1982. 6–16.

——. "Vices." *Pontifications*. Ed. Michael Lennon. Boston: Little, Brown: 1982. 32–45.

Malcolm X. "The Ballot or the Bullet." *The American Intellectual Tradition. Vol. II*. Eds. David A. Hollinger and Charles Capper. New York: Oxford UP, 2001. 437–44.

Margolies, Edward. *Native Sons*. New York: Lipincott, 1968.

Marsh, George Perkins. *Man and Nature*. Ed. David Lowenthal. Seattle: U of Washington P, 2003.

Martin, Jay. *Harvests of Change: American Literature, 1965–914*. Englewood Cliffs: Prentice, 1967.

Martin, Ronald E. *American Literature and the Universe of Force*. Durham: Duke UP, 1981.

Matthiessen, F. O. *Theodore Dreiser*. New York: W. Sloane, 1951.

Mazel, David, ed. *A Century of Early Ecocriticism*. Athens: U of Georgia P, 2001.

McCall, Dan. *The Example of Richard Wright*. Carbondale: Southern Illinois UP, 1969.

McElrath, Joseph R. *Frank Norris Revisited*. New York: Twayne, 1992.

——. "Frank Norris's *The Octopus*: The Christian Ethic as Pragmatic Response." Graham, *Critical Essays on Frank Norris* 138–52.

McElrath, Joseph R., and Jesse S. Crisler. *Frank Norris: A Life*. Chicago: U of Illinois P, 2006.

McKibben, Bill. *American Earth: Environmental Writing Since Thoreau*. New York: Library of America, 2008.

——. *The End of Nature*. New York: Anchor/Doubleday, 1989.

Meeker, Joseph W. *The Comedy of Survival: Studies in Literary Ecology*. New York: Charles Scribner's Sons, 1972.

Menand, Louis. *American Studies*. New York: Farrar, Straus and Giroux, 2002.

——. "Kael's Attack on Sarris." *Polemic: Critical or Uncritical*. Ed. Jane Gallop. New York: Routledge, 2004. 153–77.

Mencken, H. L. *A Book of Prefaces*. New York: Garden City, 1917.

———. *Dreiser-Mencken Letters: The Correspondence of Theodore Dreiser and H. L. Mencken, 1907–1945*. Ed. Thomas P. Riggio. Philadelphia: U of Pennsylvania P, 1986.

———. *The Gist of Mencken*. Ed. Mayo DuBasky. Metuchen: Scarecrow, 1990.

———. Introduction. *An American Tragedy*. By Theodore Dreiser. New York: World, 1948.

———. *The Philosophy of Friedrich Nietzsche*. London: Unwin, 1908.

———. *Prejudices: First Series*. New York: Knopf, 1919.

Michaels, Walter Benn. *The Gold Standard and the Logic of Naturalism*. Berkeley: U of California P, 1987.

Miller, J. Hillis. *Poets of Reality: Six Twentieth-Century Writers*. Cambridge: Harvard UP, 1965.

Miller, Perry. *The New England Mind: From Colony to Province*. 1953. Boston: Beacon, 1961.

———. *The New England Mind: The Seventeenth Century*. 1939. Boston: Beacon, 1964.

Mitchell, Lee Clark. *Determined Fictions: American Literary Naturalism*. New York: Columbia UP, 1989.

Mitchell, W. J. T., ed. *Landscape and Power*. Chicago: U of Chicago P, 1994.

Mizruchi, Susan L. "Becoming Multicultural: Culture, Economy, and the Novel, 1860–1920." *The Cambridge History of American Literature*. Vol. 3. *Prose Writing 1860–1920*. Ed. Sacvan Bercovitch. Cambridge: Cambridge UP, 2005. 413–739.

Moers, Ellen. *Two Dreisers*. New York: Viking, 1969.

Mohr, James C. *Abortion in America: The Origins and Evolution of National Policy, 1800–1900*. New York: Oxford UP, 1978.

Morton, Timothy. *Ecology without Nature*. Cambridge: Harvard UP, 2007.

Mott, Frank Luther. *American Journalism, A History: 1690–1960*. New York: Macmillan, 1962.

Muir, John. *Nature Writings*. Ed. William Cronon. New York: Library of America, 1997.

Mullen, Bill V., and James Smethurst, eds. *Left of the Color Line: Race, Radicalism, and Twentieth-Century Literature of the United States*. Chapel Hill: U of North Carolina P, 2003.

Musallam, Adnan A. *From Secularism to Jihad: Sayyid Qutb and the Foundations of Radical Islam*. Westport: Praeger, 2005.

Newlin, Keith. "Introduction: The Naturalistic Imagination and the Aesthetics of Excess." Newlin, *The Oxford Handbook of American Literary Naturalism* 3–17.

Newlin, Keith, ed. *The Oxford Handbook of American Literary Naturalism*. New York: Oxford UP, 2011.

———. *A Theodore Dreiser Encyclopedia*. Westport: Greenwood P, 2003.
Nordau, Max. *Degeneration*. 1895. New York: Appleton, 1995.
Norris, Frank. *Collected Letters*. Ed. Jesse Crisler. San Francisco: Book Club of California, 1986.
———. *The Complete Edition of Frank Norris*. Garden City: Doubleday, 1928.
———. *The Literary Criticism of Frank Norris*. Ed. Donald Pizer. Austin: U of Texas P, 1964.
———. *McTeague*. 1899. Norris, *Novels and Essays* 261–572.
———. *Novels and Essays*. Ed. Donald Pizer. New York: Norton, 1977.
———. "The Novel with a 'Purpose.'" 1902. Norris, *Novels and Essays* 1196–1200.
———. *The Octopus*. 1901. Norris, *Novels and Essays* 573–1098.
———. *The Pit*. 1903. New York: Penguin, 1994.
———. *The Surrender of Santiago*. San Francisco: Elder, 1917.
———. *Vandover and the Brute*. 1914. Norris, *Novels and Essays* 1–260.
Parrington, Vernon Louis. *The Beginnings of Critical Realism in America, 1860–1920*. Vol. 3, *Main Currents in American Thought*. New York: Harcourt, Brace, 1932.
Phillips, Dana. *The Truth of Ecology: Nature, Culture, and Literature in America*. New York: Oxford UP, 2003.
Pizer, Donald. *American Naturalism and the Jews: Garland, Norris, Dreiser, Wharton, and Cather*. Champaign: U of Illinois P, 2008.
———. "Bad Critical Writing." *Philosophy and Literature* 22.1 (April 1998): 69–82.
———. "Introduction: The Problem of Definition." Pizer, *The Cambridge Companion to American Realism and Naturalism* 1–20.
———. *The Novels of Frank Norris*. Bloomingdale: Indiana UP, 1966.
———. *The Novels of Theodore Dreiser: A Critical Study*. Minneapolis: U of Minnesota P, 1976.
———. *Realism and Naturalism in Nineteenth-Century American Literature*. Carbondale: Southern Illinois UP, 1984.
———. *The Theory and Practice of American Literary Naturalism: Selected Essays and Reviews*. Carbondale: Southern Illinois UP, 1993.
———. *Twentieth-Century American Literary Naturalism: An Interpretation*. Carbondale: Southern Illinois UP, 1982.
Pizer, Donald, ed. *The Cambridge Companion to American Realism and Naturalism: Howells to London*. Cambridge: Cambridge UP, 1995.
———. *Documents of American Realism and Naturalism*. Carbondale: Southern Illinois UP, 1998.
———. *The Literary Criticism of Frank Norris*. Austin: U of Texas P, 1964.
———. *Theodore Dreiser: A Selection of Uncollected Prose*. Detroit: Wayne State UP, 1977.

Poirier, Richard. *A World Elsewhere: The Place of Style in America Literature.* Madison: U of Wisconsin P, 1985.

Pollan, Michael. *The Omnivore's Dilemma.* New York: Penguin, 2006.

Powers, Martine. "For Senior, Abortion a Medium for Art, Political Discourse." *Yale Daily News* 17 April 2008. http://www.yaledailynews.com/articles/view/24513. (Accessed March 3, 2009.)

Pritchett, V. S. "The Spanish Tragedy." *New Statesman* 30 April 1938, 15.375.

"Publisher Loses Boston Test Case." *New York Times* 23 April 1927, Radio, 14.

Pudaloff, Ross. "Celebrity as Identity: Richard Wright, *Native Son*, and Mass Culture." *Studies in American Fiction* 11 (Spring 1983): 3–18.

Radway, Janice A. "Learned and Literary Print Cultures in an Age of Professionalization and Diversification." *A History of the Book in America. Volume 4: The Expansion of Publishing and Reading in the United States 1880–1940.* Eds. Carl F. Kaestle and Janice A. Radway. Chapel Hill: U of North Carolina P, 2009. 197–233.

Rahv, Philip. *Image and Idea.* Norfolk: New Directions, 1949.

Riis, Jacob. *How the Other Half Lives.* 1890. New York: Penguin, 1997.

Robinson, Cedric J. *Black Marxism: The Making of the Black Radical Tradition.* London: Zed, 1983.

———. *Black Movements in America.* New York: Routledge, 1997.

Roggencamp, Karen. *Narrating the News: New Journalism and Literary Genre in Late Nineteenth-Century American Newspapers and Fiction.* Kent: Kent State UP, 2005.

Roosevelt, Theodore. *Letters and Speeches.* Ed. Louis Auchincloss. New York: Library of America, 2004.

Rosendale, Steven. "Introduction: Extending Ecocriticism." *The Greening of Literary Scholarship: Literature, Theory, and the Environment.* Ed. Rosendale. Iowa City: U of Iowa P, 2002.

Rotundo, Anthony. *American Manhood: Transformations in Masculinity from the Revolution to the Modern Era.* New York: Basic, 1993.

Rowley, Hazel. *Richard Wright: The Life and Times.* New York: Henry Holt, 2001.

———. *Woman and the New Race.* New York: Brentano's, 1920.

Saul, Ben. "The Legal Response of the League of Nations to Terrorism." *Journal of International Criminal Justice* 4 (March 2006): 78–102.

Schama, Simon. *Landscape and Memory.* New York: Random House, 1995.

Schlesinger, Arthur M. *The Vital Center: The Politics of Freedom.* 1949. New Jersey: Transaction, 1998.

Schlosser, Eric. *Reefer Madness.* Boston: Houghton Mifflin, 2003.

Seltzer, Mark. *Bodies and Machines.* New York: Routledge, 1992.

Sherman, Stuart P. "The Naturalism of Mr. Dreiser." *Critical Essays on Theodore Dreiser.* Ed. Donald Pizer. Boston: G. K. Hall, 1981. 4–12.

Shvarts, Aliza. "Shvarts Explains Her 'Repeated Self-Induced Miscarriages.'" *Yale Daily News* 18 April 2008. http://www.yaledailynews.com/articles/view/24559. (Accessed March 3, 2009.)

Sinclair, Upton. *The Brass Check: A Study of American Journalism.* Champaign: U of Illinois P, 2003.

Sivan, Emmanuel. *Radical Islam.* New Haven: Yale UP, 1990

Smethurst, James. "Invented by Horror: The Gothic and African American Literary Ideology in *Native Son.*" *African American Review* 35 (Spring 2001): 29–40.

Sollors, Werner. "Ethnic Modernism." *The Cambridge History of American Literature.* Vol. 6. *Prose Writing 1910–1950.* Ed. Sacvan Bercovitch. Cambridge: Cambridge UP, 2002. 353–556.

Solomon, Mark. *The Cry Was Unity: Communists and African Americans, 1917–36.* Jackson: UP of Mississippi, 1998.

Soper, Kate. *What Is Nature?: Culture, Politics, and the Non-Human.* Oxford: Blackwell, 1995.

Stepp, Laura Sessions, and Ann Devroy. "Bush Cites Abortion 'Tragedy' in Call to 67,000 Protesters." *Washington Post* 24 January 1989. Highbeam.

Stimpson, Catharine R. "Foreword." *Women, Compulsion, Modernity.* By Jennifer Fleissner. Chicago: U of Chicago P, 2004. ix–xii.

Sundquist, Eric J., ed. *American Realism: New Essays.* Baltimore: Johns Hopkins UP, 1982.

Teachout, Terry. *The Skeptic: A Life of H. L. Mencken.* New York: HarperCollins, 2002.

Temkin, Moshik. *The Sacco-Vanzetti Affair: America on Trial.* New Haven: Yale UP, 2009.

Thomas, Norman. "Some Objections to Birth Control Considered." *Religious and Ethical Aspects of Birth Control.* Ed. Margaret Sanger. New York: 1926.

Thoreau, Henry David. *Walden; or, Life in the Woods.* Ed. Robert F. Sayre. New York: Library of America, 1985.

Trachtenberg, Alan. *The Incorporation of America: Culture and Society in the Gilded Age.* New York: Hill and Wang, 1982.

Trilling, Lionel. "Reality in America." *The Liberal Imagination.* By Trilling. New York: New York Review Books, 2008. 3–21.

Turner, Frederick Jackson. *The Significance of the Frontier in American History.* New York: Holt, 1921.

Veblen, Thorstein. *The Theory of the Leisure Class.* 1899. New York: Penguin, 1994.

Walcutt, Charles Child. *American Literary Naturalism: A Divided Stream.* Minneapolis: U of Minnesota P, 1956.

Waldrep, Christopher. *The Many Faces of Judge Lynch: Extralegal Violence and Punishment in America*. New York: Palgrave MacMillan, 2002.

Walker, Franklin. *Frank Norris: A Biography*. Garden City: Doubleday, Doran, 1932.

Walker, Franklin, ed. *The Letters of Frank Norris*. San Francisco: Book Club of California, 1956.

Walker, Margaret. *Richard Wright, Daemonic Genius: A Portrait of the Man, A Critical Look at His Work*. New York: Amistad, 1988.

Warnes, Andrew. *Richard Wright's* Native Son. New York: Routledge, 2007.

Warren. Robert Penn. *Homage to Theodore Dreiser*. New York: Random House, 1971.

Wexler, Alice. *Emma Goldman in America*. Boston: Beacon Press, 1984.

Whyte, Kenneth. *The Uncrowned King: The Sensational Rise of William Randolph Hearst*. Toronto: Random House, 2008.

Wilentz, Sean. *Andrew Jackson*. New York: Times Books, 2005.

Willard, James F. *The Union Colony at Greeley, Colorado, 1869–1871*. Boulder: U of Colorado P, 1918. Available online at http://www.archive.org/stream/unioncolonyatgre01willuoft/unioncolonyatgre01willuoft_ djvu.txt.

Williams, Raymond. "Naturalism." *Keywords: A Vocabulary of Culture and Society*. By Williams. New York: Oxford UP, 1983. 181–84.

Wilson, Andrew. *Norman Mailer: An American Aesthetic*. New York: Peter Lang, 2008.

Wilson, Christopher. *The Labor of Words: Literary Professionalism in the Progressive Era*. Athens: U of Georgia P, 1985.

Wilson, Edmund. *Classics and Commercials: A Literary Chronicle of the Forties*. New York: Farrar, Straus, 1950.

———. *A Literary Chronicle: 1920–1950*. New York: Doubleday Anchor, 1956.

Wilt, Judith. *Abortion, Choice, and Contemporary Fiction*. Chicago: U of Chicago P, 1990.

Wood, James. *How Fiction Works*. New York: Farrar, Straus and Giroux, 2008.

Worster, Donald. *A Passion for Nature: The Life of John Muir*. Oxford: Oxford UP, 2008.

Wright, Lawrence. *The Looming Tower: Al-Queda and the Road to 9/11*. New York: Alfred A. Knopf, 2006.

Wright, Richard. *Black Boy (American Hunger). Later Works*. Ed. Arnold Rampersad. New York: Library of America, 1991. 1–365.

———. "Blueprint for Negro Writing." *Richard Wright Reader*. Eds. Ellen Wright and Michel Fabre. New York: Harper & Row, 1978. 36–49.

———. "How 'Bigger' Was Born." Wright, *Native Son* 431–62.

———. "Introduction." *Black Metropolis. Vol. I.* Eds. St. Clair Drake and Lawrence R. Cayton. New York: Harcourt, Brace & World, 1945. xvii–xxxiv.

———. *Native Son*. New York: Harper Perennial, 2005.

———. *The Outsider. Later Works*. Ed. Arnold Rampersad. New York: Library of America, 1991. 367–841.

Yoo, John. *The Powers of War and Peace*. Chicago: U of Chicago P, 2005.

Zangrando, Robert L. *The NAACP Crusade against Lynching, 1909–1950*. Philadelphia: Temple UP, 1980.

Ziff, Larzer. *The American 1890s*. New York: Viking, 1966.

Zizek, Slavoj. *In Defence of Lost Causes*. New York: Verso, 2008.

Index